John Carroll Recovered

An oil portrait of John Carroll done by Rembrandt Peale about 1809
(Archbishops of Baltimore Collection)

JOHN CARROLL RECOVERED
ABSTRACTS OF LETTERS AND OTHER DOCUMENTS
NOT FOUND IN THE JOHN CARROLL PAPERS

THOMAS W. SPALDING

WITH THE ASSISTANCE OF PAUL K. THOMAS

Cathedral Foundation Press
Baltimore, Maryland

Library of Congress Cataloging-in-Publication Data

Carroll, John, 1736-1815
    John Carroll recovered : abstracts of letters and other documents not found in the John Carroll papers/Thomas W. Spalding
        p. cm.
    Includes bibliographical references.
    ISBN 1-885938-26-8
    1. Carroll, John, 1736-1815--Correspondence--Abstracts. 2. Catholic Church--United States. I. Spalding, Thomas W. II. Title.

Published in 2000 by

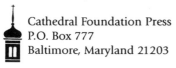

Cathedral Foundation Press
P.O. Box 777
Baltimore, Maryland 21203

Publisher: Daniel L. Medinger
Assistant Manager: Patti Medinger
Book design: Kimberly Hefner and Karen Pellegrini
Cover design: Karen Pellegrini
Printed by: Catholic Printing Services

CONTENTS

Illustrations / xiii
Preface and Acknowledgments / xv
Chronology of the Life of John Carroll / xix
A Carroll–Darnall Genealogy / xxv
Abbreviations / xxvii
Introduction / xxix

ABSTRACTS

APPENDICES

ILLUSTRATIONS

Portfolio III: Later Years . . . . Following page 188

PREFACE AND ACKNOWLEDGMENTS

John Carroll (1736-1815) is without doubt the most significant prelate in the history of the Catholic Church in the United States. The first bishop and archbishop of the American hierarchy, he provided a model, an ideal, for all the mitered leaders who followed. His was a groundbreaking role, no less than that of adjusting an ancient faith to a new configuration of secular and civic societies and institutions. As did George Washington in the secular sphere, Carroll addressed his task with a deftness and serenity that laid as solid a foundation for his church as Washington had for the nation. But for Carroll there was no retirement. Until the day he died, more than twenty-five years after he was raised to the episcopacy, he faced a succession of problems and crises that would have broken the health and spirit of almost any other man. His death caused an outpouring of genuine grief on the part of Catholic and non-Catholic alike.

The papers of most great men are eventually published. In the bicentennial year (1976) three volumes of *The John Carroll Papers*, edited by Thomas O'Brien Hanley, S.J., were published by the University of Notre Dame Press. Although a serious effort had been made to discover everything that Carroll wrote—his letters, essays, notations, sermons—such were his far-ranging activities and many contacts that a considerable number of writings were missed, enough, in fact, to fill a fourth volume. The degree to which their content may alter the contours of Carroll's life as depicted by competent biographers suggests the importance of the present effort to abstract these missing items.

First and foremost among those who have helped the compiler-abstracter-editor in his tasks of ferreting out Carroll writings and identifying the people mentioned in them is the Reverend Paul K. Thomas, archivist of the Archives of the Archdiocese of Baltimore. Without his assistance, which has gone far beyond the obligations of an archivist, the present work could not have been done.

The abstracter's negligible command of the Latin language has also placed him in the debt of the Reverend John W. Bowen, S.S., an excellent Latinist, who, without hesitation, agreed to translate the many Latin letters and other documents Carroll composed, often in almost unintelligible drafts. Father Bowen has also on numerous occasions responded to requests for identifications, for explanations of arcane facts, or for copies of documents in the Sulpician Archives of Baltimore.

In his less than perfect command of French and Italian the abstracter has also had to rely on Brother George Willenbrink, C.F.X., confrere, and on Monsignor Robert F. Trisco, former mentor. Both have offered remarkable renditions of almost indecipherable French and Italian letters. The former has also translated two Latin letters.

The present writer is also grateful to the faculty and staff of Spalding University, Louisville, Kentucky, for their unfailing encouragement and support in this as well as in his earlier writing projects. As professor emeritus he is still entitled to such indispensable benefits as interlibrary loans and copying services, which activities keep him in frequent contact with friends of long standing.

In his search for Carroll letters in the Archives of the Congregation of the Propaganda Fide he is indebted to the archivist, Dr. Wendy Schlereth, and staff, especially Sharon Sumpter and Charles Lamb, of the University of Notre Dame Archives, where can be found on microfilm all of the items described in the First Series of the *United States Documents in the Propaganda Fide Archives: A Calendar* (seven volumes edited by Finbar Kenneally, O.F.M., and published in Washington, D.C., by the Academy of American Franciscan History, 1966-1977). He is grateful for the help of Dr. R. Scott Appleby, director of the Cushwa Center for the Study of American Catholicism at the University of Notre Dame, and his assistant, Barbara Lockwood. He is also grateful for the hospitality of the Holy Cross priests and brothers at Corby Hall during his visits to the University of Notre Dame.

His gratitude extends also to Jon K. Reynolds, former archivist of Georgetown University, and Lynn Conway, his successor. He is thankful also to Rev. Hugh Fenning, O.P., of St. Mary's Dominican Priory, Dublin, for important letters from the Dominican archives in Rome and the diocese of Cloyne, Ireland, and for information supplied.

To the librarians of various collections he must likewise acknowledge his gratitude, especially to those of the Maryland Historical Society and Pratt Library in Baltimore and Maryland State Archives in Annapolis, Maryland. Father Paul Thomas has made even greater demands on these Maryland institutions.

Sisters Regina Bechtle, S.C., and Rita King, S.C., of Mount St. Vincent-on-Hudson, New York, as well as Sister Betty Ann McNeil, D.C., of St. Joseph's Provincial House, Emmitsburg, Maryland, have helped with Carroll's letters to St. Elizabeth Ann Seton in a number of ways.

The present writer is grateful likewise to Reverend Paul K. Thomas, Reverend John W. Bowen, S.S., and Dr. Christopher J. Kauffman for their willingness to peruse the manuscript before publication, not for the purpose of identifying all errors of fact or citation, for which the writer assumes full responsibility, but for the valuable suggestions they have made with regard to content and style.

He commends the patience of his computer consultant, Bryant Spalding. He thanks Mrs. Eleanor Darcy, formerly of the Maryland Historical Society, Brother Declan Kane, C.F.X., and Louis M. Mercorella for their help and many kindnesses and Brother Frank Mazsick, C.F.X., for his encouragement.

And finally he is grateful to Daniel L. and Patti Medinger of the Cathedral Foundation Press as well as Karen Pellegrini and Kimberly Hefner for their contributions to the publication of this work.

Thomas W. Spalding, C.F.X.
Spalding University
Louisville, Kentucky

CHRONOLOGY OF THE LIFE OF JOHN CARROLL

1736, 8 (or 19) Jan.	Born at Upper Marlboro, Maryland[1]
1747 or 1748	Entered Bohemia Academy, Cecil County, Maryland
1748, August	Enrolled at St. Omer's College, Flanders
1753, 8 Sept.	Entered the Jesuit novitiate, Watten, Flanders
1755, 8 Sept.	Pronounced first vows
1755-1758	Studied philosophy at the English College of Liège, the Jesuit scholasticate
1756, 12 Mar.	Received tonsure and minor orders
1758-1762	Studied theology at the English College of Liège
1760, 26 Oct.	Ordained subdeacon by Peter Louis Jacquet, titular bishop of Hippo and auxiliary to the bishop of Liège
1760, 20 Dec.	Ordained deacon by Bishop Jacquet
1761, 14 Feb.	Ordained priest by Bishop Jacquet
1762-1764	Taught philosophy at the English College of Liège
1764-1767	Taught theology at the English College of Liège
1767-1770	Taught humanities at the Jesuit College of Bruges
1770-1771	Made his tertianship at Ghent
1771, 2 Feb.	Pronounced final vows as a Jesuit
1771-1773	Continental tour as mentor of Charles-Philippe, the son of Charles, Lord Stourton

---

[1]*For the early dates see Thomas W. Spalding, "John Carroll: Corrigenda and Addenda,"* Catholic Historical Review 71 (1985): 505-18.

1772	Arrived at the Jesuit College of Nobles in Bologna, where he remained a few months
1772, 22 Oct.	Arrived in Rome
1773, Mar.	Left Rome for Liège
1773, 21 July	Ceased to be a Jesuit with the papal suppression of the Society of Jesus
1773, 14 Oct.	Arrested at the Jesuit College in Bruges
1773-1774	Chaplain for Henry, Lord Arundel at Wardour Castle
1774, 26 June	Arrived in Virginia, where he visited his sisters Eleanor and Anne and their families
1774-1786	Resided with his mother at Rock Creek, Maryland, where he established a parish and exercised a local ministry
1776, ca. 27 Mar.	Left Philadelphia with Benjamin Franklin, Charles Carroll of Carrollton, and Samuel Chase for a fruitless visit to Canada
1776, 31 May	Arrived at Philadelphia with the ailing Franklin
1783, 27 June	Met at White Marsh, Prince George's County, Maryland, with former Jesuits whom he had summoned to consider some form of government for all former Jesuits in America
1784, 9 June	Appointed superior of the American Mission by the pope (at the recommendation of Benjamin Franklin)
1784, Fall	Published at Annapolis *An Address to the Roman Catholics of the United States of America*, the first work by a Catholic author published in the United States

1784, 11 Oct.	Met at White Marsh with former Jesuits, where his plan of organization was adopted
1785	Headed the list of canvassers for the founding of St. John's College, Annapolis (see Appendix 4 for non-denominational institutions in which Carroll had a prominent role)
1785, 27 Feb.	Accepted the superiorship of the American Mission in a letter to Cardinal Leonardo Antonelli
1785, 1 Mar.	Report to Cardinal Antonelli on the church in America
1785, June	Received an honorary degree from Washington College of Chestertown, the first college in Maryland, of which he was a member of the board of visitors
1785, Oct.	Began the administration of Confirmation at Philadelphia and New York City and in New Jersey
1786, (Dec. ?)	Published his "Proposal" for the founding of Georgetown Academy (College)
1787, Oct.	Insulted by Rev. Andrew Nugent in St. Peter's Church, New York, whom he suspended
1788, Apr.	Supervised the beginning of the first building at Georgetown College
1789, 12 May	Elected to the board of visitors of St. John's College, Annapolis
1789, 18 May	Elected by fellow priests as bishop of Baltimore
1789, 14 Sept.	Election as bishop confirmed by the pope

1789, 6 Nov.	Named bishop of Baltimore by the brief *Ex hac apostolicae*
1790, 15 Aug.	Ordained bishop by Bishop Charles Walmesley, vicar apostolic of the Western District of England, at Lulworth Castle, Dorset, England
1791, Summer	Visited Boston, where he enjoyed the hospitality of John Hancock
1791, 6 Sept.	Assured the Native Americans (Indians) of Maine of his attention to their spiritual needs
1791, 7-10 Nov.	Conducted his only synod
1792, 22 Sept.	Performed the first ordination rites as bishop (see Appendix 2)
1793, 25 May	Performed his first ordination to the priesthood of Stephen Theodore Badin
1795, Dec.	Founded the Library Company of Baltimore (see Appendix 4 for civic organizations of which Carroll was a principal founder)
1795, 29 Dec.	Elected president of the newly incorporated board of trustees of the cathedral congregation
1797, 1 Feb.	Excommunicated Rev. John Goetz and Rev. William Elling of Holy Trinity Church, Philadelphia
1797, Mar.	Arrested by actions of trustees of Holy Trinity Church and humiliated in court
1798-1801	A principal founder of the Female Humane Association in Baltimore
1800	A founder of the Maryland Society for the Promotion of Useful Knowledge
1800, 7 Dec.	Ordained Leonard Neale to the episcopacy as Bishop of Gortyna and coadjutor-bishop of Baltimore

1802	A founder of the Humane Impartial Society for the relief of indigent women and of the Baltimore General Dispensary
1802, Jan.	Ended the long and demoralizing schism at Holy Trinity in Philadelphia
1803	Elected president of the board of trustees of Baltimore College
1803, 29 Sept.	Consecrated Holy Cross Church in Boston
1803, ca. 20 Oct.	Visited Maine (then part of Massachusetts)
1803, 24 Dec.	Joined in marriage Jerome Bonaparte and Elizabeth Patterson
1804, 10 Mar.	Given by the Holy See the administration of the Danish West Indies, St. Eustace, the Barbadoes, St. Kitts, Antigua, and all nearby islands not under a bishop
1805, 21 June	Named Rev. Robert Molyneux superior of the restored Society of Jesus in Maryland
1805, 20 Sept.	Given by the Holy See administration of the Louisiana Territory
1806, 25 May	Confirmed Mrs. Elizabeth Ann Seton in New York
1806, 7 July	Laid cornerstone of the Cathedral of the Assumption
1808, 8 Apr.	Named archbishop of Baltimore
1808, 16 June	Dedicated St. Mary's Chapel and welcomed Elizabeth Ann Seton to Baltimore
1810, 28 Oct.	Ordained Michael Egan, O.F.M., to the episcopacy as bishop of Philadelphia

1810, 1 Nov.	Ordained John Cheverus to the episcopacy as bishop of Boston
1810, 4 Nov.	Ordained Benedict Joseph Flaget, S.S., to the episcopacy as bishop of Bardstown, Kentucky
1810, 15 Dec.	With his suffragan bishops adopted articles of discipline for the province
1810, 17 Dec.	Sent letter and report for himself, his coadjutor, and his suffragan bishops to the pope
1811, 18 Aug.	Received the pallium from Bishop Neale
1812, 18 Aug.	Appointed Rev. Louis William DuBourg, S.S., apostolic administrator of Louisiana
1813, ca. 24 Aug.	Issued letter to all Catholics of the archdiocese to observe day of prayer requested by the president for peace
1815, 19 Jan.	Resigned as president of the Library Company of Baltimore
1815, 10 Oct.	Addressed his last report to the Congregation of the Propaganda Fide
1815, 22 Nov.	Drew his will
1815, 23 Nov.	Received the last rites from Rev. Enoch Fenwick, S.J.
1815, 3 Dec.	Died at the rectory of St. Peter's in Baltimore
1815, 5 Dec.	Buried (temporarily) in the chapel of St. Mary's Seminary

A CARROLL-DARNALL GENEALOGY

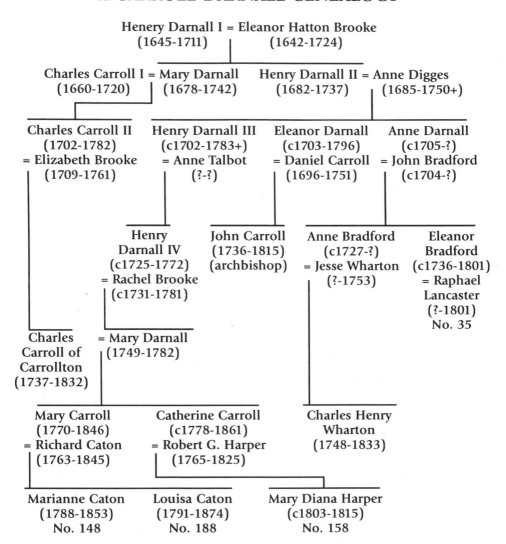

Henery Darnall I = Eleanor Hatton Brooke
(1645-1711) | (1642-1724)

Charles Carroll I = Mary Darnall   Henry Darnall II = Anne Digges
(1660-1720) | (1678-1742)   (1682-1737) | (1685-1750+)

Charles Carroll II   Henry Darnall III   Eleanor Darnall   Anne Darnall
(1702-1782)   (c1702-1783+)   (c1703-1796)   (c1705-?)
= Elizabeth Brooke   = Anne Talbot   = Daniel Carroll   = John Bradford
(1709-1761)   (?-?)   (1696-1751)   (c1704-?)

Henry   John Carroll   Anne Bradford   Eleanor
Darnall IV   (1736-1815)   (c1727-?)   Bradford
(c1725-1772)   (archbishop)   = Jesse Wharton   (c1736-1801)
= Rachel Brooke   (?-1753)   = Raphael
(c1731-1781)   Lancaster
(?-1801)
No. 35

Charles   = Mary Darnall
Carroll of   (1749-1782)
Carrollton
(1737-1832)

Mary Carroll   Catherine Carroll   Charles Henry
(1770-1846)   (c1778-1861)   Wharton
= Richard Caton   = Robert G. Harper   (1748-1833)
(1763-1845)   (1765-1825)

Marianne Caton   Louisa Caton   Mary Diana Harper
(1788-1853)   (1791-1874)   (c1803-1815)
No. 148   No. 188   No. 158

This modified genealogical chart indicates the degree of kinship of Archbishop John Carroll through the Darnalls with the family of Charles Carroll of Carrollton. (The relationship with the latter on the paternal side is unknown.) It identifies the cousins mentioned in Abstracts Nos. 35, 148, 158, and 188. It also shows the exact relationship, unknown to the Archbishop's earlier biographers, between Carroll and Charles Henry Wharton, a former Jesuit and convert to the Episcopal church, whose published apologia prompted Carroll's most ambitious literary effort.

ABBREVIATIONS

AAB	Archives of the Archdiocese of Baltimore
APF	Archives of the Congregation of the Propaganda Fide[1]
AMSV	Archives of Mount St. Vincent (Sisters of Charity)
HLC/MHS	Outerbridge Horsey Collection of Lee, Horsey, and Carroll Family Papers, MS 1974, Manuscripts Department, Maryland Historical Society Library
JCP	*The John Carroll Papers*, ed. by Thomas O'Brien Hanley, S.J. (Notre Dame, Ind.: University of Notre Dame Press, 1976)
Lemcke	Peter Henry Lemcke, O.S.B., *Life and Work of Prince Demetrius Augustine Gallitzin*, trans. Joseph C. Plumpe (New York: Longmans, Green, 1940)
Letterbook 3	Carroll's third letterbook in the Carroll Papers of the Archives of the Archdiocese of Baltimore
MPA	Maryland Province Archives of the Society of Jesus in the Georgetown University Special Collections
SAB	Sulpician Archives of Baltimore

---

[1]*For the various divisions of the Propaganda Fide archives see Introduction to Finbar Kenneally, O.F.M.*, United States Documents in the Propaganda Fide Archives: A Calendar *(Washington, D.C.: Academy of American Franciscan History, 1966), vol. 1, pp. xi-xvi. These documents were read on microfilm at the University of Notre Dame Archives.*

INTRODUCTION

I should say at the outset that the following abstracts are not the result of a determination to produce an exhaustive corpus of letters and other documents composed by John Carroll that are not found in the published *John Carroll Papers* (*JCP*). Such an attempt would demand still another piece-by-piece examination of every item in the extensive Carroll Papers in the Archives of the Archdiocese of Baltimore such as I did in my research for *The Premier See: A History of the Archdiocese of Baltimore, 1789-1989* (Baltimore: Johns Hopkins University Press, 1989). It would require also tedious and probably fruitless inquiries addressed to innumerable manuscript collections in North America and Europe. I surmise, nevertheless, that the documents here abstracted represent most (close to all) of the writings missed by the initial committee and the editor who were involved in the publication of the *JCP*.

The *JCP* had its inception in the annual meeting in 1951 of the Executive Council of the American Catholic Historical Association, which authorized the creation of the Committee on the John Carroll Papers consisting of Rev. (Monsignor in 1955) John Tracy Ellis, Rev. Henry J. Browne, Mrs. Annabelle M. Melville, and Rev. Charles H. Metzger, S.J. Ellis would be replaced by William D. Hoyt Jr., who became chairman of the committee. With no financial assistance the committee would spend some two years or more collecting, transcribing, translating, and editing, but the work soon languished. In 1969 the Raskob Foundation, through the instrumentality of Monsignor Ellis, supplied the funds for a full-time editor, Thomas O'Brien Hanley, S.J. To him the work of the committee was turned over.

"At this last phase," the editor wrote, "it was possible to enlarge the original program, which had anticipated publishing only the more important letters of Carroll. A new search was made for manuscripts in all categories and materials prepared for their publication" (*JCP*, 1: xxix). While inquiries were made of a number of repositories, the results left much to be desired. Even in the Archives of the Archdiocese of Baltimore, the Archives of the Propaganda Fide, and the Maryland Province Archives of the Society of Jesus many Carroll letters remained untouched. This may have been a result of the editor's assumption that the committee had thoroughly traversed these important terrains.

For two years and more Father Hanley and a succession of graduate students transcribed, collated, and edited the papers. No publisher could be found, however, until the Bishops' Committee on the Bicentennial was created by the National Conference of Catholic Bishops. With its support and the numerous benefactions it encouraged *The John Carroll Papers* was published by the University of Notre Dame Press in the year of the American Bicentennial.

The *JCP* has enabled scholars to push well beyond the data supplied by the principal biographers, namely, John Gilmary Shea, Peter Guilday, and Annabelle M. Melville.[1] Quite early, however, its deficiencies were noted.[2] In my own research for the era of John Carroll in *The Premier See*, which research I began not long after the appearance of the *JCP*, I frequently jotted down items not found in the three volumes but without any intention of compiling an all-inclusive list. From time to time after the completion of my work I would come across other Carroll letters quoted or cited that did not appear in the *JCP*. My conviction grew that the body of writings missed would be impressive and would touch facets of Carroll's life unremarked by his principal biographers.

---

[1]*John Gilmary Shea,* Life and Times of the Most Rev. John Carroll, Bishop and First Archbishop of Baltimore *(New York: John G. Shea, 1888); Peter Guilday,* The Life and Times of John Carroll, Archbishop of Baltimore (1735-1815) *(New York: The Encyclopedia Press, 1922); Annabelle M. Melville,* John Carroll of Baltimore: Founder of the American Catholic Hierarchy *(New York: Charles Scribner's Sons, 1955).*

[2]*For two unfavorable reviews of the work see those of John J. Tierney, former archivist of the Archives of the Archdiocese of Baltimore, "Another View of the John Carroll Papers" in the* Catholic Historical Review *64 (1978): 660-70, and my own in the* Maryland Historical Magazine *76 (1981): 296-98.*

The most serious omissions collectively were the letters in a letterbook, Carroll's third, which he filled from 1799 until shortly before his death in 1815. It contains 113 letters or notations, of which 40 appear in the *JCP* in the form of inadequate "transcripts" (actually extracts) culled from the letterbook by John Gilmary Shea, and 48 of them not at all. (The inadequacy of the Shea "transcripts" may be judged by a comparison of the abstracts that follow with the entries in the *JCP* for which the "transcripts" are the source.) Scattered throughout the Archives of the Archdiocese of Baltimore were also some twenty-seven other letters or notations.

When I finally decided to undertake the task of gathering all the Carroll writings I could find that were not in the *JCP*, I discovered some thirty in the Archives of the Congregation of the Propaganda Fide, ten in the Maryland Province Archives of the Society of Jesus, and five in family papers in the Maryland Historical Society, all of which collections had ostensibly been searched by the committee or the editor. Twelve important letters to Mother Seton were volunteered by the Sisters of Charity of Mount St. Vincent-on-Hudson from their archives. Many letters were found in published works, for example, five in Peter Henry Lemcke's *Life and Work of Prince Demetrius Augustine Gallitzin* (New York: Longmans, Green, 1940). And so it went.

Prompted largely by an unbounded admiration for John Carroll, I decided to make a place in my cluttered life for the composition of abstracts of the letters, notations, petitions, and other writings (except sermons) not found in the *JCP*. I decided also to do a number of appendices suggested by these writings and by other types of documents, such as sacramental records, ordination records, records of societies in which Carroll played a leading role, and land records, all largely ignored by his biographers.

Although I once entertained the possibility of reproducing the documents in full, this prospect I soon discarded in favor of abstracts largely because of the editorial problems that literal transcriptions would entail for one whose time constraints were narrow and inexperience in the publication of historical papers broad. At the same time I should note that I have tried to include in the abstracts all detail that could be significant. Some of the shorter abstracts, in fact, are longer than the documents themselves because of the need to change the simple pronouns I and you to Carroll and the name of the person addressed.

As a result of this effort my perception of John Carroll has changed appreciably in a number of ways. I came to admire the equanimity he brought to the crises that arose in his career, his ability to endure humiliations and rebuffs, the patience and forbearance displayed in the face of outrageous provocations. Among the offenders who find a place in the abstracts are the Revs. Andrew Nugent, Claude de la Poterie, John Ashton, John Nepomucene Goetz, William Elling, Frederic Cesarius Reuter, and Mr. James Oellers.

I came to admire Carroll's diplomacy, not artful but marked by civility and kindness, a diplomacy calculated to disarm the most refractory and win the wavering. It was a diplomacy that was flexible. The unfortunate consequences of the strong measures he took against the schismatics of Holy Trinity Church in Philadelphia led to a change of tactics, in which he would write the priest he had excommunicated some four years before, William Elling, that he "must use the privilege of an old friend" in the advice he offered (No. 63). This soft-line approach brought an end to the protracted and painful schism. At the same time he stood firm in upholding episcopal authority, as best seen in this schism and in his handling of pastor and trustees in Charleston, South Carolina, and his own see city in the case of the German congregation.

Perhaps the most telling example of his diplomacy was his relationship with Rev. Simon Felix Gallagher, the seemingly incorrigible alcoholic he had sent unwittingly to Charleston, South Carolina. If we are to believe Guilday,

Charleston became a "hot-bed of rebellion against authority in the last years of Carroll's episcopate," the scene of a "schism" and "independent church" that lasted from 1803 till the end of Carroll's life."[1] Melville concurs, insisting that Gallagher "remained insubordinate and troublesome to the end."[2] Such was far from the case, as the many letters to Gallagher not found in the *JCP* but abstracted below attest.[3] Although Carroll was never able to dislodge Gallagher from Charleston, the letters he wrote to him in his latter years show a genuine concern for the priest, whose inebriety was at least moderated. That the concern was not feigned is made clear in a letter to Dr. Edward Lynah of Charleston (No. 92). Although the Catholic community of Charleston remained sadly divided, as long as Carroll lived the cleavage never crossed the line into schism.

While Carroll's warm friendship with the Barrys of Washington is well rehearsed, especially by Melville, his equally affectionate friendship with the Marsan sisters, formerly of Baltimore but later of Charleston (Nos. 121, 126, 154, 196), as well as other families, such as the Lynah family of Charleston, find no place in his biographies. Carroll evidenced a genuine concern for the well-being of women, to many of whom he would ask to be remembered fondly in letters to others (see, for example, No. 157). Carroll lavished a special attention on young people, particularly Daniel Brent, his favorite nephew (Nos. 19, 95), and Archibald Lee, his godson (No. 133).

Carroll's ready response to those who appealed to him in times of anxiety or distress is repeatedly demonstrated. Of special concern to him was the plight of Madam

---

[1]*Guilday*, Carroll, *pp. 737-38.*

[2]*Melville*, Carroll, *p. 213.*

[3]*Carroll's earlier letters concerning Gallagher's drunkenness and insubordination were used by Archbishops Leonard Neale and Ambrose Maréchal against Gallagher (see No. 78), but his later ones praising Gallagher (Nos. 121, 126, 127, 154, 174, 175, 184) would be carried to Rome in Gallagher's defense after Carroll's death.*

Genevieve Saladin (Nos. 110, 125). His concern for others is perhaps best exemplified in the trust deeds he negotiated for their benefit, which are enumerated in Appendix 5, and in his willingness to assume the burden of caring for a troubled young man, shown in Appendix 6.

Carroll's cordial relationship with the clergy of other denominations is clearly manifest in his frank but friendly letter to Bishop James Madison of Virginia (No. 24). At the same time in a mildly facetious letter to the *Federal Gazette* he displays a moral theology at odds with Baltimore's evangelicals' (No. 141).

Two letters to Thomas Sim Lee reveal, to a greater degree than recognized before, Carroll's willingness to play a behind-the-scenes role in Maryland politics (Nos. 21, 23). Carroll's many letters to the London bankers Messrs. Wright and Company, which Shea ignored entirely in his culling of the third letterbook, give ample evidence of Carroll as a consummate businessman, careful, demanding, and conscientious (Nos. 40, 53, 70, 74, 93, 102, 106, 132, 134, 143, 146, 147, 160, 163, 191, 192). Carroll the businessman, in fact, fails to make an appearance in any of the biographies that limn his remarkable life.

While the responsibilities of creating a new church are often recognized by his biographers, the anguish that such a role often produced is seldom, if ever, a matter of note. Such an anguished moment occurred when he was called upon by Rome to recommend new sees and the persons to fill them. Carroll had little trouble in a letter he began in late 1806 in proposing the seats for new dioceses, but in the process of naming possible candidates, he was overwhelmed by uncertainty (No. 111). He sent his suggestions for new sees at that time but waited seven months before he could bring himself to send the names of priests he deemed worthy to fill them (No. 118).

Carroll handled problem priests admirably. As suggested in his dealings with the Philadelphia schismatics, however, he was occasionally tormented by the course of action he should pursue in dealing with the most notorious. Such a one was the Rev. Antonio de Sedella, or Père Antoine, of New Orleans. In her well-drawn account of Carroll's superintendence of Louisiana,[1] Melville fails to note Carroll's indecision concerning Sedella, undoubtedly because she had not seen a draft in his third letterbook, which Shea himself failed to extract (No. 120). Carroll began a letter to the dissident pastor in which he accused him of insubordination. He then proceeded to threaten him with excommunication and his parish with interdiction if he refused to obey the priest he had named administrator. He crossed out the threat in the draft, however, and probably never sent the letter at all. The memory of the unhappy Philadelphia schism may have been still too vivid.

Carroll's willingness to sacrifice ease for the service of others, a sacrifice ignored by his biographers, is seen in his refusal to employ a priest to help alleviate what he called "that insuperable antipathy to the labours of the desk" (No. 196), at which he spent long hours, because it would deprive one or more congregations of a priest (see also Nos. 126 and 135).

There are a number of other aspects of Carroll's life that were unexplored and therefore unremarked by his biographers: the extent of his pastoral ministry as revealed by the sacramental records of the procathedral; the frequency of the ordinations he performed and the character of the men ordained as revealed in the register of ordinations he kept; his possession of slaves and his attitude toward slavery as revealed in his letters and the ledger of the estate that constituted his *mensa*; the leading role he played in the foundation and operation of charitable and cultural societies as revealed in their constitutions, by-laws, and published statements; and the place in his life of the enigmatic James Du Moulin. All of these will be treated in appendices.

---

[1] *"John Carroll and Louisiana,"* Catholic Historical Review *64 (1978): 398-440.*

The above does not exhaust the many ways the contents of the missing documents and unexplored records would warrant a revision of the life of John Carroll, but they are sufficient, I believe, to suggest that whole story is yet to be told.

In the abstracts I have kept to the usage of Carroll's time by the designation of priests as "Mr." or "Rev. Mr." Rarely was the title "Father" used, even for religious priests. The correct spellings of people's names are given even though Carroll himself occasionally misspelled them. (Douglass he always spelled Douglas, for example, and Kohlmann, Kolhman.) Bracketed dates indicate either conjecture or, when specific, the date of the document on which Carroll's extract or notation appears. A bracketed question mark after a name indicates that the person can not be identified. Individuals are generally identified only once and usually by a footnote. Where this occurs is shown by bold numbers in the index. A distinction is made between "indecipherable," where the letters can, for the most part, be read but make no sense, and "illegible," where the writing is in some way obliterated.

ABSTRACTS OF LETTERS AND OTHER DOCUMENTS

1. TO CARDINAL LEONARDO ANTONELLI, Maryland, 1 March 1785

This request directed to the cardinal prefect of the Congregation of the Propaganda Fide[1] for faculties to dispense accompanied Carroll's only extensive report to Rome on the church under his care (see JCP, 1: 179-85).

> Carroll requests faculties to dispense in three matrimonial cases involving consanguinity, including that of Henry Spalding to his niece Mary Spalding.[2]

APF, America Centrale, 2: 458rv.

---

[1] *The Sacra Congregazione de Propaganda Fide was created in 1622 to oversee the work of the church in missionary lands, which the United States was considered until 1908.*

[2] *Henry Spalding (d. 1799) had some years before married Mary Ann, daughter of his older brother Thomas. In his report Carroll explained that to prevent marriages with Protestants in the colonial period dispensations had been granted as far as was allowed between blood relations (JCP, 1: 181-82).*

2. PROPOSALS FOR ESTABLISHING AN ACADEMY, AT GEORGE-TOWN, PATOMACK-RIVER, MARYLAND, [Dec.? 1786]

There can be little doubt that Carroll was the author of the "Proposals" for establishing what would become Georgetown University. On 12 January 1787 he wrote Cardinal Antonelli, "My plans [for an academy] have partly taken shape after consultation with my associates" (JCP, 1: 236).

The "Seminary" will be superintended by those having experience in similar institutions, who will see to the cultivation of virtue and to literary improvement. It will receive students who have learned the first elements of letters and conduct them through the several branches of classical learning to that stage where they may enter the university of this or neighboring states. It will receive students of every religious profession, who will be free to worship wherever they wish. The location has many advantages. Tuition will be moderate and in a few years reduced even more. Such a plan deserves public encouragement. Subscriptions will be received by Charles Carroll of Carrollton, Henry Rozer, Notley Young, Robert Darnall, George Digges, Edmund Plowden, Joseph Millard, John Lancaster, Baker Brooke, Chandler Brent, Bernard O'Neill, Marsham Waring, John Darnall, Ignatius Wheeler, Joseph Mosley, John Blake, Francis Hall, Charles Blake, William Matthews, John Tuite, all of Maryland; George Mead, Thomas Fitzsimmons, Joseph Cauffman, Mark Wilcox, Thomas Lilly, all of Pennsylvania; Col. [John] Fitzgerald and George Brent in Virginia; and

Dominic Lynch in New York. Necessary information will be given by the directors of the undertaking: John Carroll, James Pellentz, Robert Molyneux, John Ashton, and Leonard Neale.

Robert Emmett Curran, *The Bicentennial History of Georgetown University: From Academy to University, 1789-1889, Volume I* (Washington, D.C.: Georgetown University Press, 1993), p. 1 (original broadside reproduced in full).

3. *TO ALL LIBERALLY INCLINED TO PROMOTE THE EDUCATION OF YOUTH*, Maryland, 30 March 1787

Carroll himself filled in the blanks (including date) of this printed form, of which he was doubtless the author.

The undersigned has "humbly requested" [written over "appointed"] Edward Weld Esq.[1] and Lady to receive donations for the purposes set forth in the "Proposals" [No. 2], for which they will give receipts and remit contributions to the undersigned. They are also "desired" [written over "authorized"] to appoint any other person to execute the same office. Signed "J. Carroll."

Curran, *Bicentennial History*, 2 (reproduced).

---

[1]*Son of Thomas Weld of Lulworth Castle and Carroll's former pupil, he died in 1796.*

4. TO ARCHBISHOP ANTONIO DUGNANI, Maryland, 28 July 1787

Carroll had been instructed by Archbishop Dugnani's predecessor as nuncio in Paris more than two years before to send a letter of introduction with the two students Carroll would chose to be educated in Rome for their journey through France (JCP, 1: 187).

Carroll had written Dugnani probably in February—but was not sure of the precise date as he was now far from his residence—that he would soon send to Rome two young Americans to be educated at the Urban College of the Propaganda.[1] Cardinal-prince [Giuseppe] Doria-Pamphili, Dugnani's predecessor as nuncio, had asked him to address to him an open letter to be shown to the bishop or ecclesiastical superior at the place of debarkation so that they might have recourse to him if need be. He is sending them on a vessel headed to Bordeaux. Though there were other ports more convenient for going to Rome, Carroll thought it best to confide them to a ship captain who was a good Catholic [James Fenwick] rather than entrust them to a stranger and a Protestant, who might treat them harshly or impair their morals. Though the Propaganda had offered to fund the voyage to France, Carroll had committed the parents to cover this expense. Dugnani will be informed of their arrival by the delivery of this letter by the archbishop of Bordeaux or one of

---

[1] *The Urban College was founded in 1627 to educate gratis gifted students from mission lands.*

his vicars. The boys would then follow the latter's arrangements for the rest of the trip. Their parents are good Catholics. The one from Maryland, Raphael Smith age fourteen, the other from Pennsylvania, Felix Dougherty age thirteen, both have talent, especially the latter.[1]

APF, America Centrale, 2: 501rv (a copy).

5. TO [REV. JOHN THORPE ?], Baltimore, 8 May 1788

An Italian translation of a letter that Carroll wrote probably to Rev. John Thorpe, his agent in Rome, a former Jesuit, which translation was made for the benefit of the Congregation of the Propaganda Fide.

Carroll reports on a priest from the diocese of Meath in Ireland, Patrick Smyth. He had received him kindly, but after his return to Ireland he had made disparaging remarks about Carroll and other priests. He has many connections in London and could disturb the peace of the church in the United States.

APF, Congregazioni Genenerali, 892: 532r-33r.

---

[1]*Smith and Dougherty would return in 1798 without having been ordained.*

6. "CHRONOLOGICAL EVENTS RELATIVE TO THE DIO-CESS OF BALTIMORE IN THE UNITED STATES OF AMERICA," [1789]

Carroll composed a chronicle of the pre-diocesan years probably at one sitting and probably with the intention of continuing it in a ledger that would become his official "Register of Ordinations."

An account of the beginnings of the Catholic Religion in Maryland and introduction into Pennsylvania is given in papers hastily drawn up but with attention to accuracy that will be attached to this manuscript, as the writer has no time to transcribe them.[1] They tell of the United States withdrawing from the spiritual authority of the Vicar Apostolic of the London District and of the appointment of a superior for their spiritual government by Pope Pius VI and the appearance of priests in other states. [Carroll then begins his chronicle of events since then.] 1783 Nov. Several priests of Maryland and one of Pennsylvania under Rev. John Lewis, their superior, wrote a letter to the pope explaining the new political situation in the United States and the impropriety of their subjection to an authority residing in England as well as the necessity of having a superior or prefect apostolic living within the States. The pope was asked to allow them to choose one of their own and to invest him with ample powers, especially that of administering Confirmation, which had never been done before. 1784 Nov. 26. Word received of the appoint-

---

[1] *The earlier account that Carroll mentions is found, incorrectly dated, in JCP, 1: 403-8.*

ment of the writer to exercise spiritual jurisdiction in the United States. 1785 Oct. Confirmation first administered at Philadelphia, then New York, the Jersies about Mount Hope and Haycock, and Nov. 1st Goshenhoppen, Pennsylvania. 1786. Confirmation continued through most of the counties of the Western Shore of Maryland. The want of priests began to be greatly felt about this time, many parts of the country asking for them. 1787. Catholics emigrated from some of the old States to Kentucky. In the fall their first pastor, Charles Whelan, a Capuchin, went to join them. 1788. The first Catholic priest, Matthew Ryan, sent to Charleston, South Carolina, to remain nearly a year. The same year [1789 crossed out] a letter was sent to the pope through the Congregation for the Propagation of the Faith saying that the time had come to have a bishop and an episcopal see in the United States and that it would be "highly expedient" to grant the clergy the right to choose their bishop. At the same time weighty reasons suggested the founding of an academy [seminary crossed out] under priests whose religious instruction and careful discipline could ensure that the morals of Catholic youth would be preserved "from the prevailing corruption of manners & false doctrine." It would also serve as a nursery for the ecclesiastical state. Georgetown was chosen as the best location.

SAB, Register of Ordinations, pp. 1-4.

7. TO [REV. JOHN THORPE ?], Baltimore, 31 January 1789

This is the first of five letters (see also Nos. 9, 11, 12, 13) Carroll wrote about a troublesome priest in Boston probably to his agent in Rome, Rev. John Thorpe, who translated them into Italian for the benefit of the Congregation of the Propaganda Fide.

While Boston awaited the arrival of Mr. John Thayer[1] from France, a French priest, the Abbé [Claude] de la Poterie, began to minister there. He came with a French squadron. He wrote Carroll to allow him to give spiritual aid to the Catholics of Boston, who rejoicing at the hope of a permanent priest, made similar requests for the necessary faculties. These Carroll sent for a limited time. Poterie was recommended by good people known to Carroll, and his letters breathed zeal and goodness. Carroll fears that he may go to excess in the former. Poterie says he has lived in Rome two years and knows important people there, especially Cardinal York.[2]

APF, America Centrale, 3: 121r.

---

[1]*Rev. John Thayer, a former Congregational minister of Boston whose conversion to the Catholic Church in Rome created a stir, entered the Sulpician Seminary in Paris and was ordained a priest in 1787.*

[2]*Henry Benedict Stuart, Duke of York, was last of the Stuart heirs to the throne of Great Britain.*

8. TO ARCHBISHOP ANTONIO DUGNANI, Maryland, 23 February 1789

Carroll wrote again to the nuncio in Paris, responding to a letter sent some nine months before.[1]

Carroll received on 28 January the nuncio's letter of 27 May 1788 and attributes the delay to the suspension of the packet boat of the [indecipherable] due to the meddling of Mr. Jefferson.[2] If the nuncio can not send his letters to Carroll immediately, he asks that they be sent to Mr. [Joseph] Fenwick,[3] an American merchant at Bordeaux. The scandal in New York mentioned in Carroll's last letter [see *JCP*, 1: 278] was caused by a sacrilegious priest [Andrew Nugent], who after suspension for his crimes took forcible possession of the church with a band of ignorant people but was soon after excluded himself. Carroll appreciates all the nuncio is doing for the good of the church in America, which he hopes in time can compensate for the losses in Europe. The pope has just consented to the erection of a diocese and allowed the priests to name the first bishop to fill it. Although dated the past July, Cardinal Antonelli's letter announcing this was not received until 12 February. Plans are now being laid.

AAB, 8A-I-4 (inside letter of Dugnani to Carroll).

---

[1]*JCP, 1: 349, says letter of 23 February 1789 to Giuseppe Doria-Pamphili [sic] "Not found." Dugnani had replaced Doria-Pamphili in 1785.*

[2]*Thomas Jefferson was then American minister to France.*

[3]*Joseph Fenwick was then or later American consul in Bordeaux. He was the younger brother of Captain James Fenwick (see No. 4), John Ceslas Fenwick, O.P. (see No. 164, n. 2), and Colonel Ignatius Fenwick, father of Edward Dominic Fenwick, O.P. (see No. 105, n. 1).*

9. TO [REV. JOHN THORPE ?], Baltimore, 14 March 1789

This is the second of the letters Carroll sent probably to Rev. John Thorpe concerning Rev. Claude de la Poterie (see No. 7).

In his last Carroll praised too soon M. de la Poterie, to whom he had sent the usual faculties at the request of flattering letters from himself and others. Poterie hardly had them in hand before he published a letter in the form of a Lenten Pastoral in which, among other titles that filled half a sheet, he called himself Vicar Prefect Apostolic of the Catholic Church of Boston. And in the pastoral are things likely to make Americans laugh and other things outside his competence. In poor English he shows a great spirit of independence. What he has written of the charges against Mr. Thayer, who is expected daily, makes Carroll uneasy.

APF, America Centrale, 3: 121 rv.

10. TO [REV. JOHN THORPE ?], n.p., 25 May 1789

This is another Italian translation of a letter of Carroll to probably Rev. John Thorpe concerning Rev. Patrick Smyth (see No. 5).

Carroll speaks of a work published by Smyth, in which he and Rev. William O'Brien, O.P., are slandered.[1] He intends to do a rebuttal of

---

[1] *The work was entitled* The Present State of the Catholic Missions Conducted by the Ex-Jesuits in North America, *published in Dublin in 1788. It accused the former Jesuits of luxuriating on large estates while neglecting their poor parishioners, of abusing their slaves, and of other such calumnies.*

the work and perhaps publish it.[1]

APF, Congregazioni Generali, 892: 533r.

11. TO [REV. JOHN THORPE ?], Baltimore, 1 June 1789

This is the third of the letters Carroll wrote probably to Rev. John Thorpe concerning Rev. Claude de la Poterie (see No. 7).

Carroll admits that Poterie's early letters had charmed him. With an apostolic zeal he was concerned only with the welfare of others. With similar effusions of holiness he had also deceived the bishop of Quebec into recommending him. At first Carroll had attributed some extravagances to imprudence, but he came to see Poterie's conduct as dishonorable to a priest. He assigned Mr. O'Brien,[2] curate of New York, the task of investigating all, and finding no other remedy Carroll suspended him. Poterie then came to New York to find Carroll but swindled several people along the way. Finding out in time, Carroll took from him at least some of the things he had appropriated. It will not be easy for Mr. Thayer or anyone to undo the bad impression Poterie had left in Boston.

APF, America Centrale, 3: 121v-22r.

---

[1]*Carroll's rebuttal is in JCP, 1: 337-46. At the advice of Archbishop John Thomas Troy, O.P., of Dublin it was never published.*

[2]*William O'Brien, O.P., who was in Philadelphia as early as 1785, would be Carroll's principal agent in investigating and solving difficult problems, having acted in such a capacity in New York two years before.*

12. TO [REV. JOHN THORPE ?], n.p., 13 July [1789]

Fourth of the letters Carroll wrote concerning Rev. Claude de la Poterie.

This priest whom Carroll had suspended is now spreading the usual clamors against Carroll and others that under the pretext of promoting religion they were trying to establish the Society of Jesus[1] and similar calumnies. Skilled and tireless in his intrigues, he may try to influence the patrons he claims to have in Rome. "But no hypocrite has known better how to feign the style of a real apostle." His name is Claude Bouchard de la Poterie of the diocese of Angers,[2] about 35 years old, rather short but good-looking, not lacking in talent, and versed in ecclesiastical matters, especially the rites and ceremonies of the church. He had recently written Carroll an insolent and outrageous letter from New York.

APF, America Centrale, 3: 122r.

---

[1]*Poterie published in Philadelphia* The Resurrection of Laurent Ricci: or a True and Exact History of the Jesuits. *It was dedicated to "The new Laurent Ricci in America, the Rev. Fr. John Carroll, Superior of the Jesuits in the United States, also to the friar-inquisitor, William O'Brien." Lorenzo Ricci was the Jesuit general at the time of the suppression of the Society in 1773.*

[2]*In his next letter (No. 13) Carroll will say he was from the diocese of Blois.*

13. TO [REV. JOHN THORPE ?], n.p., 18 October 1789

Fifth of the letters Carroll wrote concerning Rev. Claude de la Poterie.

Carroll has received a testimonial from the vicar general of the diocese of Blois, from which Poterie comes. He confirms the impressions in America of an insinuating [illegible] and accomplished scoundrel. But he has not been seen in Boston for five months, a boon for religion in that city, where Mr. Thayer is expected soon.

APF, America Centrale, 3: 122v.

14. NOTATION FOR REV. MARMADUKE STONE, [16 August 1790]

Carroll outlined the principal points of his reply to a letter from Rev. Marmaduke Stone, president of the Liège Academy conducted by former Jesuits, dated 16 August 1790.

Speak to Mr. Strickland[1] about expenses and talents of Messrs. Delvaux and Erntzen.[2] Literary talents of Mr. Brosius.[3] Account of Maryland and office.[4] German affairs.[5] Carroll's own account. Mrs. [Katherine] Heneage.[6]

AAB, 7-V-1.

---

[1]*Rev. William Strickland was the financial agent of the former Jesuits.*

[2]*Nicholas Delvaux and Paul Erntzen, two recently ordained students at the Liège Academy who volunteered for America.*

[3]*Francis Xavier Brosius, another student at Liège Academy (see No. 15).*

[4]*Corporation of the Clergy and English Province Fund. See AAB, 8-A-5.*

[5]*Carroll may have been referring to an arrangement made to have Germans educated at the Liège Academy for the American missions and to two young Germans from Liège who arrived in England while he was there (JCP, 1: 466).*

[6]*Mrs. Heneage was the widowed mother of two children at the Liège Academy.*

15. TO REV. FRANCIS XAVIER BROSIUS, London, 14 September 1790

On a letter from Rev. F. X. Brosius dated Louvain 9 August 1790 and sent to Lulworth Castle, Carroll penned a notation in English and the draft of a response in Latin.

[Notation:] Answered September 14, London, 1790. Carroll can not send dispensation of age or an act of reception until Brosius is "excorporated" by his own bishop. He will send Brosius an act of reception into the Diocese of Baltimore on condition that his bishop allows it. He hopes to provide for his coming next spring.

[Draft:] "John, by the Grace of God, and the Apostolic See, Bishop of Baltimore, to Rev. F. X. Brosius, greetings."[1] Looking forward most seriously to the care of souls in the United States, Carroll embraces Brosius, assuming that the Most Reverend Bishop, in whose jurisdiction Brosius was born, will give him permission to transfer to his diocese. [A last sentence is illegible.]

AAB, 2-B-2.

---

[1]*This may have been the first time Carroll used this expression in his official correspondence after his ordination as bishop on 15 August.*

16. To [?], n.p., 15 September 1790

Carroll wrote from England to someone in the United States about an interview with the Sulpician Francis Charles Nagot.[1]

Providence seems to favor "our" views. As a consequence of correspondence between the nuncio in Paris [Dugnani], Mr. Emery,[2] and Carroll, Mr. Nagot, superior of the petit seminaire, came to England to see him. They agreed that two or three priests selected by Emery will come to Baltimore next spring. They have the means to buy ground for buildings, and, Carroll hopes, of endowing a seminary for young ecclesiastics. They will probably bring three or four seminarians with them who either are English or speak it. They will be amply provided with books, church furnishings, and professors of philosophy and divinity. Carroll intends to place them near his home at the cathedral so that they may be, as it were, the clergy of the church and contribute to the dignity of divine worship. This is an auspicious event for "our" diocese, but it is sad to think that "we" owe so great a blessing to the "lamentable catastrophe" in France.

[Daniel Brent], *Biographical Sketch of the Most Rev. John Carroll, First Archbishop of Baltimore, with Select Portions of his Writings*, ed. by John Carroll Brent (Baltimore: John Murphy, 1843), p. 125.

---

[1]*Francis Charles Nagot, S.S. (1734-1816), would become the first president of St. Mary's Seminary and superior of the Sulpicians in the United States.*

[2]*Jacques-André Emery, S.S. (1732-1811), was superior general of the Society of St. Sulpice from 1782 until his death.*

17. TO BISHOP CHARLES WALMESLEY, Baltimore, 22 March 1791

Seven months and a week after Bishop Charles Walmesley, O.S.B., Vicar Apostolic of the Western District of England, had raised him to the episcopacy Carroll wrote him a letter of esteem and congratulations.

Carroll congratulates Walmesley on the prospect of an end to the commotions that agitated English Catholics.[1] His many friends among them render him deeply interested in the outcome. He attributes much of the tranquility they are likely to enjoy to Walmesley's authority and pastoral solicitude. The prospects are due in some degree to the calamities in France. Mrs. [?] Plowden has written Carroll that Walmesley was well enough to perform the consecration of two new bishops in Advent at Lulworth.[2] "The chapel of that noble castle will be remembered in the future ecclesiastical history of the United States," as well as in that of England when the late events are recorded. Carroll wishes the bishop a long life.[3]

Catholic Historical Review 1 (1915): 253-54.

---

[1]*After a bitter dispute over a controversial loyalty oath that was waging when Carroll was in England, in which he carefully avoided taking sides, a Catholic Relief Act satisfactory to all won acceptance at this point and passed in June. Perhaps the best recent account of the controversy from the Cisalpine (lay Catholic) point of view is that of Mark Bence-Jones,* The Catholic Families *(London: Constable, 1992), pp. 66-74.*

[2]*William Gibson and John Douglass, vicars apostolic of the Northern District and the London District respectively.*

[3]*Vicar apostolic since 1756, Walmesley died in 1797.*

18. JOHN CARROLL'S PRAYER FOR CHURCH AND CIVIL AUTHORITIES, 10 November 1791

At the synod of 7-10 November 1791 this prayer composed by Carroll was adopted 10 November and prescribed to be said after the gospel on Sundays and feast days.

Carroll prays that the church, being spread throughout the world, may "continue with unchanging faith in the confession of Thy name." He prays that Pope N.N., Bishop N.N., and all bishops and pastors in the church be endowed with knowledge, zeal, and holiness. He prays that the administration of the president of the United States be conducted with righteousness in the encouragement of virtue, execution of the laws of justice, and the restraint of vice, and that Congress "shine forth" in its laws promoting peace, happiness, industry, and equal liberty. He prays that the governor, members of the Assembly, judges, magistrates, and other officers may discharge their duties with honesty and ability. He prays for all fellow citizens of the United States that they may be blessed in knowledge, sanctified in the observance of the laws, and preserved in union and peace. He prays for all who have gone before, particularly those lately deceased, and for benefactors of the church.

John Tracy Ellis, ed., *Documents of American Catholic History*, 3 vols. (Chicago: Henry Regnery, 1967), 1: 174-75.

19. TO MR. DANIEL BRENT, Baltimore, 22 January 1792

Carroll wrote his favorite nephew, then employed in the Treasury Department, in order to introduce a friend and to tell his nephew of family matters.[1]

Carroll wants his nephew to know Mr. Robert Walsh,[2] bearer of the letter, and one of Carroll's best friends in Baltimore. He is on business in Philadelphia, and Carroll wants his nephew to recommend him to Secretary [Alexander] Hamilton as a man capable of serving the secretary well. Carroll had left Rock Creek last Tuesday, where the serious illness of his mother had called him.[3] There he found also Daniel's mother, sister [Catherine Digges], and brothers George and Robert, all proud of Daniel's good conduct. Carroll is certain Daniel will continue in the same line of conduct but advises him to keep in close contact with Mr. Fleming.[4] Carroll believes Billy[5] will enter Georgetown Academy.

HLC/MHS.

---

[1]*Daniel Brent (c1770-1841) was the son of Robert Brent of Woodstock, Virginia, and Anne Carroll. In Chester Horton Brent,* The Descendants of Coll° Giles Brent, Cap¹ George Brent, and Robert Brent, ᴳᵉⁿᵗ, Immigrants to Maryland and Virginia *(Rutland, Vt.: The Author, 1946), p. 136, the nephew's name is given as Daniel Carroll Brent (hereafter Brent,* Descendants*). There is no documentary evidence, however, for the middle name. See also No. 95 below and Appendix 6.*

[2]*Robert Walsh (c1750-1831), a wealthy Baltimore merchant, was a trustee of the cathedral congregation from 1795 to 1805 and the future father-in-law of Daniel.*

[3]*Eleanor (Darnall) Carroll would live for four more years, dying in 1796 at the age of 92 according to her tombstone in the Carrolls' Chapel cemetery, St. John's Church, Rock Creek (Forest Glen).*

[4]*Rev. Francis Anthony Fleming, pastor of St. Mary's Church in Philadelphia and one of Carroll's vicar generals, would die the next year in an epidemic of yellow fever.*

[5]*William Brent (1775-1848), Daniel's youngest brother, attended Georgetown Academy (College) 1792-1796.*

20. TO THE CATHOLICS OF VINCENNES, KASKASKIA, AND CAHOKIA[1], Baltimore, 23 January 1792

On the same day he wrote Rev. Pierre Gibault at Vincennes (JCP, 1: 8) Carroll addressed also the people of these French-speaking villages of the Illinois Country.

Carroll tells his "very dear Brothers in Jesus Christ" that he learned with regret that the carrier of letters they had written him in response to his of December 1790 had been captured by the savages. He had written of learned and virtuous pastors destined to serve them but who were delayed by a total ban of emigration from France except for sailors and merchants.[2] He will do all in his power to see that they are never again abandoned. He thanks God that they are still attached to the faith of their fathers and to the Holy See, to which they profess with heart and mouth an inviolable fidelity, honoring their belief by the sanctity of their lives and observance of all the commandments.

AAB, 9-A-4.

---

[1]*Carroll spells these latter two Kaskaskias and Kaokias. JCP, 2: 10, says this letter is not found.*

[2]*Carroll is speaking of the Sulpicians, one of whom, Benedict Flaget, would be sent to Vincennes in 1792.*

21. TO MR. THOMAS SIM LEE,[1] Baltimore, 5 March 1792

Carroll wrote this close friend about an approaching election.

Carroll is happy to hear through Lee's servant that his family is in good health despite a severe winter and embraces the opportunity to tell him that some gentlemen the past week had asked him to prevail upon Lee to allow them to promote his candidacy for governor. Mr. Campbell[2] had first mentioned it, but Col. Samuel Smith[3] pledged not only his vote but all his efforts in Lee's favor. Smith was active and decided and his influence considerable. It would be "very pleasing" to Carroll to see Lee again at the head of the government especially as there seems to be some intention of extending the powers of the governor, but only if the prospect is agreeable to him. It would place him closer to all his friends.

HLC/MHS.

---

[1]*Thomas Sim Lee (1745-1819) had served as governor of Maryland from 1779 to 1783 and had become a Catholic, probably through Carroll's influence, in 1788. He was a first cousin of Patrick Sim, who married Carroll's niece.*

[2]*Archibald Campbell (c1747-1805), a prominent Baltimore businessman.*

[3]*General Samuel Smith (1752-1839), Revolutionary War officer and congressman, at this time a Federalist, would later become a leader of the Jeffersonian Republican Party.*

22. NOTATION FOR REV. WILLIAM O'BRIEN, O.P., [29 July 1793]

On a letter from Rev. William O'Brien, O.P., of New York dated 29 July 1793 Carroll commented:

> Respecting Capt. Sullivan's death and the letter of Patrick McLaughlin from Amsterdam of 16 April 1793.[1]

AAB, 5-U-1.

23. TO GOVERNOR THOMAS SIM LEE, White Marsh, 4 November 1793

Lee became Maryland's first popularly elected governor in 1792. Carroll wrote him from White Marsh, the ex-Jesuits' largest estate in Maryland, concerning business matters and politics.

> Carroll wanted to reach Annapolis the previous Saturday but was detained by the fever and ague in St. Mary's County longer than he expected, and after his recovery he heard the distressing news of the death of two of his priests in Philadelphia,[2] which obliged him to return immediately to Baltimore. He had fully inquired about Mr. Wilfrid Neale's[3] land. It was well situated, well suited to farming, with a sufficient amount of timber, and the price was

---

[1]*McLaughlin's letter can not be found in AAB. O'Brien's letter to Carroll indicates that McLaughlin, not actually mentioned by name, claims to have been a "brother officer of Mr. Sullivan" in the Dutch service.*

[2]*William Fleming and Christopher Keating were both stricken by yellow fever, but Keating recovered. Laurence Graessl, who had been chosen coadjutor bishop to Carroll, would die of the same yellow fever epidemic in October.*

[3]*Of St. Mary's County (d. 1808).*

£5.10 per acre. Carroll asked Lee to ask Mr. Magrath of the College[1] to inform the visitors of his disappointment that his illness would prevent his attending their meeting. Carroll heard in St. Mary's County that Mr. Plater and Mr. Kilgour,[2] both under the same influence, wanted to displace Lee and hoped "their puny efforts, or the more vigorous efforts of their principals," would be unsuccessful, although he knew Lee to be "superior to the gain or loss of public favor" since he always acted on right principles. Carroll offered his most affectionate compliments to Mrs. Lee and love to his young family.[3]

HLC/MHS.

24. TO BISHOP JAMES MADISON, Baltimore, 23 April 1794

To Bishop James Madison of the Episcopal diocese of Virginia, who had sailed on the same ships as Carroll to and from England to be raised also to the episcopacy, Carroll wrote of a former priest who wished to be an Episcopalian clergyman.

Carroll had been handed that morning Bishop Madison's letter of the 16th. Since last autumn he had made several inquiries about Mr.

---

[1]*Carroll was elected to the board of visitors of St. John's College, Annapolis, in 1789. See Appendix 4.*

[2]*George Plater III (1766-1802), son of George Plater II (1735-1792), governor of Maryland 1791-1792, and William Kilgour (d. 1796) were both wealthy planters of St. Mary's County.*

[3]*Lee married in 1771 Mary Digges (1745-1805), with whom he had by 1793 five surviving sons and two daughters.*

Delvaux [see No. 14] but had heard nothing more until reception of the Bishop Madison's letter. To answer "with the candor due to truth & to my friendship with you," Delvaux was ordained a Roman Catholic priest, but his moral conduct was not agreeable to the canons of his church. Carroll had suspended him last summer for having seduced a young woman and having had with her a child and lived with her for some time. An accusation of intemperance was unfounded. The last time Carroll saw him he agreed to return to Europe, with the passage to be paid by Carroll, but he heard that he had for a short time still lived with the young woman. Carroll owed it to Bishop Madison to say that Delvaux had promised to reform and had requested Carroll to assign him to a parish in North Carolina asking for a priest, but Carroll was reluctant to send him to a place so remote from supervision. Carroll believed his application to Bishop Madison the result of poverty more than conviction and that the bishop would later feel "inconvenience" by accepting him. But the bishop could judge best after weighing Carroll's remarks.

AAB, Letterbook 2, pp. 83-84.

25. PETITION TO THE HOLY SEE, 3 July 1794

This petition for certain indulgences accompanied Carroll's letter of the same date to the Propaganda Fide (JCP, 2: 117-19) that included a copy of the statutes of the diocesan synod.

> Carroll asks that the altar in the chapel of the Carmelite Sisters [of Port Tobacco] be declared privileged and that indulgences be granted to those who visited the chapel.[1]

APF, Udienze, 32: 429r.

26. TO REV. STEPHEN THEODORE BADIN,[2] Baltimore, 2 August 1794.

Carroll wrote this only active missionary in Kentucky at that time concerning his difficulties there.

> Badin's letters of 5 and 10 May from Lexington brought Carroll both joy and sadness. Badin displayed in them both courage and confidence in God and a distrust in his own strength that would make him a fit instrument for the salvation of many. On the other hand, the vices he found among many of his flock and the distressing decision of Mr. Barrière[3] to depart almost as soon as he arrived filled him with a concern that "went near to my heart." The patience of the good Catholics of Nelson

---

[1] *The petition was granted in a papal audience of 30 November 1794.*

[2] *Stephen Theodore Badin (1768-1853), who came over with the Sulpicians as a seminarian, was in 1793 the first priest Carroll ordained. He sent him immediately to the neglected Catholics from Maryland who had settled in Kentucky.*

[3] *Rev. Michael Barrière left almost immediately for Louisiana and later Arkansas.*

County[1] having been tried for many years, Carroll "after many fruitless endeavors" was happy that Barrière would fill that duty. Instead he left them for reasons which Carroll now found in his letters to him that he had entered into an agreement at Fort Pitt to follow certain persons over the Mississippi. Carroll ratifies the authority [vicar general] with which Barrière thought he could invest Badin. Badin was to exercise authority over any priest there or any priest who comes into the state until Carroll determines otherwise. He does not know if any provisions have been made for him by his flock. Mr. Fenwick[2] had made promises to Carroll, and he expects that he and his neighbors will soon buy land and build a house for a priest, without which Badin's situation would be precarious. But Badin is free to seek a place where he may receive better support. As regards the first of the disorders Badin mentioned, Carroll advised him to stress the cruelty of masters' hiring or selling their slaves when the latter would have no means of practicing their religion. The second and third [unnamed] disorders should be treated as any other inveterate habit of vice by reproof, counsel, and exhortation, public and private. For the fourth use all means to banish laziness, the fruitful source of vice and misery. Make frugality and industry frequent subjects of his instructions because they make good citizens and promote unity and piety in

---

[1]*Whose county seat was Bardstown, seat of the first diocese west of the Alleghenies.*
[2]*Joseph Fenwick of Scott County would about 1796 lead a number of Catholics to Missouri.*

Catholic families. "When I performed for the first time the awful ministry of priestly ordination, I besought Almighty God that you . . . might be a pledge of the blessings intended by Providence on this infant Church. I now humbly pray that Providence has heard my prayer, and that divine faith, through God's goodness and your instrumentalty, will spread itself through all our Western territory, and raise up children of Abraham, that is, endowed with the faith of Abraham, in the wilderness of America." May Badin increase in every virtue needful in his situation, and may grace be showered plentifully on those for whom he labors, for whom Carroll offers daily his "most affectionate and paternal wishes."

(Cincinnati) *Catholic Telegraph and Advocate,* 19 March 1853.

27. TO REV. MICHAEL MacCORMICK, O.F.M., n.p., 20 August 1795

On a letter of 15 March 1795 from Michael MacCormick, an Irish Franciscan then in Naples, Carroll penned an extract of his reply concerning his offer to come to America.

Carroll hardly knows what to answer. If all the priests arrive who have offered their services, or have been invited, he will have no place left to give MacCormick. Several offer but fail to come. He will leave it to MacCormick's own determination but he must bring evidences of

good conduct, especially from his own religious superiors, and from Cardinal Gerdil[1]
and Mr. Connell[2].

AAB, 5-C-3.

28. NOTATION FOR REV. LAURENCE SILVESTER PHELAN, [9 October 1795]

On the letter of a lawyer to Rev. Laurence Silvester Phelan dated 9 October 1795 concerning title to land left by Rev. Theodore Brouwers[3] Carroll wrote a formula for Phelan to use.

"That the members of the religious Society of
R[oman]. C[atholics]. inhabiting within (limits here described) & attending divine worship
at [blank] shall be & they are hereby erected
into & declared to be one body politic and cor-
porate, in deed and in law, by the name
[blank] stile and title of the 'Trustees &c.'"

AAB, 8-S-1.

---

[1]*Giacinto Sigismondo Gerdil had in February been named prefect of the Congregation of the Propaganda Fide.*

[2]*Rev. James Connell, a former Jesuit, was at the time Carroll's agent in Rome.*

[3]*Brouwers willed "Sportsman's Hall," the future site of St. Vincent's Archabbey, Latrobe, Pennsylvania, to Francis Fromm, O.F.M., who proved unworthy of his charge. A Pennsylvania court case upheld Carroll's right in 1798 to eject him.*

29. TO REV. JOHN FRANCIS RIVET, n.p., 26 September 1796

On a letter from Rev. John Francis Rivet of Vincennes to Carroll dated 2 May 1796 Carroll wrote the following:

> "Ans^d Sep. 26 but to be referred to when I write a letter to the several cong^{ns} in the W.T. [Western Territory]"[1]

AAB, 8B-D-1.

30. TO REV. JOHN BURKE, n.p., 2 March 1797

On a letter from Rev. John Burke in Cork, Ireland, dated 1 November 1796 Carroll wrote:

> "Ans^d 2 March 1797. Accept his services & those of his friend. One of them probably will be stationed at [blank] N.Y. the other at Albany. I advise them to take passage to N.Y."

AAB, 2-D-8.

---

[1] *If Carroll wrote such a letter, it has not been found.*

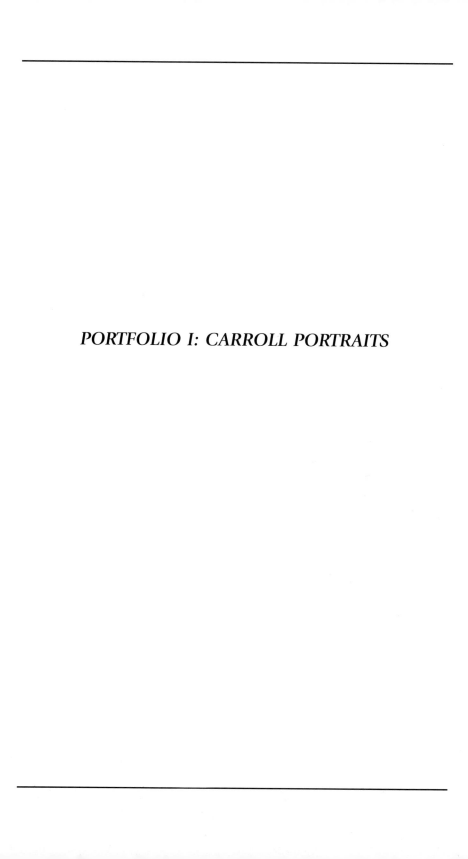

PORTFOLIO I: CARROLL PORTRAITS

1. Portrait of 1790 by Thomas Peat. An oil painting on silverplate done by this London painter was found in a rectory in Liverpool, England. It was a gift in 1991 of the bishop of Plymouth, in whose diocese the chapel at Lulworth is located, to the archbishop of Baltimore. Since the portrait that is the frontispiece for Volume 1 of *JCP* is suspect, this is the earliest portrait of Carroll known for certain. (Archbishops of Baltimore Collection)

The Right *Rev.ᵈ John*

BISHOP OF **BALTIMORE.**

2. Engraving of 1790 by Lovelace (?). Based on the Peat portrait, this engraving was commissioned by James P. Coghlan of London for an account of Carroll's episcopal ordination that Coghlan published later that year. In the legend it has the earliest known representation of Carroll's episcopal coat-of-arms. (Shea, *Life*, p. 370)

3. Portrait of 1795 (?) by unknown artist. This somewhat primitive oil painting was preserved in the Carroll family. When presented to the archbishop of Baltimore, it was said to have been painted about 1795. (Archbishops of Baltimore Collection)

4. Portrait by Gilbert Stuart. This oil painting by the artist best known for his paintings of George Washington was, in all probability, done during the years 1803-1805, when Stuart went to Washington to do the portraits of a number of leading statesmen. It is perhaps the most reproduced of the Carroll portraits. (Georgetown University Art Collection)

5. Engraving by John Sartain. Though done later in the century, this engraving was copied from a miniature of Carroll, now lost, painted by Joseph Peter Picot de Clorivière about the time he entered St. Mary's Seminary in 1808. (Sulpician Archives of Baltimore)

6. Portrait by Joshua Johnson. Originally attributed to Jeremiah Paul, this oil painting, done perhaps around 1810-1812, is now thought to be the work of Joshua Johnson, a resident of Baltimore, the first important African-American artist in the United States, and apparently a Catholic. (Archbishops of Baltimore Collection)

Eng.d by S. Hollyer

MOST REV. JOHN CARROLL,

ARCHBISHOP OF BALTIMORE.

Copyright by John G. Shea, 1888.

7. Engraving by Samuel Hollyer. This likeness, commissioned by John Gilmary Shea in 1888, was done from an engraving by William S. Leney and Benjamin Tanner of 1812 based on a painting by Jeremiah Paul now lost that combined features of the Gilbert Stuart and the Joshua Johnson portraits. The Leney/Tanner engraving has been used by many later engravers. (Shea, *Life*, opposite p. 208)

8. At the University of Notre Dame (1). This was the section of the Bishops' Hall devoted to the archbishops of Baltimore assembled by the noted librarian James F. Edwards. To the left of Archbishop Martin John Spalding (at right) is a bust of Carroll with a miter, smaller oil paintings of the six archbishops who preceded Spalding with Carroll on the lower left, and at the far left a full-length portrait of Carroll matching that of Spalding. (University of Notre Dame Archives)

9. At the University of Notre Dame (2). This full-length oil portrait of Carroll by an unknown artist at the far left in the previous illustration is a late nineteenth-century perception of how Carroll looked. It was commissioned by Edwards the librarian. It is now in a vault of the Catholic Center in Baltimore. (University of Notre Dame Archives)

31. TO REV. WILLIAM O'BRIEN, O.P., n.p., 8 November 1797

This extract of a reply on a letter of O'Brien dated 27 October 1797 concerns Carroll's involvement in the long and painful schism in Holy Trinity Parish in Philadelphia.[1]

Carroll says that Goetz[2] must make reparation as public as the offence for the scandal he has given. By his assertions in sermons and in print he has led the unlearned to resist ecclesiastical authority. He must publicly disavow the principles of independence he espoused. He is absolved from his ministry after notification of the withdrawal of his faculties, suspension, excommunication, etc. If he consents to Carroll's terms, his censures will be removed. After a term of penance he must make an explicit act of faith and declaration of principles because in one of his sermons he spoke as a Deist and Latitudinarian, advocating the policies of Joseph II[3] and freemasonry. Carroll concludes by mentioning the well-grounded report of his allegat[ions?] at Philadelphia. If reparation is satisfactory, he need not come to Baltimore. O'Brien or another can act in Carroll's name.

AAB, 5-U-6.

---

[1]*O'Brien was often chosen by Carroll as his agent in the handling of difficult cases (see Nos. 10 and 11, n. 2).*

[2]*Revs. John Nepomucene Goetz and William Elling, O.S.B., of Holy Trinity Church, Philadelphia, were excommunicated by Carroll for refusing to submit to his authority and for other "sacrilegious" acts. For this protracted schism see Vincent J. Fecher,* A Study of the Movement for German National Parishes in Philadelphia and Baltimore (1787-1802) *(Rome: Gregorian University Press, 1955).*

[3]*Joseph II of Austria had advocated a policy of state control of all church affairs.*

32. TO REV. DEMETRIUS GALLITZIN,[1] n.p., 20 October 1798

Carroll wrote Gallitzin, then pastor of Taneytown, of complaints that had been made against him.

Carroll tells Gallitzin that some of his parishioners at Taneytown had come to him to complain of his high-handed manners, especially in the disposition of church affairs in which he wholly ignored the trustees. When they tried to remonstrate with him Gallitzin rebuffed them with insulting language. As Carroll knew "both sides of my people," he had put them off with general remarks, telling them it was their duty to obey their pastor. In the course of his visitation, however, he would soon come to Taneytown and investigate affairs. Carroll had often told Gallitzin to try to win the affection of his congregation with a mild temper, occasionally overlooking things that were not as they should be, correcting by gentle persuasion instead of carrying his authority to extremes. If [their] yielding to his every opinion without reservation was the proper course, why were bishops placed over priests, archbishops over bishops, and over all the pope, except to render acts subject to revision?

Lemcke, pp. 96-97.

---

[1]*Prince Demetrius Gallitzin (1770-1840) of the Russian nobility came to America in 1792, entered the seminary in Baltimore, and in 1795 was the first priest ordained by Carroll to have made all his clerical studies in the United States (see Appendix 2).*

33. TO REV. DEMETRIUS GALLITZIN, Washington, 1 March 1799

Carroll responded to Gallitzin's wish to take up residence among the growing number of Catholics settling in western Pennsylvania, whom Gallitzin had visited often from Taneytown.

Carroll doubts that Gallitzin would prove up to so arduous an undertaking but grants the request. He should not live with a private family, however, longer than was needed to build a house on the land granted by Mr. McGuire[1] or, if more convenient, on land Gallitzin had acquired if he intended to keep it.[2] Carroll instructs Gallitzin to include in all his services a prayer for the pope that he was sending to him.

Lemcke, p. 115.

34. TO MONSIGNOR CHARLES ERSKINE, Baltimore, 20 August 1799

In his frustration over the breakdown of communications with Rome due to the French invasion of Italy Carroll wrote to Monsignor Charles Erskine, papal envoy extraordinary to England.

Carroll's principal embarrassment in the administration of his diocese proceeded from the want of communications with the Holy

---

[1]*Capt. Michael Maguire, for whom Maguire's Settlement was named, the future site of Loretto.*
[2]*Lemcke remarks at this point that Carroll spoke also of other things of no special interest to the reader.*

See, which he hoped would be an apology for his imposition on Erskine, who probably had avenues of contact that Carroll did not. The secretary of the Congregation [of the Propaganda Fide] had written 23 April 1798 that the pope had put him in charge during the dispersion of the cardinals who were members of the congregation, and Carroll believes he [Cesare Brancadoro] was compelled to leave soon after.[1] Nearly three years ago the briefs for his coadjutor [Leonard Neale] had been sent and a duplicate not long after, but both had miscarried. "My advanced age is a constant monitor to me of mortality & increasing anxiety [about what] my death before a successor would involve this diocese." If Erskine could have other copies sent by way of England, it would be of great benefit to a very extensive diocese. Other matters of utmost importance in the United States require the immediate attention of Brancadoro. Carroll will leave the accompanying letter to him unopened so that, if need be, Erskine can submit the substance of it to Brancadoro.[2]

Letterbook 3, pp. 1-2.

---

[1]*In February 1798 Napoleon's troops occupied Rome. The Roman Republic was proclaimed and Pius VI taken prisoner, dying at Valence, France, in 1799.*

[2]*For the enclosed letter to Brancadoro of the same date see JCP, 2: 270-75. A note, however, says: "Any possible letter to Erskine in this connection has not been found."*

35. TO REV. STEPHEN THEODORE BADIN, Baltimore, 17 October 1799

A brief extract from one of Carroll's letters to Badin appeared in the Catholic weekly cited below.

Carroll feels great consolation for having ordained Badin and having appointed him to Kentucky. He asks to be remembered "in a most affectionate manner" to his worthy cousin Mrs. Lancaster[1] and her family. He writes also to Badin's fellow laborers, Messrs. Salmon and Fournier.[2]

(Cincinnati) *Catholic Telegraph and Advocate*, 19 March 1853.

36. TO REV. JAMES GRIFFIN, n.p., 3 March 1800

This is an extract of a letter Carroll wrote as a follow up to one he had written earlier (but not found).

Carroll supplies facts on which accusations against Griffin in a former letter were founded: 1) a party with public performers at which Griffin's intoxication made him an object of derision, giving non-Catholics a bad impres-

---

[1]*This is one of many times Carroll asked Badin to remember him to his cousin, Eleanor Bradford, daughter of John Bradford and Anne Darnall, sister of Carroll's mother, and the wife of Raphael Lancaster, who brought his family to Kentucky even before the first of the annual treks of Maryland Catholics in 1785.*

[2]*Rev. Michael Fournier sent by Carroll to Kentucky in 1796 died in 1803. Rev. Anthony Salmon sent in 1799 died a tragic death soon after his arrival, the first priest to die in Kentucky.*

sion of the church; 2) many of his congregation had withdrawn their confidence; 3) burial
of an irreligious young man in a Protestant
churchyard with Catholic rites.

Letterbook 3, p. 12.

37. TO REV. STEPHEN THEODORE BADIN, n.p., 20 March 1800

This is a brief extract of a letter to the Kentucky priest.

Carroll promises to send Badin a light altar
stone, and, when in his power, a missal and
breviary.

Letterbook 3, p. 12.

38. TO REV. MATTHEW CARR, O.S.A.,[1] Baltimore, 28 April 1800

Carroll wrote this Augustinian priest in Philadelphia concerning the schism at Holy Trinity Church in Philadelphia (see No. 31).

From statements of Messrs. Heartley and
Tilghman [?] it seems to Carroll that the court
wishes to avoid a decision in the case of Helbron vs. Trustees.[2] The latter must show cause

---

[1]*In JCP, 2: 309, the name is incorrectly given as William Carr. Dr. Matthew Carr, O.S.A., pastor of St. Augustine's Church, came to America in 1795 with the intention of founding an Augustinian province.*

[2]*Rev. Peter Helbron, O.F.M.Cap., whom Goetz and Elling (see No. 31) had ousted as pastor of Holy Trinity Church, sued the trustees for a restoration of his pastorate. Peter signed his name Helbron, his brother John Charles, Heilbron. Peter had been associated with his brother at Holy Trinity.*

why Helbron should not be restored to his care of Trinity Church. To do this two things must be ascertained: 1) if Helbron was indeed pastor and recognized as such by the trustees; 2) if it was consonant with the discipline of the church to remove him of their own authority, for the laws of Pennsylvania uphold all churches in the exercise of their government unless it is repugnant to the Constitution and the laws of the state and United States. What are the specific points, Carroll asks, that Oellers[1] pretends to refer to the Holy See? Carroll doubts that he has done so, but no engagement can be made until they are known, and even then, according to the Council of Trent and the brief creating the see of Baltimore, Carroll's decision would be final. Should the court decide that Catholics, as other religious societies, have a right to govern themselves by their own regulations and discipline, Carroll would submit to a declaration of the Holy See concerning the laws of the church on that point but would decide himself how to apply the declaration to the facts. He makes this reservation not as doubting the issue of Rome's decision but in order to surrender none of the prerogatives of the episcopacy with which he is burdened. But it must also be understood that such a submission would not mean he was withdrawing from the jurisdiction of the court in temporal matters. Carroll is surprised that the court took no notice

---

[1]James Oellers, the owner of a hotel, was president of the board of trustees.

of Oellers' assertion that the trustees' cause was being carried to Rome. Had such a claim been made on Helbron's side they would have accused him of resorting to a foreign tribunal. Carroll believes that Oellers' claim was a snare and that Helbron should not agree to remove the cause from the court so that it could be adjudicated elsewhere. It should be determined by arbiters mutually acknowledged. Carroll has no doubt that Oellers and his party are seeking approval for their schism in Europe as well as America. Should any German bishops countenance attempts so ruinous to episcopal authority, it would have to be the result of misrepresentation. Carroll believes the Congregation of the Propaganda to be in possession of the history of this wicked business, so many means having been tried to open communication with it. Carroll is much obliged to Carr, nevertheless, for offering the services of his friend in Rome, who may have returned there since that city was rescued by the French [?]. Carr will render service to religion by making his friend master of the subject.

Letterbook 3, pp. 13-14 (see *JCP*, 2: 309).

39. TO REV. FRANCIS CHARLES NAGOT, S.S., Baltimore, 29 April 1800

In this letter to Nagot, superior of the Sulpicians in the United States, Carroll responded to points raised by Nagot in his last letter.

In response to Nagot's of 26 April Carroll makes a number of points: 1) Nagot's assurance that no ecclesiastic of the diocese will be admitted to the Society [of St. Sulpice] without the bishop's approval is satisfactory; 2) complaints about Cuddy and Poole[1] were true of the first but Poole asserts he was never approached by DuBourg,[2] only Flaget,[3] but perhaps at DuBourg's suggestion; 3) the proposal that David[4] and DuBourg become members of the Corporation of the Clergy[5] was immediately turned down by them; 4) Nagot had already told Carroll of Mr. [Roger] Smith's failure to imbibe the spirit of the society; 5) the suspicions about Mondésir[6] came not from Carroll's "brethren" [the former Jesuits at Georgetown] but from Mondésir himself.

Letterbook 3, pp. 15-16.

---

[1]*Michael Cuddy and Thomas Poole were seminarians at St. Mary's Seminary.*

[2]*Louis William DuBourg, S.S. (1766-1833), was founder of St. Mary's College in 1799. For the achievements of this talented but unpredictable Sulpician in the development of the Catholic Church in early America see Annabelle M. Melville,* Louis William DuBourg: Bishop of Louisiana and the Floridas, Bishop of Montauban, and Archbishop of Besançon, 1766-1833, *2 vols. (Chicago: Loyola University Press, 1986).*

[3]*Benedict Joseph Flaget, S.S. (1763-1850), was a professor at St. Mary's Seminary when named bishop of Bardstown, Kentucky, in 1808.*

[4]*John Baptist David, S.S. (1761-1841), then a missionary in Charles County, would later become coadjutor to Flaget in Bardstown.*

[5]*In 1792 a General Chapter that was created under Carroll's prodding in 1783 was incorporated by the state of Maryland as the Corporation of Roman Catholic Clergy. The General Chapter had been created for the support of former Jesuits and the maintenance of their properties. The Corporation of the Clergy would admit members who had never been Jesuits. The title, however, would be appropriated by the Maryland Jesuits when the Society of Jesus was restored.*

[6]*John Edward Pierron de Mondésir, one of the original seminarians brought from France, taught for a time at Georgetown College before being ordained in 1798.*

40. TO MESSRS. THOMAS WRIGHT AND COMPANY, Baltimore, 9 May 1800

Messrs. Wright and Company, Catholic bankers of London with ties to some of the prominent Catholic families of England, including the Plowdens, were Carroll's agents for the conduct of his financial affairs in England.

Bishop Douglass[1] or Mr. Strickland is to pay this month on Carroll's account £59.10.8, and the bankers have received directions from Sir Thomas Moore,[2] to whom Carroll encloses a letter to answer the drafts for his nephew's expenses. Carroll has this day drawn on the bankers for William Walton [?] for £9.12.2, of which consequently £52.9.4 is on Sir Thomas's account. In a P.S. Carroll adds that if in consequence of the death of Rev. Mr. [Thomas] Talbot Sir Thomas Moore's annual payment on his nephew's account has not been made to please add a line to the enclosed letter. In any event Carroll is sure Mr. Strickland will credit him for £66 rather than suffer Carroll's bill to be returned.

Letterbook 3, p. 18.

---

[1]*William Douglass as vicar apostolic of the London District was charged with the distribution of the Sir John James Fund created in 1740 for the support of Jesuit missionaries in Pennsylvania outside of Philadelphia.*

[2]*For Sir Thomas Moore and his nephew, James Du Moulin, see Appendix 6.*

41. TO REV. WILLIAM STRICKLAND, n.p., 9 May 1800

At the same time he wrote to Wright and Company Carroll wrote to Rev. William Strickland about his account with the English procurator.

Carroll has examined Strickland's account with Maryland [the Corporation of the Clergy] and himself and is at a loss to understand why he charged Maryland with £155 at the death of Mrs. White.[1] Not being conversant in bookkeeping, Carroll may have misunderstood. In a few days he will meet with a "Committee of our Brethren" [Corporation of the Clergy] and call their attention to Strickland's demands on them, but he hopes Strickland will pay as usual to Wright and Company the annuity for the German Pennsylvania fund,[2] for which Carroll draws on them this day. Keep the money mentioned in Carroll's note to Anthony Carroll [see No. 136] unless provision has not been made since the death of Mr. Talbot, his intermediary with Wright and Company for Sir Thomas Moore's payments for his nephew's expenses [see No. 40]. Carroll hopes Strickland will pay the £66 rather than suffer his bill to be protested.

Letterbook 3, p. 18.

---

[1] *A Miss Elizabeth Shepheard, later Mrs. White, of Pennsylvania had made a contribution to the missions there in exchange for an annuity of £100 for herself.*

[2] *This was undoubtedly the Sir John James Fund. For this and the White annuity as bones of contention between the Maryland Corporation of the Clergy and the former Jesuits in England see Thomas Hughes,* History of the Society of Jesus in North America: Colonial and Federal, Documents, *vol. 1 in 2 parts (London: Longmans, Green, 1908, 1910), pp. 239, 261-63, 640-41, 657-58, and passim.*

42. TO REV. JACQUES-ANDRÉ EMERY, S.S., n.p., [August 1800]

Carroll wrote this long letter to the superior general of the Sulpicians in Paris on the possibility of their American members being recalled to France.[1]

Carroll received Emery's letters, that of 21 April four months ago and that of 9 August a few days ago. He is not surprised at his chagrin that the seminary to which he had given so much and for which he had such hopes has been so long without students. Like Emery Carroll is persuaded that little reliance can be placed on recruits from Europe but much on products of the seminary. He has always said that he has never known men more capable of forming the kind of clergy needed today than the Sulpicians. He was stunned to read of the possibility of Emery's recalling them. Banish the thought and never doubt that they will finally achieve the aim Emery had in sending them. His last letter pained Carroll in another way. He seems to have been led to believe that Carroll no longer favored his priests. "Never!" He has the same respect even if he disapproves a few measures adopted by a few of them, whose purity of motives he never doubted. Carroll does not know if Emery has been told what happened after Mr. DuBourg stepped down from the presidency of Georgetown College after difficulties with the five directors. Perhaps DuBourg acted imprudently

---

[1] *Carroll's draft is very labored, filled with deletions and marginal and interlinear additions.*

in some ways and the directors, carried away by some ill-founded prejudices, interfered too much in his administration. Upon his return [to Baltimore] he raised the question of a college at the seminary. Some of the Sulpicians favored it but others were so opposed it did not happen then, and DuBourg left for Havana. The Georgetown directors felt that another college would be harmful because of the small number of Catholic boys whose parents could afford to send them. After their having spent 150,000 pounds [livres tournois] on Georgetown, Emery can understand how painful it would have been to see it fail. DuBourg's trip to Havana was not successful.[1] Incessantly the question of a college in Baltimore came up. Carroll opposed it as productive of division and distrust, but Mr. Nagot, whose merits Carroll respects, was all for it and kept telling him of its usefulness to the diocese. Finally Nagot proposed twelve boarders and use of income for the seminary. So as not to assert "absolute authority" Carroll agreed, but immediately they took in twenty-four boarders and put up a building to hold fifty. People were angry because it was thought the young men who would go to the seminary in the fall would be too distracted and that DuBourg, the object of the resentment, would use them to staff his school. Carroll agrees that these ideas are based on prejudice, which he has fought to overcome. Six or seven Georgetown pupils were destined

---

[1]With Benedict Flaget and Peter Babad [also Babade] DuBourg tried to establish a school in Havana.

for the seminary in September, but while Carroll was away the Corporation of the Clergy decided not to pay room and board for the seminarians [at Georgetown] who could not afford it and also decided to begin a course in philosophy to keep them at Georgetown. Nagot has informed Emery of the pain Carroll felt, not from the erection of a chair of philosophy but from the delay it would mean for the seminary. Carroll has already told Emery of the fears of the old clergy who thought the best candidates would be induced to join the Sulpicians. Mr. Mondésir [see No. 39] on leaving the seminary was indiscreet enough to accuse Nagot of a proselytizing zeal, which was seen in the case of Mr. Gallitzin. Carroll is concerned for the loss of the ministry to the congregations. The Sulpicians always stress their special goal, saying that ministry to outsiders puts them out of their proper calling. Then what, Carroll had asked, would be the condition of the diocese if the best seminarians were likely not to be under the direct authority of the bishop? But now Carroll is satisfied in that regard. Nagot has reassured him, and Emery's letters have put him fully at ease. Emery had finished his last letter by asking how, after having sent his best men to Baltimore, has it all come to naught? There were, Carroll replies, various answers: 1) Georgetown, just begun and made up of different teachers, lay and cleric, has followed no system and inspired no love for religion or performance of exercises, defects corrected so that several pupils were ready to come to the seminary except for the misunderstanding caused by Georgetown; 2) the lack of means to educate seminarians, the clergy having been impoverished by huge sums to build Georgetown College; 3) the unfortunate nationalistic spirit in the old clergy, all subjects of England, who by their indiscretion had alarmed candidates by telling them that customs at the seminary were very different from what they were used to, as well as did the English seminarians who came with the Sulpicians, [Francis] Tulloh, [John Edward] Caldwell, etc.; 4) when DuBourg had proposed a college, some hotheads had supposed this a plot to harm Georgetown and spread the word to others. All this will give Emery some idea of the extreme opposition shown, some [Sulpicians] even shouting that it would emasculate the seminary. Carroll has played for time, hoping to calm tempers. He has more hope than ever after Emery's second letter, who leaves the fate of the college to Carroll's discretion. Carroll has proposed to let it continue for two or three years in order to reimburse the seminary. Carroll wants people to believe this proposal was made by the Sulpicians, who are here out of love for peace, and so has not told a single old missionary of the discretion Emery has entrusted to him. The Sulpicians seem content with the proposal. They are all deserving of Carroll's esteem and gratitude, especially Mr. Garnier,[1] than whom Carroll has not seen a

---

[1]*Anthony Garnier, S.S. (1762-1845), would become superior general of the Sulpicians.*

more virtuous or learned man. Carroll would ask that he be Nagot's successor if he were not afraid of taking him away from so many brilliant activities. Earlier he had thought of Mr. Levadoux,[1] but the illnesses of which he writes make him perhaps even unable to make the long trip from Detroit. Carroll esteems all of Emery's men but especially Garnier, Maréchal,[2] and [Peter] Babad. It would break Carroll's heart to see Nagot leave and would hurt him too. Mr. Tessier[3] is admirable and never gives offense but stays close to the seminary and does not adjust to American ways. Of DuBourg's zeal, virtue, and talent he has already spoken but some think he has a spirit of intrigue and that he dominates Nagot. Carroll thinks he should be sent elsewhere. If Emery should agree, he would send him to Natchez, fifty leagues north of New Orleans, where he could teach seminarians and minister to the numerous Catholics. They are well off and have two Spanish-style churches. Since DuBourg knows English, French, and Spanish, he could serve the area well. Carroll was about to stop at this point but has just spoken to Nagot, who surprised and alarmed him. Until now he has given Carroll the impression that he would try to get Emery not to recall his men from the diocese. Now he says he has written the general to recall all, there being no

---

[1] *Michael Levadoux, S.S. (1746-1803), was a missionary at Cahokia and Detroit.*
[2] *Ambrose Maréchal, S.S. (1768-1828), would become the third archbishop of Baltimore.*
[3] *John Mary Tessier, S.S. (1758-1840), would be named the second superior in Baltimore.*

prospect of success with the seminary. His turnabouts must come from the deterioration Carroll has already written Emery about. Some around him have convinced him there is no hope. Carroll can not understand his conduct. While he urges recall, he still works to finish the new college, and instead of the two or three years Carroll proposed he wants to keep it for at least six.

Letterbook 3, pp. 19-25 (see *JCP*, 2: 313-14).

43. TO REV. [?] DOYLE, Baltimore, 9 December 1800

In this letter Carroll wrote to a religious (but otherwise unidentified) priest in Pennsylvania.

Doyle had received his faculties under express limitation of their being revocable whenever the bishop judged it expedient, which is now the case. He must cease the ministry after receipt of this letter, whose deliverance Mr. Brosius will certify. He should leave Conewago and had two courses open to him, either to return to Europe and the direction of a religious superior of his order, or with the latter's concurrence to devote himself [in America] to the instruction of youth in the learned languages.

Letterbook 3, p. 24 (see *JCP*, 2: 329).

44. TO MR. JEREMIAH TARLTON, n.p., 29 January 1801

Carroll wrote this resident of Scott County, Kentucky, and former Marylander of scandal involving Rev. John Thayer, whom Carroll had sent to Kentucky in 1799.

> Carroll has received Tarlton's of 24 December and another from Badin on the same subject, on which he can say little more at present than he hopes Tarlton had seriously considered such grievous charges, which if true would subject the person charged to the severest censures in Carroll's power.[1] Thayer had told Carroll of Tarlton's not only discrediting him in darkest colors but also Mr. Dubois[2] back in Frederick, Maryland, which Carroll had investigated about three years ago and found it a malicious calumny. If Tarlton has committed calumny, he should retract and make reparation.

Letterbook 3, p. 26 (see *JCP*, 2: 346).

45. TO REV. JOHN THAYER, n.p., 30 January 1801

Carroll wrote Thayer the day after he had written Jeremiah Tarlton, Thayer's accuser (No. 44).

> Carroll has empowered Badin to investigate charges against Thayer with the help of Mr.

---

[1]*Tarlton and others accused Thayer of improper conduct toward a woman penitent.*
[2]*Paris-born John Dubois, S.S. (1764-1842), was pastor in Frederick before he founded Mount St. Mary's Seminary and College in Emmitsburg, Maryland. He was later bishop of New York.*

[Michael] Fournier. They are much like charges in Boston and in Zachiah [Maryland], which Thayer had persuaded Carroll to overlook. He has received a letter from Tarlton, which is no more than a confirmation of Badin's letter.

Letterbook 3, p. 27 (see *JCP*, 2: 346).

46. TO A GENTLEMAN OF NATCHEZ, n.p., 7 February 1801

Carroll wrote to a "G" of Natchez...Sir"[1] concerning his request for a priest.

Rev. Mr. [Matthew] O'Brien's long uncertainty about going to Natchez has kept Carroll from complying with the gentleman's wishes and his own duty. O'Brien has now decided he is not going. As soon as a proper subject can be found Carroll will honor the request. He will not send an unfit priest. He has asked the bishop of Louisiana[2] to allow some of his priests to attend Catholics of that territory [transferred to the United States in 1798] and to invest them with the proper powers on Carroll's behalf.

Letterbook 3, pp. 28-29 (see *JCP*, 2: 348).

---

[1]*Perhaps William Vousdan. See* JCP, *2: 280.*
[2]*Luis Peñalver y Cárdenas (1749-1810), bishop of Louisiana and the Floridas from 1795 until named archbishop of Guatemala in 1801. See* JCP, *2: 346-47.*

47. TO REV. JACQUES-ANDRÉ EMERY, S.S., Baltimore, 13 February 1801

Carroll wrote again to the superior general of the Sulpicians on the problems of the Society in Baltimore (see No. 42 and JCP, 2: 343-44).

Carroll wrote Emery a very detailed letter on the 6th and 12th of January[1] of this year by way of London. Since he sent it in duplicate, at least one should have reached Emery before this, which will explain [in greater detail] the main reason for the lack of confidence on the part of several older priests of this diocese with respect to the undertakings of Mr. Nagot, namely, the establishment of a college attached to the Seminary. Carroll has indicated how he intends with respect to the continuation of the college to use the authority Emery vested in him in his letter of 9 August 1800. The more Carroll thinks about it, the more he is persuaded that there is no other way to reconcile the reestablishment of harmony with the necessary restoration of well-being to the Seminary. The expenses incurred by the Sulpicians require that the college be allowed to continue for two or three years, limiting the number of pupils to twenty-four at the most. After that only ecclesiastical students will be sought, unless it is desired to offer there a free education in the humanities to a small number of young men who would declare themselves disposed to a clerical vocation. Mr. Nagot

---

[1] *For Carroll's letter of 6 and 12 January 1801 see JCP, 2: 343-44, for which the source is given as Joseph W. Ruane,* The Beginnings of the Society of St. Sulpice in the United States (1791-1829) *(Washington, D.C.: Catholic University of America Press, 1935), pp. 47-49. Ruane's source is not indicated.*

seems very attached to this arrangement, and Carroll is reluctant to press the matter further for fear of upsetting him too much, especially since he has informed Carroll of his intention to resign as superior. Carroll is persuaded that he will with his usual humility submit to whatever is decided. They say he is asking Emery to name as superior Mr. David, a man of distinguished merit but, it is believed, entirely devoted to the plans for the new College, and Carroll is certain this is enough to make this nomination unacceptable to some Sulpicians, especially those who have the soundest ideas about the customs and natives of the country. On the other hand, the nomination of Mr. Tessier would please everyone. Carroll has no more to add to his last letter but can not close this one without begging Emery again not to even think of recalling the priests who are the glory and the edification of the diocese. In a postscript Carroll says that after having written the above, he had a talk with Mr. Nagot, during which he denied he had written Emery in favor of recalling the Sulpicians, as Carroll mentioned in his last. Carroll was very surprised at this. He insists absolutely that Carroll misunderstood him. It is hard for Carroll to believe he misunderstood so completely. He still remembers some of Nagot's expressions, which indicated his fear of displeasing Carroll. But Carroll must necessarily attribute this mistake to his own misunderstanding or absent-mindedness. He is grateful Nagot did not ask to be recalled.

Letterbook 3, pp. 29-30 (see *JCP*, 2: 348).

48. TO REV. FRANCIS BEESTON,[1] Baltimore, 3 March 1801

Carroll wrote this short note to the rector of the cathedral congregation, then on business at Elkton, Maryland.

"For special reasons," Carroll declines sending the cover letter of a certificate he forwards to Beeston this afternoon.

MPA, box 30, folder 4, no. 103R1¾.

49. TO REV. CHARLES SEWALL,[2] n.p., 10 March 1801

Carroll did an extract of this letter to Sewall, then the secretary and fiscal agent of the Corporation of the Roman Catholic Clergy.

Carroll asks Sewall as agent of the Corporation to have Strickland's Maryland account [see No. 41] corrected as a result of instructions Carroll sent the trustees at Newtown last May. As agent Sewall could decide on it himself or lay it before the Corporation. It contains a pledge of £70.18.8 to Carroll plus £10 he advanced 4 November 1794 to pay [Rev.] Mr. Peter Jenkins's[3] annuity due from the college. Debit Mrs. White's annuity £300 to 1794 and £50 for half of 1794. Credit the Pennsyl-

---

[1]*English-born Francis Beeston (1751-1809) entered the Society of Jesus on the eve of its suppression. After ordination he came to America in 1786. After some years in Philadelphia, he served for a brief period as pastor on the Eastern Shore before being called by Carroll in 1793 to be rector of St. Peter's Procathedral. This letter was addressed to Beeston, "& in his absence, Hugh Matthews Esqʳ - Attorney at Law."*

[2]*Charles Sewall (1744-1806), a former Jesuit, was pastor of St. Peter's Procathedral 1782-1793, before his transfer to St. Thomas Manor.*

[3]*A generous English benefactor of Georgetown College.*

vania fund for 1791-1794 £350. See Strickland's letter.

Letterbook 3, p. 30.

50. TO BISHOP JOSEPH-OCTAVE PLESSIS, Baltimore, 8 April 1801

In this letter Carroll wrote[1] the bishop of Quebec concerning certain problems they shared in their adjoining jurisdictions.

Carroll is happy to hear in Plessis's letter of 18 September that he has received papal approval for a coadjutor. He too has received bulls sent four years ago for his coadjutor's consecration, done 7 December last, Leonard Neale,[2] first pastor of St. Mary's, Philadelphia, and now at Georgetown College. Carroll would love to meet Plessis in Detroit and commends the priests there to him: Mr. Levadoux, grand vicar and pastor of Detroit, Mr. Richard,[3] his vicar, and Mr. [John] Dilhet, parish priest at River Raisin. Carroll accepts the bishop's kind offer to administer confirmation in this area, of which Levadoux had written him. Carroll was mortified to hear that he had not received his answer to Plessis's of 10 October 1798.

---

[1]*The letter is in French, the conjecture of JCP, 2: 352, that it was in Latin notwithstanding.*

[2]*Leonard Neale (1746-1817), a native of Charles County, Maryland, and former Jesuit, would succeed Carroll as archbishop of Baltimore.*

[3]*Gabriel Richard, S.S. (1767-1832), would serve Detroit with distinction from 1798 until his death from cholera.*

Despite his wish to proceed as one with the bishop, especially in places adjoining his, he has not been able to do so as regards dispensations of consanguinity and affinity. His faculties from Rome [see No. 1] and the prejudices of Protestants requires him to grant these dispensations gratis, but he will write again to Rome and consult his priests in the western parishes. Long ago he had allowed Levadoux to approve the priests approved by Plessis; if he has not done so, Carroll asks that he use his authority in this matter. Catholics in England marry before their pastors but to legalize the union go then to a minister of the dominant religion. Here Catholics are under no such humiliating obligation, but to have to marry a Protestant before a Protestant minister Catholics consider a "crime." Carroll has submitted his way of proceeding to Rome, which has approved, and has kept the documents so attesting.

Letterbook 3, pp. 33-34 (see *JCP*, 2: 351-52).

51. TO REV. JOHN ASHTON, Baltimore, 10 June 1801

Ashton, a former Jesuit, was dismissed as fiscal agent and manager of the Corporation's largest estate, White Marsh, for living in concubinage.[1]

Carroll acknowledges Ashton's resignation and transfer of White Marsh to [Rev.] Mr.

---

[1]*For Carroll's relationship with Ashton and other problem priests see Spalding,* Premier See, *pp. 42-45.*

[John] Bolton. Ashton may select his own residence. The other trustees request Carroll to ask Ashton for statements on property necessary for his successor. As Ashton has often asked to retire, an opportunity is now afforded that must lead to "pleasing effects after a life of agitation and vexation of late."

Letterbook 3, p. 38.

52. TO REV. JOHN ASHTON, Baltimore, 2 July 1801

Carroll responded with restraint to several angry and unseemly letters of Ashton concerning the latter's resignation and removal from White Marsh (see No. 51).

Carroll's return from Cecil and Harford counties on the last day of June is the reason he has not yet responded to Ashton's of 13, 19, and 22 June. He encloses his direction to Wright and Company on Ashton's annuity. He is sorry to see in Ashton's of 13 June that he thought Carroll cool and unfriendly when he was last in Baltimore and assures him it was inadvertent. After sending the trustees the purport of Ashton's letters on the resignation of his faculties and other matters, further action will rest with the trustees. Since Carroll does not wish these matters brought up again, he has suffered the impudence of Cahill[1] and others to pass, but some things have happened afterwards that make him anxious. The trustees'

---

[1] *For Rev. Denis Cahill's impudence see Spalding,* Premier See, *p. 43.*

decision to appoint Bolton manager [of White Marsh] was sent Carroll from Newtown. He had not ordered Ashton's removal in March. If there was no house in the district [that would take him] then let the rule stand Ashton had urged in Mr. Diderick's[1] case. The time of Bolton's going [to White Marsh] could not be ascertained until Ashton's answer was received. Ashton's personal kindness to him and his services to the common cause deter Carroll from commenting on certain passages in his last two letters.

Letterbook 3, pp. 38-39.

53. TO MESSRS. THOMAS WRIGHT AND COMPANY, n.p., 2 July 1801

Carroll wrote to his London bankers about Ashton and other matters.

Carroll has never included his credit for the £5 pounds paid annually since 1791 by Mr. Strickland for the use of John Ashton.[2] For several years Carroll's bills on the bankers were only for so much as came from Bishop Douglass through Strickland and for the use of Sir Thomas Moore's nephew, whose annuity should be transferred to him [the bishop ?].

Letterbook 3, p. 40.

---

[1] *Rev. Bernard Diderick, former Jesuit, was, in effect, ostracized for his opposition to Carroll and the Corporation on the establishment of Georgetown Academy and other matters.*
[2] *The result of a legacy left Ashton by James Carroll. Bishop Carroll wrote but crossed out at this point that he wished Ashton's account had not been "blended" with his own.*

54. NOTATION FOR REV. STEPHEN THEODORE BADIN, 16 July 1801

This was simply a notation in the letterbook that he had written Rev. Stephen Theodore Badin.

"Wrote to Mr. Badin, Balte., 16 July 1801 by Mr. Solomon Hayes."

Letterbook 3, p. 41.

55. TO REV. JOHN ASHTON, n.p., 24 July 1801

In this extract Carroll wrote Ashton again but with obvious exasperation.

This is the real story of the communication of the paper from the trustees written by Mr. Molyneux[1] and given to Carroll by the coadjutor [Bishop Neale] as the joint opinion of the other four trustees. It gave Ashton a full account except for Article 4 (which was offensive). As to entering into a plot to replace Ashton, Carroll spoke of it last fall in his own house. Bishop Neale had not acted through malevolence as imputed by Ashton, and Carroll can not fail to notice the coarseness and indecency of Ashton's expressions concerning him.

Letterbook 3, p. 41.

---

[1]*English-born Robert Molyneux (1738-1808) was sent by Jesuit superiors to British North America as early as 1771. There during the American Revolution he was pastor of St. Mary's Church in Philadelphia, a position much to his liking, but in 1793 Carroll persuaded him to accept the presidency of Georgetown College. This he resigned when chosen by Carroll in 1805 to become the first provincial of the restored Society of Jesus in America.*

56. TO REV. JOHN THAYER, n.p., 31 July 1801

This is an extract of a letter Carroll wrote to Thayer (see No. 45).

> Carroll had informed Thayer 30 January of: 1) Badin's having been invested with full powers to render sentence; 2) there being no need to investigate when the facts were certain. Censures were incurred not only by Thayer's indecent conduct but also by the time and place it was committed. Carroll admits he may have gone too far in imputing "perpetual irregularity," but he is surprised at Thayer's saying he made light of affairs in Charles County. Carroll recommends that he leave Kentucky.

Letterbook 3, p. 42.

57. TO MR. BENNET HAMILTON, Baltimore, 4 November 1801

Carroll called this a copy of a paper delivered to Hamilton concerning an unnamed priest (except for an initial) accused of an unnamed crime (except by implication).

> Carroll has received that morning an undated letter with several signatures of persons in Charles County delivered by Mr. B. Hamilton. Carroll had told Bishop Neale to conduct an inquiry but no accusers appeared. He must therefore consider the priest innocent until proven guilty, especially when his character seems blameless, but he will give due attention to what they have written. The deposition they got under oath from Mrs. G. precluded

further investigation. If Mr. M. makes one of a contrary tenor, what can the bishop do without causing one side or the other to complain?

Letterbook 3, p. 42.

58. TO MR. SAMUEL CORBETT, Baltimore, 10 November 1801

Carroll responded to Corbett, secretary of the vestry of Charleston, South Carolina, concerning his intended replacement of Rev. Simon Felix Gallagher.[1]

Carroll welcomes such letters as Corbett's. Replacing Gallagher is not the result of misrepresentation. Dr. Gallagher knows of Carroll's readiness to make allowance for failings not habitual or scandalous, but his decision was based on the reports of disinterested persons. He can not foresee the final issue of the new arrangement, but he is "disposed to great and long forbearance, rather than incur the danger of schism." It is sad to hear of the lack of piety, neglect of the sacraments, and other abuses. Carroll must assume some of the blame for having postponed a visitation of Charleston some years ago when he was able to do so.

Letterbook 3, p. 43 (see *JCP*, 2: 367).

---

[1]*Rev. Simon Felix Gallagher, a learned and eloquent priest from the archdiocese of Dublin and a graduate of the University of Paris, was sent by Carroll to Charleston in 1793 but was soon found to be an unreliable alcoholic. This was the first of a number of unsuccessful attempts to dislodge Gallagher from Charleston. Corbett had written on 18 October 1801 that Carroll was misinformed, that, in fact, Dr. Gallagher had won the affections of his flock (AAB, 2-U-4). The intended replacement was Rev. Matthew Ryan.*

59. TO THE WARDENS AND VESTRY OF CHARLESTON, Baltimore, 16 November 1801

This is a copy of Carroll's letter to the vestry of Charleston sent later by Archbishop Leonard Neale (but in the hand of Ambrose Maréchal) to the Congregation of the Propaganda Fide. In large part the wording is the same as in the letter to Samuel Corbett (No. 58).[1]

Dr. Gallagher has been informed of the motives which induced Carroll to think of a change for him, which were not suggested by willful misrepresentations. "Far from seeking for causes of dissatisfaction with the clergymen my Brethren, dispersed through the United States, nothing gives me more pain [than] to hear of any." Dr. Gallagher knows how ready Carroll is to make allowance for failings that are neither habitual nor scandalous, but Carroll's proceedings with him were based on reports of disinterested persons. Gallagher has perhaps made known to the trustees what passed recently between them. The language of the sentiments expressed in Gallagher's letter was not calculated to remove any unfavorable impressions Carroll may have had. Carroll can not foresee the final issue of the new arrangement, but he is disposed to great forbearance rather than incur the danger of a schism. It is sad to hear of the lack of piety, neglect of the sacraments, and other abuses.

APF, America Centrale, 5: 609v-610r.

---

[1]*Archbishop Neale signed his name after "Vera Copia" at the end of the last of three letters of Carroll transcribed by Maréchal, which also include No. 78 below.*

60. TO MR. JAMES OELLERS, n.p., 19 November 1801

Carroll wrote that he still wished for a reconciliation of differences at Holy Trinity Parish (see Nos. 31 and 38).

> Oellers' letter of 11 October reached Carroll at Washington after a visitation through parts of Virginia, where an indisposition detained him. He is willing to go to all lengths to restore harmony but wishes more particulars and appoints Mr. Carr [see No. 38] to confer with Oellers. The charge that he had not given them a chance to be heard was unfounded. Once when Carroll went to Philadelphia for the purpose of reconciliation he was brought into court to hear from Oellers' lawyers the foulest abuse of the church he had ever heard, as if they had ransacked all Protestant libraries to defame it.[1] Oellers had not tried to moderate the rancor of their invectives. His lawyer had denied in Oellers' name that Carroll was his bishop and that Holy Trinity was in his jurisdiction. But burying the past in oblivion, Carroll asked that Oellers let him know the present disposition of his friends.

Letterbook 3, pp. 44-45 (see *JCP*, 2: 367).

---

[1]*When Carroll went to Philadelphia in 1797, the trustees had him arrested and subjected him in court to such humiliating treatment that Melville, Carroll, p. 207, was moved to remark: "It seems inconceivable that any man subjected to such indignities could go on negotiating with his persecutors, but the Bishop of Baltimore was too big a man for them all."*

61. TO REV. FREDERIC CESARIUS REUTER, O.F.M.CONV., n.p., 19 November 1801

Carroll wrote (in Latin) to Reuter, pastor of the German church in Baltimore, setting down the conditions for reconciliation.[1]

Mr. Carr will explain to Reuter why Carroll's response has been so long delayed. It is a matter of waiting for the Congregation of the Propaganda Fide to sort out all the various claims involving the jurisdiction of the ordinary and the rights of religious, all without detracting from the Holy See. "From my heart I desire peace and concord with the Germans of Philadelphia, and I would surrender my life for such a blessing." In the face of all the letters he has received about this case, Carroll has come to the following conclusion. As soon as Reuter has subscribed in writing to the enclosed articles Carroll will make provision and provide an office for him: 1) that he recognizes no other ecclesiastical jurisdiction in the diocese than that of the Sovereign Pontiff and the bishop of Baltimore; 2) that all Catholics of the diocese of whatever nationality are subject to that jurisdiction; 3) that no priest can without the approval of the bishop exercise any function in the diocese, or beyond those limits prescribed by the bishop; 4) that in giving Christian doctrine classes Reuter use no catechism but what the bishop prescribes and least of all the one Reuter has composed;

---

[1] *Fecher, German Parishes, pp. 143-44, cites a letter of Reuter to the Propaganda of 30 December 1801 for the contents of this letter.*

5) Reuter will employ himself in the care of souls only where the bishop decides.

Letterbook 3, pp. 45-46 (see *JCP*, 2: 367-68).

62. TO MR. JAMES OELLERS, Baltimore, 4 December 1801

Carroll wrote Oellers again on attempts at reconciliation (see No. 60).

In a P.S. dated 30 November in his letter of 25 November [AAB, 11B-W-8] Oellers said that Rev. William Elling had a conference with Rev. [Matthew] Carr. Although Carroll has not heard from Carr, Carroll must respond now because he is going to Port Tobacco tomorrow, disagreeable at this season and inconvenient, and will be gone about ten days. Carroll agrees to all but one of the conditions Oellers proposes in behalf of the trustees for reunion. The first, that the trustees will be involved in no new lawsuits, meets his full approval. To the second, that all suits be withdrawn, Carroll says that he had never brought suit and that he had not heard whether the suit brought by the trustees against him and Mr. [Leonard] Neale for contempt had been concluded. He was in no way concerned with this condition as he always wanted to keep church matters out of civil courts and earnestly recommends that every dispute of that kind be ended. The third condition, to show how anxious he was for reconciliation he would appoint Mr. Elling pastor if he would submit to the doctrine of the church and authority of the bishop, which could be done privately in such a way he would describe to Carr. The fourth condition, when reunion is agreed upon consonant with the doctrine and government of the church, public notice must be given of the termination of the dissension. The fifth condition, it having been publicly asserted that the bishop of Baltimore had no jurisdiction over Holy Trinity Church, it must be acknowledged in writing by Elling and the trustees that they are subject to his spiritual authority and that he has the same right to visit Holy Trinity as any other church in his diocese, the condition that required further explanation. Herein is required nothing but what every bishop is obliged by duty to demand. To do less would offer only a "treacherous peace." No one in Carroll's situation could be more moderate; he grants such favorable terms from a wish for the reconciliation of all for whose salvation Carroll is responsible to God.

Letterbook 3, pp. 46-47 (see *JCP*, 2: 368).

63. TO REV. WILLIAM ELLING, O.S.B., Baltimore, 4 December 1801

Carroll wrote to Elling on the same matters as in Nos. 60 and 62.

Carroll was glad to see Elling's handwriting again, but how could he say Carroll would not correspond with him when he had tried but Elling had not answered? He had even gone to his house. Carroll is disposed to forget all past differences and as far as anything personal freely to forgive. All shall be done privately. Carroll "must use the privilege of an old friend" to expostulate with Elling, when he speaks of the members of Holy Trinity Church as being subject only to the laws of God and the land in which they live, and reprobates the pretensions of Mr. Charles [Peter ?] Helbron. By the laws of God Carroll hopes he means likewise those of His Church.

Letterbook 3, pp. 47-48 (see *JCP*, 2: 368).

64. TO REV. LAURENCE SILVESTER PHELAN,[1] n.p., 27 December 1801

Carroll wrote Phelan, a former priest of Philadelphia then at Bohemia, about a transfer back to Philadelphia.

Mr. Beeston has informed Carroll of Phelan's refusal to leave Bohemia to go to Philadelphia before he received full value for the crop on the ground. This is not Carroll's concern. Mr. Fitzpatrick[2] alone has the right to the house. If Phelan stays, he must pay rent.

Letterbook 3, p. 48 (see *JCP*, 2: 368).

---

[1] *The priest signs all of his letters to Carroll as "Laur. Silv. Phelan."*
[2] *Rev. R. FitzPatrick, Phelan's replacement, may not have gone to Bohemia since he is still found at St. Mary's in Philadelphia in 1802.*

65. TO [?], n.p., [6 January 1802]

Carroll wrote this Latin extract on the back of a letter to which it has no bearing.

> Carroll writes this letter of recommendation for an unnamed person as he leaves for Europe on business. He also adds best wishes "before and after the reception of priestly ordination." He commends him first to the divine mercy and then to the prelates and pastors with whom he comes in contact.

AAB, 5-C-1.

66. TO REV. LAURENCE SILVESTER PHELAN, n.p., 11 January 1802

Carroll wrote again to Phelan about his transfer (see No. 64).

> Carroll is surprised that Phelan has not gone to Philadelphia. He had not insisted, but Phelan had written he would return to live there, this before he had sown any wheat for the next crop. Carroll never told anyone that Phelan might remain at Bohemia if he liked, and he is determined not to retract the promises he made in Philadelphia. The rest of Phelan's letter is a matter for the Corporation of the Clergy, to whom it will be referred. The opinion of Phelan's lawyer's may have some effect upon the Corporation but not upon Carroll.

Letterbook 3, p. 49 (see *JCP*, 2: 372).

67. TO MR. JAMES OELLERS, n.p., 22 January 1802

Carroll wrote Oellers in still another attempt to end the protracted schism at Holy Trinity (see Nos. 60, 62, 63).[1]

Oellers' letter dated both 31 December and 5 January [AAB, 5-Y-5] offers continued hope of a restoration of harmony, with Mr. Carr having withdrawn the suit instituted by Mr. [Peter] Helbron. The trustees must adhere to the conditions already specified, including reconciliation in the tribunal of confession. Carroll can make no further concessions without a written submission of the trustees to the authority of bishop of Baltimore and supplies a formula for the same. In it the trustees acknowledge for themselves and their constituents that they hold themselves subject to the jurisdiction of the bishop of Baltimore "for the time being"[2] according to the brief of the late pope erecting the see of Baltimore.

Letterbook 3, pp. 49-51 (see *JCP*, 2: 372).

68. TO REV. JOHN ASHTON, n.p., 22 January 1802

Another letter to Ashton concerning his replacement (see Nos. 51, 52, 55).

If Mr. Vergnes[3] introduced such a subject as Ashton said he did in his of 6 January, he

---

[1]*This is a labored draft with many deletions and additions.*

[2]*What Carroll undoubtedly meant here is that another bishop might in the future be placed over them.*

[3]*Rev. William Vergnes was pastor at Upper Marlboro.*

stands in need of much advice, but if he said the quality of the sin was changed by the quality of the accomplice as regards incest, adultery, sacrilege, etc., Carroll would agree. As to Ashton's return to White Marsh Carroll will not bind himself in the manner Ashton wishes. "Our brethren" will discover in Ashton's extraordinary requisition only a pretense to secede from his engagements with them. Carroll thanks Ashton for not believing him capable of sending [Bolton] to White Marsh to spy on him. He went there with Ashton's consent and to his entire satisfaction.

Letterbook 3, p. 52.

69. TO REV. WILLIAM ELLING, O.S.B., n.p., [probably 22 January 1802]

This draft was Carroll's last attempt to end the schism in Philadelphia (see No. 63), in this case successful.

Carroll received Elling's letter of the 6th with great pleasure, which brought to mind the many testimonies of his personal regard and of his adhesion to the true principles of religion. Nothing remains but for him to complete the work happily begun. The only obstacle, according to Carr, is Elling's telling his adherents that they must rectify their confessions, the principles of which he had imbibed in Rome[1] and outside Carroll's powers

---

[1]*Elling had lived in Rome prior to his coming to America and had been recommended to Carroll, with reservations, by Rev. John Thorpe.*

to dispense. This may be done as privately as possible. The sooner he does it the greater will be the benefit to those who rely on him. Delay increases the difficulty. Dishonor springs from persistence in a wrong course, not in retraction. Elling's own conscience is involved as well as that of others. How joyfully will Carroll then meet him when this is done.

Letterbook 3, pp. 52-53 (see *JCP*, 2: 370-71).

70. TO MESSRS. THOMAS WRIGHT AND COMPANY, Baltimore, 11 February 1802[1]

This is another of Carroll's routine letters to his London bankers.

Carroll draws this day in favor of George [Peter ?] Jenkins for £9.8.1 partly due by Sir Thomas Moore for his nephews's account of £59.10.8 due from Bishop Douglass May 1801. The balance of Sir Thomas's account being only £29.9.4, this draft is inadequate to the necessary expenditures of his nephew, for which he will soon have to draw more.

Letterbook 3, p. 53.

---

[1] *A duplicate was sent 26 February.*

71. TO DR. EDWARD LYNAH, Baltimore, 14 February 1802

This is the first of five letters (see also Nos. 80, 81, 84, and 92) Carroll wrote to Dr. Edward Lynah, a prominent Catholic of Charleston, that were taken to Rome by Rev. Robert Browne, O.S.A., in 1819 as evidence in his case against Archbishop Ambrose Maréchal.[1]

Replying to Lynah's letters of 20 November and 2 January Carroll says that he has decided that Mr. [Matthew] Ryan is not suitable for Charleston for a number of reasons. Rev. [John Edward] Mondésir will be appointed but for the time being Dr. Gallagher's removal is not contemplated. Carroll speaks of provision for Mondésir, who is about thirty-three and of good health and though French born has received most of his education in America. Carroll hopes to visit Charleston. Mr. Beeston sends regards to Lynah's family, as does Carroll. In a postscript Carroll reveals that Rev. Mr. Lemercier[2] is in Baltimore waiting to return to France.

APF, America Centrale, 5: 634r-40r.

---

[1]*The letters were translated into Italian and the originals returned to Lynah at his request. Large parts of the translations are almost impossible to read on microfilm because of bleeding. The summations of Kenneally, Calendar, 1, Nos. 519-523, are helpful.*

[2]*Rev. Angadreme Lemercier, an exile from Saint Dominque, went to Savannah, Georgia, in 1796 and built a church there in 1799.*

72. TO REV. WILLIAM STRICKLAND, S.J., n.p., 26 February 1802

On the same day Carroll sent his duplicate to Wright and Company (No. 70) he penned the extract of a more detailed letter to Rev. William Strickland.

Carroll has submitted Strickland's reduced demand for £70 to the Corporation of the Clergy as promised, but his examination of their correspondence induces him to believe there are mistakes in Strickland's statement. Carroll concludes that a balance was struck between the English ex-Jesuits and the American Corporation and all demands liquidated, mentioning a legacy of Mr. [Joseph] Howe[1] and the account of Anthony Carroll,[2] and quoting a letter of 1795. The mistake was in not having credited the Americans with the Howe legacy. Another and convincing proof that Strickland considered the American debt as discharged is that he placed to Carroll's credit the Pennsylvania annuity[3] which Strickland had appropriated to his office as security. Carroll will depend upon Strickland's seeing the accuracy of his elucidation and draw therefore as usual upon Wright and Company.

Letterbook 3, pp. 53-54.

---

[1]*Joseph Howe, an English Jesuit, died prior to June 1792. See AAB, 6-O-4 and 8-G-8.*
[2]*Anthony Carroll, an English Jesuit, as executor of the will of James Carroll in Maryland, still had responsibilities for certain legacies. See below No. 136.*
[3]*The Sir John James Fund. See No. 41.*

73. TO REV. LAURENCE SILVESTER PHELAN, n.p., 15 March 1802

Carroll wrote Phelan on his failure to follow through on earlier instructions (Nos. 64 and 66).

> In consequence of Phelan's failure to abide by Carroll's arrangements and earlier directives he is to consider himself as no longer having a pastoral charge and his faculties "for the present" are withdrawn.[1]

Letterbook 3, p. 54 (see *JCP*, 2: 386).

74. TO MESSRS. THOMAS WRIGHT AND COMPANY, Baltimore, 3 May 1802

This is a follow-up to Carroll's letter of 11 February (No. 70).

> Carroll refers to his letter of 11 February and duplicate of 26 February. Bishop Douglass for Mr. Strickland had paid for him in May 1801 £59.10.8 and the additional sum in Carroll's draft of £21.9.4 was for the support of Sir Thomas Moore's nephew. Carroll had mentioned that he would call for an additional sum, and, since the annuity from Bishop Douglass falls due this month, Carroll had drawn

---

[1]*Phelan would later be named pastor at Chambersburg, Pennsylvania.*

that day for £124 in favor of Mr. Luke Tiernan[1] of Baltimore. Besides their honoring this draft Carroll wishes Messrs. Wright to pay the superior of the Carmelites at Canford House £15.9, being the amount received by their prioress, Mrs. Dickenson,[2] in Maryland. Carroll provides figures that show a balance of £1.7.8, which will be settled in the next account.

Letterbook 3, p. 54.

75. PETITION TO THE HOLY FATHER, [30 May 1802]

Carroll applied to the Holy Father for a series of favors.

Carroll asks for marriage dispensations, for the validation of marriage dispensations granted after the expiration of his faculties, for an extension of the jubilee indulgences, and for a dispensation from the customary *ad limina* visit to Rome.[3]

APF, Udienze, 40: 355r-56r.

---

[1] *Irish-born Luke Tiernan (1757-1839) settled first in western Maryland but moved to Baltimore to become a wealthy merchant. He was a trustee of the cathedral congregation (1796-1839) and a prominent member of the Hibernian Society. He would often be employed by Carroll for business transactions abroad.*

[2] *English-born Mother Clare Joseph Dickenson (1755-1830) came to Maryland in 1790 and succeeded Mother Bernardina Matthews as prioress of the Mount Carmel community in 1800.*

[3] *The favors were granted in an audience of 30 May 1802.*

76. TO REV. MICHAEL LACY,[1] Baltimore, 12 July 1802

Carroll wrote to this priest in Philadelphia about a new appointment.

> The unhappy disagreement between Lacy and
> Mr. Rossiter[2] reduces Carroll to the necessity
> of telling Lacy that he must leave St. Mary's.
> Carroll greatly esteems Lacy's service and will
> soon propose another station, which he hopes
> will be more durable, afford him decent sub-
> sistence, and provide an opportunity for him
> to exercise his zeal.

Letterbook 3, p. 55 (see *JCP*, 2: 393).

77. TO BISHOP WILLIAM COPPINGER, Baltimore, 23 September 1802

In this letter Carroll wrote to the bishop of Cloyne, Ireland, about the bishop's brother and Rev. Cornelius Mahony.

> Carroll was truly mortified that he had no op-
> portunity to help Bishop Coppinger's brother.
> He landed at New York and went immediately
> to the Mississippi. Carroll wishes him well in
> his new residence, where he hopes he will re-
> ceive no molestation from the other side of the
> river now that Louisiana is ceded by the
> Spaniards to the French. Since his brother's

---

[1]*Rev. Michael Lacy was in Boston as early as 1781. From there he moved to Philadelphia and would be assigned by Carroll to Norfolk, Virginia, where he died in 1815.*

[2]*John Rossiter, O.S.A., came to America to establish the Augustinian province mentioned in connection with Matthew Carr, O.S.A. (see No. 38, n. 1).*

arrival he has not heard from Dr. Matthew O'Brien,[1] at which he is surprised, as he was to tell Carroll of Coppinger's answer concerning Rev. Mr. Mahony. Coppinger had written that he was deserving of censure. On his coming to America O'Brien had sent a favorable account of him except that he had left Cloyne without obtaining Coppinger's consent, which he was sure he would receive in three or four months. Carroll had refused to allow him to serve the congregation at Albany that had invited him over until he had the consent. O'Brien wrote again that Coppinger had refused the consent until Mahony made certain concessions, which Carroll has now forgotten. Carroll had written that if Mahony in conscience felt that he was under no censure he could continue to say Mass rather than see the congregation dispersed and had heard nothing since. "The cruel & treacherous treatment, to which the Catholics of Ireland have been so long sacrificed, always excites my sympathy, and not infrequently, my indignation." Never was the treachery more exemplified perhaps than in the late maneuvers for effecting the union.[2] But the comfort of a Christian is that "divine justice will hereafter order all things."

Diocesan Archives of Cloyne.

---

[1] *Rev. Matthew O'Brien, a brother of William O'Brien, O.P., had come to Albany in 1798 with a reputation for preaching but soon after moved to New York City, where he received Elizabeth Ann Seton into the church. See also No. 46.*

[2] *Irish Catholics were led to believe that Catholic emancipation would follow the Act of Union [of Britain and Ireland] passed in 1800.*

---

78. TO REV. SIMON FELIX GALLAGHER, Baltimore, 3 November 1802

Carroll wrote Gallagher concerning instructions he had received from the Congregation of the Propaganda Fide.

> Carroll has received from the cardinal prefect of the Propaganda Fide a copy of Gallagher's appeal to the pope occasioned by Carroll's request for his resignation at Charleston. The cardinal wanted Carroll to set a time limit for Gallagher's presenting his case, which Carroll sets as the last day of July 1803, during which time Gallagher may present such documents in Rome as may be useful to his case.

Letterbook 3, p. 55, and APF, America Centrale, 5: 610rv (see *JCP*, 2: 396, where the addressee is incorrectly given as Cardinal Hyacinth [Giacinto] Gerdil, the cardinal prefect).

79. TO THE GERMAN CONGREGATION OF BALTIMORE, n.p., 3 November 1802

This is a copy of a paper delivered to the Germans of the new church of St. John the Evangelist.

> The bishop of Baltimore declares that within twelve months of the time of writing he will allow parochial services to be performed in the new church provided Mr. [Cesarius] Reuter, who is appointed to say Mass there, or some other priest in default of Reuter, prove himself deserving of that confidence.

Letterbook 3, p. 55.

80. TO DR. EDWARD LYNAH, Baltimore, 1 February 1803

This is the second of Carroll's five letters to Dr. Lynah of Charleston that were carried to Rome (see No. 71).

> Replying to Lynah's letters of 27 December and 6 January Carroll speaks of Lynah's venerable mother and his amiable son James at Georgetown College. Mr. Lemercier is disposed to go to Charleston. Two things discourage Carroll from sending him there, the difficulty of retiring Gallagher and the want of fluency in English of Lemercier, but Carroll wants a person of zeal and virtue as pastor. Mr. Beeston joins Carroll in presenting their respects to Lynah's family.

APF, America Centrale, 5: 660r-62v.

81. TO DR. EDWARD LYNAH, Baltimore, 13 April 1803

This is the third of Carroll's five letters to Dr. Lynah of Charleston that were carried to Rome (see No. 71).

> Carroll has just received Lynah's letter of 21 March, with its regards from his mother. Carroll explains his shortage of priests and the difficulties of finding one for Charleston. He suggests Mr. Dunlevy [?]. There is little possibility of finding a priest in the neighboring states. Carroll unites with Beeston in extending best wishes to Lynah's family.

APF, America Centrale, 5: 642r-44r.

82. TO CARDINAL STEFANO BORGIA, Baltimore, 16 May 1803[1]

Carroll wrote to the cardinal prefect of the Propaganda Fide regarding the stratagems of Rev. Simon Felix Gallagher.

Borgia has asked that a copy of previous letters be sent to him again. Rev. Felix Gallagher had written almost three weeks ago that for health's sake he would leave Charleston for a few months and perhaps forever but that he was not yet giving up the congregation committed to him there. Then he wrote again that he had left for Rome to defend his cause. Carroll doubts that he will because he must know that no verdict has been reached against which he can appeal. Carroll patiently awaits the judgment of the Holy See. He will send no further testimony from Charleston on the poor reputation Gallagher has among the good people there. Gallagher may bring documents from those he has bound to himself and perhaps petitions from friends in France where he studied sacred and profane letters. But Carroll is persuaded the Holy See will not "change the order of administering this diocese" by a judgement before it is first argued before the bishop. He hopes this letter will clear up his differences with Gallagher. [Carroll then adds a paragraph renewing his request for faculties for marriages especially those involving disparity of cult. Though with

---

[1]*Under the same date Carroll sent a second version with the added clause that clergy in charge of souls in the United States were only missionaries, not parish priests [with parochial rights].*

less detail he makes the same requests he will
later make in a letter of 14 February 1804 in
JCP, 2: 433-35.]

APF, America Centrale, 5: 608rv; Letterbook 3, p. 58 (see *JCP*,
2: 414).

83. TO FATHER GENERAL GABRIEL GRUBER, S.J., n.p., [16/25 May 1803][1]

*To the superior general of the remnant of the Society of Jesus that
had survived in Russia Carroll began a letter that would initiate the
process of the restoration of the Society in the United States.*

On 10 March of this year Carroll and the bishop of Gortyna [Leonard Neale], his coadjutor,
had written a letter to the superior general of
the Society of Jesus, whose name they did not
know at the time, but he afterwards learned
that the votes of the Society had been cast for
"Your Paternity," now father and director. "We
do not doubt that this has been accomplished
by the highest blessings of divine mercy; therefore [the letter ends at this point]."[2]

Letterbook 3, p. 58.

---

[1] *This Latin extract follows immediately, at the end of the page, Carroll's letter to Cardinal Borgia of 16 May 1803 in Letterbook 3 (No. 82). It may have been the date given in the following footnote.*

[2] *Carroll at this point evidently decided to continue the letter elsewhere than in his letterbook. The continuation may be the same as the letter whose beginning is missing in JCP, 2: 414-15, which itself, as well as the date 25 May 1803, is found in Hughes, Documents, pp. 818-19, where no source is indicated.*

84. TO DR. EDWARD LYNAH, Baltimore, 19 May 1803.

This is the fourth of Carroll's five letters to Dr. Lynah of Charleston that were carried to Rome (see No. 71).

> Dr. Gallagher has written to Carroll that he will be absent from Charleston for some months owing to ill health. Carroll believes that he is on his way to Europe in connection with his appeal to Rome and its antecedents [see No. 82]. He adopts Lynah's suggestion for a joint statement on Gallagher's conduct signed by Mr. Murphy [?] and recommends that it be sent directly to the secretary of Propaganda Fide. And again he presents the usual respects from Mr. Beeston and himself to Lynah's family.

APF, America Centrale, 5: 646r-50r.

85. TO REV. SIMON FELIX GALLAGHER, Baltimore, 11 January 1804

Carroll wrote to Gallagher concerning the latter's plans.

> Carroll had received Gallagher's letter of 24 December. It was not clear when Carroll left New York whether Gallagher would return to Charleston since he had so many times spoken of the danger of a residence in Charleston and had voluntarily surrendered his pastoral charge there. Gallagher then told Rev. Mr. Lemercier [whom Carroll had sent to replace

him] that he had not resigned nor been deprived of his charge. He had, Carroll reminded him, resolved to live in retirement for one or two months before accepting the charge of Albany in the hope that it would renew his zeal and improve his health. When Carroll returned to Philadelphia he wrote the vestry of this decision, but it appears the letter had not reached Charleston when Gallagher wrote. He and the vestry must see the impropriety of removing Lemercier without cause. It is natural that Gallagher's friends would want to keep him and that Gallagher would want to complete work on the church he had begun, but this could not be done without the danger of his renewing his disorder and of injuring another person [Lemercier]. The sentiments of humility, piety, and true zeal with which he had edified Carroll in New York offer assurance of his acquiescence.

Letterbook 3, p. 60 (see *JCP*, 2: 431).

86. TO THE GERMAN CONGREGATION OF BALTIMORE, Baltimore, 16 January 1804

Carroll scolded the German congregation. The conduct of both the congregation and Rev. Cesarius Reuter had worsened (see Nos. 61 and 79).

Carroll informs Mr. J. Shorb and others that, as they have shown no remorse for having prevented him from entering St. John's the day before, he would listen to no proposals from them until they offered reparation. Although his answer will probably be misrepresented to many of the ignorant of the congregation, he can send no other.[1]

Letterbook 3, p. 60 (see *JCP*, 2: 431).

87. TO THE WARDENS AND VESTRY Of CHARLESTON, n.p., 30 January 1804

Carroll wrote the wardens and vestry in an effort to avert a crisis in Charleston (see No. 85).

The failure of a packet boat to bring a letter to the vestry and to Mr. Lemercier has been the cause of difficulty. The vestry was told of Carroll's having met Dr. Gallagher in New York and of his having freely resigned his claim to their church in the presence of Mr. [William or Matthew ?] O'Brien, agreeing that it would be prejudicial for him to return. At his wish Carroll had assigned him to Albany when his strength was restored, but he decided there was business in Charleston he must transact first. Carroll had told the vestry that he had sent Lemercier as their pastor but with instructions to have no contention with Gallagher public or private. It now pained him to

---

[1]*At the same time Carroll sent a statement for Reuter to sign acknowledging Carroll's jurisdiction, apologizing for his role in Carroll's exclusion from the church, and promising he would accept any appointment made for the church. See JCP, 2: 432-33. Carroll eventually had to take Reuter to court in order to remove him.*

hear Lemercier exhibited hostility to the vestry claiming exclusively the pastoral functions. The vestry had always shown attachment to the discipline of the church and a personal regard for Carroll, and he hoped it would agree to whatever appointment he would make.

Letterbook 3, pp. 61-62 (see *JCP*, 2: 433).

88. TO REV. SIMON FELIX GALLAGHER, n.p., 6 February 1804

Carroll wrote Gallagher concerning his untoward conduct in Charleston.

Carroll's letter of 11 January explicitly stated his determination regarding the pastoral charge of Charleston, and Gallagher can see why he can not deviate from it. If he had received that letter in time the scene of 22 January, when he prevented Lemercier from saying Mass, would not have occurred. Lemercier withdrew rather then cause a public scene, which Carroll had instructed him to do. Carroll hopes that Gallagher retroceded to Lemercier the use of the altar as soon as he received his letter. He requests him again to go to Albany.

Letterbook 3, p. 62 (see *JCP*, 2: 433).

89. TO THE WARDENS AND VESTRY OF CHARLESTON, n.p., 6 February 1804

This is a follow-up to Carroll's letter of 30 January (No. 87).

Carroll had omitted one observation in his letter of 30 January. When Gallagher said he was leaving last April and that it was necessary to find another pastor, those approached declined, fearing the return of yellow fever to the sea ports. But Lemercier accepted. He wrote the 23rd saying he withdrew from the altar rather than have an open conflict. Carroll hopes Gallagher will honor his pledge.

Letterbook 3, pp. 62-63.

90. TO REV. SIMON FELIX GALLAGHER, n.p., 28 February 1804

Carroll penned an extract of a letter to Gallagher indicating a change of mind.

If the great majority of the congregation in Charleston are so opposed to Mr. Lemercier as to leave him no peace of mind or to render his ministry useless Carroll will adopt such measures as the good of religion will require.

Letterbook 3, p. 64 (see *JCP*, 2: 438).

91. TO MR. PIERRE-CLEMENT LAUSSAT, n.p., [between 28 February and 16 April 1804]

The transfer of the Louisiana Territory from Spain to France occasioned this response to the French colonial prefect there.

> M. Pichon [?] had forwarded Laussat's instructive letter of 28 January. In the name of the church in the United States Carroll thanks Laussat for his interest in the good conduct of its ministers, and for the homage he renders to the principles owed the respective rights of the spiritual power and of the state. As regards the conduct of the Rev. [Michael] Barrière [see No. 26], however, Carroll's commission does not extend to the Louisiana Territory. After the departure of the last bishop of Louisiana his authority passed to the cathedral chapter [of New Orleans] until the Holy See determines otherwise.

Letterbook 3, pp. 64-65 (see *JCP*, 2: 429).

92. TO DR. EDWARD LYNAH, Baltimore, 15 March 1804

This is the last of the five letters Carroll wrote to Dr. Lynah in Charleston that were carried to Rome (see No. 71).

> This is a confidential letter. Carroll regrets he has not written since his long trip to the state

of Maine,[1] concerning which he will relate certain events that he leaves to Lynah's discretion, because even Mr. Lemercier has not been told everything. In New York he found Dr. Gallagher in a wretched state of mind and body that stirred Carroll's compassion. He seemed ready to recognize the principles of religion and the ill effects of his own intemperance. He had been in England and Ireland and there had seen the wickedness of his ways, and encouraged by Carroll's words of consolation made an absolute renunciation of his office in Charleston. If he continues his abstemious life he could be "an ornament to our ministry." The wardens and vestry of Charleston wrote 25 February indicating their complete submission to episcopal authority but they complain of the inordinate conduct of Mr. Lemercier. Carroll asks for Lynah's impartial opinion. Mr. Beeston joins him again in extending best wishes to his family.

APF, America Centrale, 5: 652r-58v.

---

[1] *On 29 September Carroll had consecrated Holy Cross Church in Boston. In October he went with Rev. John Cheverus of Boston and Rev. Jacques-René Romagne, who was returning to his mission among the Indians, to visit the Catholic congregations in Maine (Robert H. Lord, John E. Sexton, and Edward T. Harrington,* History of the Archdiocese of Boston in the Various Stages of Its Development, 1604-1943, *3 vols. [New York: Sheed and Ward, 1944], 1: 605).*

93. TO MESSRS. THOMAS WRIGHT AND COMPANY, Baltimore, 16 April 1804

This is another of Carroll's letters to his London bankers.

Wrights' last, 2 September 1803, showed a balance of £34.17.4, to which would be added £59.10.8 to be paid by either Rev. William Strickland or Bishop Douglass and £50.9.4 by Sir Thomas Moore, totalling £110 drawn that day in favor of Luke Tiernan and Company, which Wrights' is asked to honor. Of the £34.17.4 Wright should pay £32.4.4 to Mrs. Smith, abbess of the Poor Clares of Rouen now at Haggerston, which Carroll had received for Mrs. Sarah Edelen's account.[1]

Letterbook 3, p. 66.

94. TO BISHOP WILLIAM COPPINGER, Baltimore, 23 September 1804

Carroll wrote the bishop of Cloyne again (see No. 77) concerning the status of Rev. Cornelius Mahony and other matters.

After a long interruption Carroll assures Coppinger of his concern and pain at seeing the bishop's efforts to instill in his flock princi-

---

[1] *Sarah Edelen (Sister Mary Teresa) and possibly also the abbess were natives of Maryland. The Poor Clares, who attracted a number of Marylanders, including Archbishop Neale's sister, were forced by the French invasion to move to Haggerston, in county Northumberland, England.*

ples of subordination and peace so misconstrued by the lord chancellor.[1] Carroll read with pleasure Coppinger's vindication of the "foul aspersion" cast on him and on all Irish Catholics. The proceedings of the Irish government towards Catholics, whom they have in their power to unite "hand & heart" in the national defense, are the worst symptoms of the danger hanging over Ireland. The old maxim, "Whom God wishes to destroy he first makes mad," points to a danger greater than the armies of the Emperor Napoleon. In his last Coppinger had said he would accept any satisfaction made by Mr. [Cornelius] Mahony that Carroll deemed sufficient and then allow Carroll to employ him. In consequence Mahony had shown a copy of his humble submission to Coppinger to Rev. [Matthew] O'Brien in New York, which induced Carroll to give him employment, but he would resign him again to Coppinger if the bishop thinks otherwise. After a short stay in New York Coppinger's brother had been persuaded to go to Kentucky to begin a business that required more capital, Carroll fears, than the brother could raise and for which that country is hardly ripe. He had wanted Carroll to obtain advances from a house in Baltimore, but failing in this he had not heard from him for eighteen months.

Diocesan Archives of Cloyne.

---

[1]*John Freeman-Mitford, Lord Redesdale, chancellor of Ireland, had accused Coppinger of trying to "kindle fanaticism in the popish multitude" when he restored a priest who had been involved in the Rebellion of 1798 to his former parish after his return from exile.*

95. TO MR. DANIEL BRENT, Baltimore, 1 November 1804

Brent had moved from the Treasury Department in 1793 to the State Department, where he would become first secretary. Carroll wrote him on family matters.

Carroll received that day Daniel's letter of 29 October telling him that Daniel's mother had recovered from a long fever.[1] Carroll hoped also that Kitty's[2] indisposition was transient. The boys had dined with him and expected to recover lost time. Robert was not taking logic but it was no great loss because of the poor way it was being taught.[3] Carroll regretted, however, that Robert's attention was confined to Spanish, with some French and mathematics, to the exclusion of Latin. He would occasionally suggest the best way to employ his time. Robert and Dudley told Carroll that Daniel and his brother William believed that Daniel could dispose of several [lottery] tickets now that the drawing had started.[4] Carroll believed Aunt Betsy should purchase the land Daniel mentioned but with certain cautions.[5] Carroll would have to sell one of his shares of

[1]*Ann Carroll Brent, Carroll's sister, died soon after, in November 1804, and was buried in the Carroll cemetery, Rock Creek (Forest Glen).*

[2]*Catherine Brent (d. 1837), Daniel's sister, married George Digges of Warburton and Green Hill (Chillum).*

[3]*Brent, Descendants, pp. 136-37, maintains that Daniel married in April 1813 Eliza, daughter of Robert Walsh of Baltimore, with whom he had only two children, Anne and Robert Walsh, both of whom died in infancy. If so, "the boys" were probably Daniel's nephews. Robert was likely Robert Young Brent (1789-1855), son of Robert, who was at the time a student at Georgetown College.*

[4]*The lottery tickets were for the building of the Cathedral of the Assumption.*

[5]*Elizabeth Carroll (1743-1821), Carroll's youngest and unmarried sister.*

the Potomac stock to help.[1] At Daniel's brother's suggestion Alexius took Carroll's bay horse to someone to prepare him for sale in the spring.[2] Alexius also has a coat that could be given to George Carroll.[3] Nora Carroll[4] is also well. Daniel is asked to send letters to Georgetown.

The Catholic Mirror, 2 November 1889.

96. TO THE CONGREGATION OF CLEARFIELD SETTLEMENT (LORETTO), n.p., 30 November 1804

When dissension arose in Gallitzin's congregation at Loretto, Carroll commissioned the nearest priest to investigate and composed a letter to be posted on the church door.

Carroll tells the congregation that he has known for some time of the uneasiness between the Rev. Mr. Smith [Gallitzin][5] and some individuals in the parish. He was convinced that the pastor had acted with the best of motives and insisted that nothing stood in the way of a complete reconciliation, that the pastor was willing to act towards all with fatherly tenderness, and that they in turn should give him proofs of their confidence in him. They

---

[1]*Carroll had purchased at $400 per share a large amount of stock in the Potomac Company, the forerunner of the Chesapeake and Ohio Canal.*

[2]*Alexius was Carroll's man servant (slave). The brother in this case was probably Robert Brent (1764-1819), first mayor of Washington, D.C. For Alexius see Appendix 3.*

[3]*Probably George Attwood Carroll (1788-1844), the archbishop's great-nephew.*

[4]*Probably Nora Carroll (1791-1861), the daughter of Daniel Carroll of Duddington and Anna Brent, daughter of William Brent and Eleanor Carroll (1737-1788), sister of the archbishop.*

[5]*Gallitzin was known to most by his alias, Augustine Smith.*

should, moreover, be grateful to him for the many hardships that he was undergoing for them and the deprivations of many temporal advantages that he might elsewhere have enjoyed.

Lemcke, p. 150.

97. TO REV. NICHOLAS ZOCCHI,[1] n.p., 5 December 1804

This is an extract Carroll wrote on a letter of Zocchi's dated the same day Carroll penned his response.

Zocchi should not be surprised to find Carroll using "the language of discontent and almost reproach" for Zocchi's having misconstrued Carroll's letter of 10 November [not found]. Though he had said he would not use his authority to compel Zocchi to go to Zachiah,[2] it was impossible for him to mistake Carroll's meaning by supposing he would be allowed to stay in charge of Taneytown and Winchester. Zocchi knew that he had assigned these congregations to Dr. Caffry.[3] What was Carroll to think if he should continue in their neighborhood after the clear manifestation of his will that Zocchi should not be their pastor?

AAB, 8-T-6.

---

[1] *Rev. Nicholas Zocchi (1773-1845) was the only member of the Fathers of the Faith, or Paccanarists, an attempt to continue the Society of Jesus under another name, to come to the United States. Arriving about 1803, he took up residence at Taneytown, where he would remain the rest of his life.*

[2] *St. Mary's, Bryantown, Charles County.*

[3] *Rev. Anthony Caffry (or Caffrey), O.P., who began St. Patrick's Parish in Washington, D.C., in 1794.*

98. PETITION TO THE HOLY SEE, [1805]

Probably in early 1805 Carroll sought a special permission from the Congregation of the Propaganda Fide.

> **Carroll asks permission to request the clergy of Maryland [Corporation of the Clergy?] to assign him a part of the funds of Georgetown College so that he can set up five sources of episcopal income [mensae].[1]**

APF, Udienze, 43: 324r.

99. TO REV. DEMETRIUS GALLITZIN, n.p., 2 January 1805

Prince Gallitzin was deprived of his family inheritance by the Russian government for having been ordained a priest. Carroll sent him the documents concerning this unfortunate turn of events with the following letter.

> **The letter of Gallitzin's mother to Carroll is discouraging.[2] Gallitzin will find that he is a victim of his faith and of his relatives in Russia, who used anti-Catholic legislation to enrich themselves. This distresses Carroll because he knows that Gallitzin, relying on remittances from Europe, has incurred large debts. Carroll wants to relieve him by the sale**

---

[1] *There is no record of a response to this petition.*
[2] *The German-born Countess Amalia von Schmettau, the mother, was a Catholic.*

of properties at Huntingdon and by other means. But Carroll is unable to help much because of his own straitened circumstances. He is sorry because he knows Gallitzin's distressed condition was the result of his charity and zeal, but it should teach him to temper his zeal with prudence, "to mix some of the serpent's qualities with the simplicity of the dove." He hopes that God will grant Gallitzin peace of mind and freedom from worry and anxiety.

Lemcke, pp. 152-53.

100. TO REV. SIMON FELIX GALLAGHER, Baltimore, 19 April 1805

Carroll wrote Gallagher of a plan to bring peace to the congregation in Charleston.

The restoration of peace and unity to the congregation at Charleston has for months past employed Carroll's chief attention. He waives all discussion regarding the past. Since Gallagher [and Carroll] is weary of dissension, he presents a plan: 1) he will encourage the resignation of Mr. Lemercier; 2) he will substitute as parish priest Mr. [Louis] Sibourd, whom Gallagher wished to have as his companion; 3) since emoluments were of little concern to Sibourd, he could leave most such to his assistant [Gallagher]; 4) he is not ambitious for the title of rector and will serve Gallagher in a subordinate role. The alternatives now are to confirm Lemercier or reappoint Gallagher, either of which would tend to perpetuate disunion. To complete all this Gallagher's cooperation is essential and would be the test of judging his past and his candor. Gallagher will reconcile his friends to the plan by explaining its advantages and will prevail upon the vestry to make reasonable compensation to Mr. Lemercier. No new appointments will be made. Its adoption will allay Carroll's suspicion that prejudice and passion were the reason for the list of charges against Lemercier. Sibourd would live with Gallagher, who could use his services as he pleased. This plan, Carroll expects, will conciliate the Irish and satisfy the French.

Letterbook 3, pp. 66-67 (see *JCP*, 2: 477).

101. TO REV. FRANCIS IGNATIUS NEALE,[1] Baltimore, 6 June 1805

Carroll wrote to Francis Neale, fiscal agent of the Corporation of the Clergy, regarding land held by Jesuits in the middle of the eighteenth century and other matters.

Mr. Bitouzey[2] thought the defect was in Mr. Thorold's[3] will but Neale now writes Carroll

---

[1]*Francis Ignatius Neale (1754-1836), a younger brother of Bishop Leonard Neale and Charles Neale, would enter the restored Jesuits in 1806. Charles Neale (1751-1823), chaplain of the Carmelite nuns, would reenter the Jesuits in 1805 and eventually be named their superior.*

[2]*Rev. Germain Barnaby Bitouzey, though not a former Jesuit, would be admitted to the Select Body of the Corporation of the Clergy and in 1801 entrusted with the management of White Marsh. He would later complain against the invasion of the "Russian Association," as he called the restored Jesuits, and eventually return to France.*

[3]*George Thorold, S.J. (1670-1742), was superior of the Maryland Mission 1725-1734. In his will of 16 June 1737, and proved 22 November 1742, Thorold left all [Jesuit] estates to Richard Molyneux, and should he predecease him to James Quin. He also willed to Quin an estate in England deeded him by Lord Cardigan. For the problems arising from their wills or want thereof see Hughes, Documents, pp. 207-9, 254-55, 270, and passim.*

that it originated with Mr. Richard Molyneux,[1] which is more likely and unfortunately embraces more of "our" estates. Mr. [James] Quin [S.J.] died in 1746 or 1747, killed by his horse dragging him on the gunwhale of the ferry at Choptank River. He was, as Neale suggests, an Englishman. Of his will Carroll knows nothing. Neale may defer his journey to Bohemia. Pasquet[2] will be at the Marsh [White Marsh] tomorrow or next day with Dr. Scannell [?], nephew of Dr. Matthews [?]. Carroll intends to go to the Marsh the 1st or 2nd of July so that the trustees may meet in that or the following week. He will "indite" three Masses to be said by all members of the Select Body [Corporation of the Clergy] to beg the direction of the Holy Ghost on "our" deliberations. Francis's brother [Leonard] will give this notice. Mr. Richmond [?] has been asked to make "entreats" at Easton. In a postscript Carroll sends his compliments to "good Mr. Bitouzey" and says that Pasquet sent 500 bushels of corn to him that had been expected at Baird's Point, South River, last Monday. Mr. Beeston will attend to Bitouzey's business. [There follows in another hand a judgment of the court of 29 May 1805 regarding Richard Molyneux's will and in still another hand questions about the present holders of estates. Then in Carroll's hand:] Thorold died at St. Thomas Manor, Charles County. Quin died

---

[1]*Richard Molyneux, S.J. (1696-1766), was named superior of the Maryland Mission in 1736 and again in 1743.*
[2]*Rev. William Pasquet, a secular priest, was admitted to the Select Body of the Corporation of the Clergy and in 1802 entrusted with the management of Bohemia.*

1747. Richard Molyneux returned to England 1749. James Carroll died at Newtown 15 November 1756. [Lightly in pencil in Carroll's hand is part of the will of George Thorold.]

MPA, box 23, folder 11, no. 90R3.

102. TO MESSRS. THOMAS WRIGHT AND COMPANY, Baltimore, 9 June 1805

This is another of Carroll's letters to his London bankers.

Rev. [Anthony] Caffry had disposed of the £20 Carroll mentioned in his March letter. In a former letter he wanted the bankers to answer a draft of £20 of Rev. Peter Jenkins on Carroll's credit. Carroll just drew for £130 favor of Luke Tiernan and Company, of which £50 on the account of Sir Thomas Moore and £59.10.8 on credit of the payment due last month from Bishop Douglass through Mr. Strickland. The rest of the draft will be made up by the balance of Carroll's last account.

Letterbook 3, p. 67.

103. TO REV. JOSEPH HERMAN STÖCKER, n.p., 25 November 1805

This is an extract of a letter to the pastor of Lancaster, Pennsylvania.

Carroll will tell the German supplicants of Baltimore who wish Stöcker as their pastor that he will not ask him to leave Lancaster unless he is unhappy there, a promise he made to Stöcker earlier. The bearer of the petition, however, is going to Lancaster in the hope of inducing him to come back to Baltimore with him and after staying there a few days for Stöcker to make his decision. Carroll says come or not as he pleases. He is not at a loss to secure necessary assistance for the Germans of Baltimore.

Letterbook 3, p. 67 (see *JCP*, 2: 499).

104. TO REV. ESMENARD SCHNELL, n.p., 5 January 1806

Carroll penned an abstract of a letter sent to a priest in Fulda, Nassau, in Germany, about his coming to America.

Carroll is grateful for Schnell's offer to labor in America and to bring with him a few young men who wish to become priests. He would readily accede to both propositions if he had enough money at hand for the expenses of the journey, which is far from so. His means are modest and uncertain, so that he dare not assume also to pay the seminary every year for their food and clothing. But as regards Schnell he does agree and will assign him to a station among the Germans provided he arrives near the end of this year [?]. Carroll will pay the expenses of a journey from Hamburg or another port in Germany or Holland, from which ships leave frequently for Baltimore or Philadelphia. He urges Schnell to seek an honest and experienced ship captain and agree on the price, food, and other accommodations.

Letterbook 3, p. 68 (see *JCP*, 2: 503).

105. ENDORSEMENT FOR DOMINICAN FOUNDATION, Baltimore, 25 April 1806

Carroll endorsed the plan of Rev. Edward Dominic Fenwick, O.P., and three English Dominicans to establish a college in Kentucky.

Rev. Edward D. Fenwick[1] and other priests connected with him, having proposed the establishment of a college or academy in Kentucky for the education of youth, Carroll not only approves but greatly rejoices at their resolution, which, if carried into effect can not fail to produce the most beneficial effects for the rising generation. Believing that God inspired them with this design, Carroll recommends and exhorts all his brethren and children in Christ to grant it every encouragement.[2]

AAB, 3-R-6.

[1]*Edward Dominic Fenwick, O.P. (1768-1832), of an old Maryland family (see No. 8, n.3), was the founder of the Dominicans in the United States and first bishop of Cincinnati.*

[2]*St. Thomas of Aquin College, connected with St. Rose Priory, began classes in 1806, the first Catholic college in the West.*

106. TO MESSRS. THOMAS WRIGHT AND COMPANY, Baltimore, 16 May 1806

Another business letter Carroll addressed to his bankers in London, this one shorter than most.

> Carroll signs this day three bills of exchange, one for £9.11.2 in favor of Tiernan and Company, of which £9.5.3 is charged to Sir Thomas Moore on credit of payment made annually by Bishop Douglass and Strickland.

Letterbook 3, p. 68.

107. TO REV. DEMETRIUS GALLITZIN, n.p., 6 October 1806

Carroll forwarded a letter from Gallitzin's sister Marianne, the Princess Gallitzin.

> Carroll says he is sending directly to Gallitzin a letter from his sister announcing the death of their mother[1] despite the advice of Count Stolberg[2] to prepare him for the news gradually. He offers his condolences and assures Gallitzin of the prayers of himself and others.

Lemcke, pp. 154-55.

---

[1]*Countess Amalia von Schmettau died 27 April 1806.*
[2]*Count Frederic Leopold von Stolberg was executor of the mother's estate and one of Gallitzin's agents in Europe in pressing his suit for the legacies of his mother.*

108. TO MR. LOUIS-FRANÇOIS LELOUP, Baltimore, 29 October 1806

Carroll wrote to the French consul in Baltimore to thank him for services rendered.

Carroll thanks Leloup for the letters the minister of cult had directed him to forward to Carroll from the Cardinal Legate [Giovanni Battista] Caprara in Paris. Carroll takes the opportunity to renew his felicitations to the consul's family.

Letterbook 3, p. 68.

109. TO MESSRS. P. SIMOND AND J. P. HANKEY, Baltimore, 6 November 1806

Carroll wrote to Messrs. Simond and Hankey, the London bankers who handled the financial affairs of Rev. Demetrius Gallitzin in Europe.

As instructed in the bankers' letter of 28 July 1806 Carroll drew on them a bill in favor of Mr. Luke Tiernan for thirty days dated 31 October for £158.2.11. Prince Gallitzin has been advised that Carroll holds the money, subject to his order, which is soon expected, together with letters to his sister the princess and other friends. According to their directions, Carroll encloses acknowledgments for their favors to him.

Letterbook 3, p. 69.

110. TO REV. RICHARD LUKE CONCANEN, O.P.,[1]
Baltimore, 21 November 1806

Carroll wrote this long letter to the Dominican Richard Luke Concanen, whom he now wishes to be his agent in Rome. Carroll's description of the church in America in it will be quoted in full.

When he wrote by way of Mr. [Daniel] McHenry Carroll did not see the propriety of writing a separate and private letter or he would have transferred his "confession" to this one, of which please consider it a part. Opportunities of maintaining a regular correspondence with Rome have not been wanting for the last four years via Leghorn, France, Holland, Hamburgh, and even England, so the long delay is entirely Carroll's fault. Enclosed is a letter from Rev. Edward Dominic Fenwick, who with three others of his order have begun their establishment in Kentucky and enjoy much good will there. Carroll had long encouraged their coming from England, which offered no great prospect for the extension of their order; as long ago as 1802 [?] he had urged Mr. [William Benedict] Short, the English provincial, to make an advantageous settlement in America, but he was too old and infirm to engage in new undertakings. By this Concanen will see that he was prepared to give them the best reception in his power. Rev. Mr. [Robert] Angier has remained at Carroll's request to

---

[1]*The Irish-born Concanen (1747-1810) spent most of his ecclesiastical life in Rome. He was at this time living at the Minerva, the Dominican generalate. He would be consecrated bishop of New York on 24 April 1808 but would die in Naples on the eve of departure.*

serve the mission [Zachiah in Charles County] given him on his arrival until his presence in Kentucky is indispensable. He is greatly beloved by his flock, and the rest of Concanen's brethren give equal satisfaction. Mr. Fenwick naturally wished to make his establishment in Maryland, where his property and family are, but after considering that the colleges of Georgetown and St. Mary's were amply sufficient for the Catholic youth of this and neighboring states he visited Kentucky and returned with the resolution of fixing himself there. Mr. Wilson[1] will be a great help, and as long as Carroll has jurisdiction over that part of the diocese nothing will be wanting to favor their object. A division of it into several other dioceses has long been proposed to Rome and now approved. Kentucky with Tennessee will probably be one of them, about which Carroll will write the Propaganda Fide. For it Prince Demetrius Gallitzin will probably be nominated. Having traveled to this country with a letter to Carroll from the prince bishop of Paderborn, he wished to enter the seminary, for which he obtained the consent of his mother and father. He was ordained in 1795 at age twenty-six and since then has served the poorest Catholics whom he formed into a large congregation in the Allegheny Mountains. Carroll asks Concanen to mention these details to the cardinals and secretary of the Propaganda Fide. He will go on loading him with commissions since he has not heard from

---

[1]*Samuel Thomas Wilson, O.P. (1761-1824), president of the new college, had held the same position at the Dominican college in Bornheim, Belgium.*

his former correspondent, Mr. [James] Connell, for some ten years. He knows he is still alive because the Propaganda recommended him to perform the *ad limina* visit for Carroll. Will Concanen tell him it is Carroll's earnest desire to hear from him and ask this former Jesuit to perform that pious office. If he is unable to do so, would Concanen do him the favor? As Carroll is ignorant as to what is involved, would Concanen let him know? Concanen had indicated the readiness of the Propaganda to contribute to the education of one or two young men for Carroll's diocese. Their education could be completed at less expense here than in Rome. In this expectation Carroll has placed a young man at Georgetown college. Two hundred Roman crowns annually would suffice for him and another. This matter Carroll also commits to Concanen. A French Visitation nun, whose name is Saladin, fled the revolution to America, where she was used by one of her countrymen. In her confusion she married him and went to Saint Domingue. When the husband died, she went to Cuba and led a penitential life. She implores forgiveness and asks to be absolved from her vows except chastity. Carroll pleads for her [see No. 125]. He will mention the matter briefly in a letter to the Propaganda but asks Concanen to supply the details and send him the dispensation if granted. As compensation for all the troubles he has imposed on Concanen Carroll wishes to supply him with some points on the church in America. "The cause of religion seems to progress rapidly in

Boston, thro the instrumentality and zeal of two eminent French ecclesiastics [John Cheverus and Francis Matignon] in that town: a wonderful phenomenon in the eyes of all, who have any knowledge of the frightful ideas formerly there of the monster, Popery. At New York, your old venerable friend Dr. [William] ô Brien, tho vigorous in mind last summer, when I visited him, can render no service in the ministry. But three other priests are fully employed, yet cannot do full justice to that immense congregation, which some estimate as high as ten or twelve thousand souls. But for want of labourers, little or no progress is made in forming new congregations in the interior country. In Philadelphia, three large churches hardly suffice for our numerous brethren in faith; and many other churches are settled throughout Pennsylvania. In Baltimore there are three churches, besides the Chapel of the Seminary; and we have begun to raise a cathedral which, if ever completed, will be a phenomenon in this country for size (though diminutive in Europe) and elegance - Its length upwards of 170 feet; & width in the transept, being in the shape of a Latin cross, 115 feet, with a nave and two aisles. It would cost too much time to recapitulate all the other places of worship in this state. In our extensive W[est]. Country nothing prevents the growth of Religion, but the scarcity of good clergymen. - Some few Jesuits have come from Russia, & if under present circumstances the reestablishment of the Society could be granted to the United States, many would enter into it. But on the other hand, little is done hitherto to the Southward of Virginia, & not much even there." Carroll was asked about a year ago to recommend a priest as bishop of Louisiana, but none who were qualified in his diocese to conciliate and govern that medley of nations would consent to go, and none in Louisiana was known well enough. Carroll has waited too long. Disorders have increased. Rev. Patrick Walsh, the most prominent, died. He would have been nominated except that Bishop Coppinger charged him with leaving his diocese without an *exeat*. Cardinal Caprara has sent from Paris instructions from Rome for Carroll to superintend the church of Louisiana. His own government is displeased at this being done at the instigation of a foreign power, France, and as soon as this is explained to the government he will proceed to execute his commission from the pope. Concanen will be tired of reading this long letter, but it is easier to write all this fully in English than in Latin, and Concanen will be able to supply the details when Carroll soon writes the Propaganda. "May heaven preserve you!" and the pope and the holy city so grievously threatened.

Archivum Generale Ordinis Praedicatorum, Series 13, Volume 031250 (through the courtesy of Rev. Hugh Fenning, O.P.).

111. TO CARDINAL MICHELE DI PIETRO, n.p., [22 November 1806][1]

Toward the end of November 1806 Carroll composed a letter much emended in his letterbook concerning the location of new dioceses and the candidates for them, as well as other matters, a large section of which was not sent to Rome at this time.

Carroll speaks of correspondence with Rev. Richard Luke Concanen, O.P., especially one Concanen wrote in September 1805, from Cardinal Gerdil 3 July 1802, Cardinal Borgia 12 March 1803 and 13 June 1804, the bishop of Myra 27 August 1803, Pietro 20 September 1805, and one sent three weeks ago via Cardinal Caprara in Paris. He reiterates the difficulties in communications at both ends with its consequent misunderstandings. A minimum of four dioceses ought to be erected in the United States: one at Boston with jurisdiction over the [then] five New England States; a second at New York City embracing New York and East Jersey; a third at Philadelphia including the states of Pennsylvania, Delaware, and West Jersey; and a fourth in Kentucky to include Tennessee. The see city for the last is dubious, Frankfort, the capital, or Lexington, the largest city? Rev. S. T. Badin says it should be

---

[1]*This is the version in Carroll's third letterbook, which contains an important section on the selection of candidates for the proposed sees that he did not include in the version he actually sent to Cardinal Pietro, which carries the date here given. (This APF version is improperly placed in the Atti of America Settentrionale.) There are significant differences in his recommendation for candidates from those of the letter he finally wrote 17 June 1807 (No. 118). JCP, 2: 537, in a very confusing notation says this letter of 23 [sic] November 1806 sent to Stefano Borgia [sic] can not be found.*

Bardstown, near which the most Catholics live. A fifth diocese is needed for the region between the Ohio and the Great Lakes to the Mississippi, but the priests there are few, so that it should be left under the jurisdiction of the bishop of Kentucky. To the bishop of Baltimore should be left jurisdiction over the remaining eastern states down through Georgia. There, "whether because of the unworthiness of the bishop," lack of priests, or low morals of the people, "almost all that has been tried has failed." There are only three missions in Virginia, one in Charleston, South Carolina, and one in Georgia. It would not be fitting or necessary for them to have a bishop. There are also states south of Tennessee over to the Mississippi that could well be entrusted to the bishop of New Orleans, where someone could assist the widowed church there.[1] On his recommendation for candidates Carroll writes that "for this task, I, the most unworthy of men, find it so foreign that I approach so dangerous an obligation with only a desire to obey; may God pour out the spirit of wisdom on me as I write." For Boston there are two outstanding candidates of the secular clergy: [Francis] Anthony Matignon,[2] a doctor of the Sorbonne and professor of sacred language at

---

[1]*At this point there is a marginal note: "omitted but [the rest] to be forwarded on account of the ship's departure." Carroll also omitted in his final version to Rome what follows on candidates because of paralyzing doubts about a number of the priests that might be considered. The "widowed church" referred to the fact that Bishop Peñalver of the diocese of Louisiana had been promoted in 1801 to the archiepiscopal see of Guatemala.*

[2]*Paris-born Francis Anthony Matignon (1753-1818) arrived in Boston in 1792, where he was highly regarded until the day he died.*

the College of Navarre in Paris, and John Cheverus,[1] a former pastor in the diocese of Nantes [Mans], of "marvelous ease and skill." Matignon is outstanding but Carroll fears he would leave America rather than accept a bishopric. For New York Carroll dares to recommend no one. One, whom Carroll might have once considered [William O'Brien], lacked "what is needed for a priest much less a bishop." The rest of the clergy of New York are young and unproved. Either the see should not be erected or it should be placed temporarily under Boston. For Philadelphia Carroll offers several names. Rev. Matthew Carr, "once of great repute for his outstanding eloquence and learning and attractive manner," has slipped in Carroll's estimation. Rev. Michael Egan,[2] "truly pious, learned, and a preacher of outstanding humility," he believes would uphold the episcopal dignity "on account of his vigor, his firmness of spirit, and his greater experience in handling affairs." Of Rev. Demetrius Augustine Gallitzin, a prince and secular priest, son of the imperial ambassador to the court of the Hague and of a most noble princess who died recently in a monastery in Westphalia, Carroll has asked Rev. Mr. Concanen to convey to the cardinal

---

[1]*John Louis Anne Magdalen Lefebvre de Cheverus (1768-1836) fled to England in 1792 and came to America in 1796, where he ministered to the Penobscot Indians of Maine and the Catholics of Massachusetts. He would later be transferred to the bishopric of Montauban in France and archbishopric of Bordeaux, where he was made a cardinal.*

[2]*Irish-born Michael Francis Egan, O.F.M. (1761-1814), came to America 1802 and was chosen pastor of St. Mary's in Philadelphia in 1803.*

what he has told him. Rev. Louis [De] Barth[1] seems to have much ability but is too severe with priests and laypeople. Gallitzin, with all his abilities and talents, would be better suited to Kentucky or Louisiana. Thus he feels that Egan would be the best suited to Philadelphia.[2] Carroll expects that an administrator will soon be appointed for Louisiana. He has named Rev. Henry Kendall prefect of St. Croix and adjacent islands and Rev. Matthew Hérard vice prefect and commends the work of both. The angelic Cistercian [Trappist] monks[3] have decided to move to Kentucky, but Carroll will avail himself of their example and counsel as long as they are near him. So also for the Dominicans [see No. 110]. Carroll mentions the plight of religious expelled from the monasteries by the revolutions in France and Saint Domingue and asks the Holy Father to respond to the tears of one of them and absolve her from her religious vows [see Nos. 110 and 125]. He mentions the needs of two students he is sponsoring at Georgetown College. [There is also a reference to the archdiocese of Santiago de Cuba that is too illegible to read.]

Letterbook 3, pp. 71-75, compared with his letter in APF, Atti (America Settentrionale), 145: 106r-9r, which is difficult to read. (See *JCP*, 2: 537.)

---

[1]*Son of Count Joseph de Barth de Walbach, Louis De Barth (1764-1843) would be named administrator (1814) and bishop (1818) of the diocese of Philadelphia, which latter honor he declined.*

[2]*What follows would be included in the letter actually sent to Rome.*

[3]*Trappists under Dom Urban Guillet arrived at Baltimore in 1803. They were housed at the seminary until they went to the Sulpician farm at Pigeon Hill, Pennsylvania, from which they migrated to Kentucky in the fall of 1805.*

112. TO REV. ROBERT MOLYNEUX, S.J., Baltimore, 24 November 1806

Carroll wrote to Molyneux, whom he had named provincial of the restored Society of Jesus in Maryland on 21 June 1805, on matters that required immediate action and on the spirit of the Society.

In his last via Rev. [Notley] Young Carroll reminded Molyneux of two things, one depending on Molyneux, the second to be executed by Rev. Francis Neale, agent of the Corporation of the Clergy. The first was Molyneux's signature on a bond for the conveyance of "your" estate near White-Clay Creek, Delaware, to Rev. Patrick Kenny. The second was for a power of attorney in behalf of the Corporation of the Clergy empowering Rev. Mr. John Rossiter of Philadelphia to receive the interest accruing on the stock of the Corporation mentioned in his transfer to them. Carroll has letters from both Kenny and Rossiter complaining of the delay. Molyneux will perhaps complain also of Carroll's delay in sending the money in Mr. [John] Dorsey's hands, but the fault is not Carroll's. He had gone to Dorsey's office but he was not to be found. Two courts have been in session, the Criminal Court, of which Dorsey is chief judge, and the District Court, in which he is an active lawyer. Last week Carroll was "uninterruptedly engaged" from morning till late at night, but he assured Molyneux that the business will not sleep. Mr. Young wrote in Molyneux's name that he could not spare Mr.

PORTFOLIO II: EARLY YEARS

Above 1. Carroll's birthplace. This sketch of the home in which Carroll was born in Upper Marlboro, Maryland, was done in 1884. Though a marker beside the court house indicates that as its location, the exact site is in dispute. (Shea, *Life*, p. 25)

Right 2. Eleanor Darnall Carroll. Educated by the Sepulchrine nuns of Liège, the mother of John Carroll was not only a woman of refinement but a competent manager of her estate. Carroll resided with her from 1774 till 1786. She died in 1796 at the age of ninety-two. (Georgetown University Art Collection)

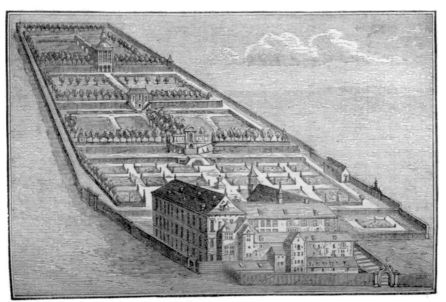

3. English College of Liège. At this Jesuit scholasticate Carroll resided from 1755 to 1767 for seven years as a student and five as a teacher. After the suppression of the Society of Jesus it became the Liège Academy. (Shea, *Life*, p. 33)

4. St. Peter's Procathedral. This sketch of Rev. J. Alphonse Frederick is based on a watercolor of 1801. To the central portion, built in 1770, was added in 1784 the larger church extension to the left and the rectory to the right. The puzzling foreground (not in the watercolor) may suggest a regrading of what would become Saratoga Street soon after the watercolor was done. (Riordan, *Cathedral Records*, p. 10)

5. Francis Beeston. An English novice of the Society of Jesus at the time of its suppression, Beeston would be the second of the three pastors of St. Peter's (1793-1809) Carroll appointed to serve in that position. His death was for Carroll a matter of genuine grief. (Riordan, *Cathedral Records*, p. 28)

6. Chapel at White Marsh. In this older portion of the Sacred Heart Chapel at White Marsh, built between 1729 and 1741, Carroll was elected the first American bishop by his fellow priests on 18 May 1789. (*The Bicentennial Celebration of the Election of Archbishop John Carroll on May 18, 1789*, p. 50)

7. Chapel at Lulworth Castle. In this private chapel of the Weld Family Carroll was ordained bishop on 15 August 1790. The chapel still stands though the castle was destroyed by fire. (Shea, *Life*, frontispiece)

PIVS PP. VI.

AD FVTVRAM
REI MEMORIAM

Ex hac apostolicae servitutis specula
ad Universas Orbis Terrae partes ani-
mum intendentes, ut impositum Nobis
licet immerentibus, munus regendi,
ac pascendi Dominicum gregem
quantum in Domino possumus, exe-
quamur; ad id potissimum curas, solli-
citudinesque Nostras convertimus, ut
Christi fideles, qui in diversis Provinciis
Religioni Catholicae Nobiscum communio-
nec

8. The bull of erection. This is the first page of the bull *Ex hac apostolicae* creating the diocese of Baltimore and naming John Carroll its first bishop. (Archives of the Archdiocese of Baltimore)

9. St. Mary's College and Seminary. Between St. Mary's College to the left and the seminary to the right is the chapel designed by Maximilian Godefroy. Over the roof of the seminary can be seen that of One Mile Tavern, the original seminary building. (Sulpician Archives of Baltimore)

10. Francis Charles Nagot. This ascetic member of the Society of St. Sulpice was in 1791 the true founder of the first Catholic seminary in the United States. (Sulpician Archives of Baltimore)

Kohlmann,[1] whom he had assigned to the master of novices to give German lessons. "Bless me!" What need was there for keeping a man of his talents as companion to a master of a few novices, when there was need for a professor of philosophy? How many novices would have occasion to use German? Carroll asked that he be allowed to offer one piece of advice "suggested by a most ardent wish not only for the restoration of the Society, but the restoration of it with all that energy of enterprise for promoting the divine honour, & exertion in the service of religion, which characterized it, even to its downfall, especially there [Maryland], where its spirit was best preserved." Nothing will dampen this spirit more than to restrain the vigor and zealous exercises of those who might do credit to the Society, and wonderfully benefit the faithful, and allow no theater for exercising them to their full extent. From Mr. Young's letter it seems that Mr. Epinette[2] will have no theology students this year, only a lesson on Holy Scripture to the novices and preparation of candidates for the novitiate, an employment unheard of before. Carroll highly approves the Scripture lesson but questions the need of the novice master for a companion. Molyneux's own unbiased judgment will see the fatal tendency of leaving so little unemployment to a man of Kohlmann's character.

---

[1]*Anthony Kohlmann, S.J. (1771-1836), was sent over that year by the Russian general of the Society of Jesus.*
[2]*Peter Epinette, S.J., was another member sent over that year by the Russian general.*

"How would he raise the character of the Society, what services would he not render to many souls, what an insight would he not obtain into the habits, management & best methods of serving religion here, by performing a kind of mission thro all the German congregations; Baltimore, little Winchester, Conewago, York, Lancaster, Eliz^th Town, or Echerodts [?], Tolpehoken [?], Cushehopen [Goshenhoppen ?], Haycock, Philad^a &c?" After that he would be ready to take up your course of philosophy. This Carroll earnestly entreats "for the glory of God above all things; and next for the honour of the Society." Mr. Malevé[1] longs to be actively employed. Do not overwhelm the College or the fund which is to pay for him with useless expense. Do not let habits of indolence, "too natural to our climate," be cherished by inaction. Set both these good gentlemen free from a life of inactivity. "*Dum tempus habemus* [While we have the time] &c." What news of Mr. Sewall? Has the good Bishop returned? If so Carroll asks that his best respects be presented to "our excellent Brethren."

MPA, box 57.5, folder 13, no. 203S12.

---

[1]*Francis Malevé, S.J., was sent over by the Russian general in 1805.*

113. TO REV. NOTLEY YOUNG, n.p.. 10 December 1806

In this extract Carroll wrote the stepson of his sister Mary about arrangements to serve the congregations of the city of Washington.

Carroll suggests the only way to avoid the inconvenience of holding services alternately in the east and west divisions of the city, to which Mr. Matthews[1] [of St. Patrick's] can make no reasonable objection. Young may say Mass at St. Mary's Chapel[2] whenever he pleases, since it has been blessed. He may say Mass there once or twice a month on Sundays if he accompanies the services with religious instruction and catechism for children. But none who holds a pew at St. Patrick's may withhold their contributions from its pastor, though an agreement may be made with him as to baptisms, marriages, and burials. If Young performs those ceremonies, he is to keep accurate records and report them to Mr. Matthews to place in his register.

Letterbook 3, p. 77 (see *JCP*, 2: 538).

---

[1]*William Matthews (1770-1854), the first native-born priest ordained by Carroll, succeeded Rev. Anthony Caffry as pastor of St. Patrick's in 1804, a position he would hold until his death fifty years later.*
[2]*St. Mary's Chapel at Greenleaf Point was a family chapel built by James Barry.*

114. TO REV. H. LE SAGE, Baltimore, 20 December 1806

For his letter to this French-speaking priest living at 4 High Street, St. Giles, London, Carroll provided a brief extract.

> Carroll will pay Le Sage £30 on his arrival and the same for another priest younger and healthy provided they know English well enough to catechize and hear confessions. Le Sage will probably be appointed to Detroit and the other to Vincennes.

Letterbook 3, p. 75.

115. TO ARCHBISHOP BARTOLOMEO DE LAS HERAS NO-VARRO, Baltimore, United States, 6 March 1807

Carroll wrote a letter of introduction to the Archbishop of Lima for his nephew.

> Carroll has hesitated writing the archbishop but he was finally persuaded by a reliance upon that benevolence of Catholic prelates, though their sees be far apart in distance and dignity, with which they are accustomed to care for one another. His nephew Thomas Brent[1] is about to go to Spain on business and from there sail to Peru if he wins the favor of the king of Spain, which Carroll has no doubt he will. He has asked for letters of introduction in case there is any difficulty in that unfa-

---

[1] *Actually a great-nephew, Thomas Ludwell Lee Brent (1784-1847) was son of Daniel Carroll Brent (1759-1815) and grandson of William Brent (1737-1782) and Eleanor Carroll (1737-1788).*

miliar region. Carroll decided to commend him to the archbishop because the nephew is not a Catholic, and Carroll hopes the examples of virtue and the piety Hispanics bring to their sacred celebrations will impress him, plus the contrast between indifferent Protestants in America with their profane concerns and a flock devoted solely to their Creator. Carroll declares himself the only Catholic bishop in these vast regions but hopes soon others will be created by the Holy See. He asks forgiveness for intruding upon the archbishop's "sublime ministry and grave concerns."

Letterbook 3, pp. 77-78 (see *JCP*, 3: 12).

116. TO REV. EDWARD DOMINIC FENWICK, O.P., n.p., 14 April 1807

This is an extract of a letter in which Carroll tried to reconcile differences of opinion among the clergy of Kentucky.

Carroll has recommended to Rev. Messrs. [Stephen] Badin and [Charles] Nerinckx[1] to hold a conference with Fenwick and the other Dominicans and submit their opinions to the soundest authors, such as Antoine [?], on the subjects in which there is a variation of practice. There is no need to cite any particular divine, however, but merely to conform to principles universally accepted. Carroll has

---

[1]*Belgian-born Charles Nerinckx (1761-1824) came to America in 1804 and was sent by Carroll the next year to Kentucky. He was the founder of the Sisters of Loretto.*

told Badin that to forbid the marriage privilege while the wife is pregnant or throughout
Lent is not only an erroneous opinion but exceedingly dangerous for the salvation of the
married persons. Counsels are not to be con-
founded with precepts or even attempted
when there is danger of occasion of grievous
sin. Carroll has also told Badin that it is in-
comprehensible to him on what grounds he
can delay for years the reconciliation of those
who have married outside the church when
there are true signs of repentance. When any
such penitents apply to Fenwick from any congregation, he ought to absolve them and in-
struct them to tell their parish priest that they
are absolved and are ready to acknowledge
their guilt before the congregation and beg
God's forgiveness. This is the reparation required by the statutes of the diocese.

Letterbook 3, p. 78 (see also *JCP*, 3: 17).

117. TO REV. RICHARD LUKE CONCANEN, O.P., Baltimore, 17 June 1807

Carroll wrote to his newly acquired agent in Rome (see No. 110) concerning choices for proposed bishoprics.

Carroll was well into copying a letter to the
cardinal prefect of the Propaganda when he
heard of the almost immediate sailing of Mr.
[Robert ?] Purviance for Leghorn, but another
ship for there will leave in two days, which will

give him time to finish that letter. If this one should reach Rome before it, Concanen is asked to mention to the prefect or the secretary of the Propaganda that a full list of priests proposed for the new dioceses will follow immediately. Amongst others Carroll will mention Rev. [Samuel Thomas] Wilson for Kentucky, not with any expectation of his being appointed now but to bring his name to notice for some future occasion. His short residence in America, the desired success of his college, and a dispute over moral principles with the older priests [Badin and Nerinckx] argue against his choice as bishop now. Concanen may be surprised that no mention is made of their old friend, Rev. William O'Brien, for New York, but he is sorry to say he cannot in conscience recommend him. Though tortured by gout he is vigorous enough but is rarely seen in church and is accused of drinking too much. His disqualification leaves no one in the state who ought to be appointed. In his last to Concanen of December he asked for his protection and direction in his studies of young Daniel McHenry. While [quarantined] at the Lazaretto in Leghorn he had forwarded Carroll's letters to Rome. In his letter to the Propaganda Carroll has a full account of the steps he had taken to settle the church in Louisiana. Enclosed are letters from Rev. Edward Fenwick received some weeks ago. In a P.S. Carroll says he is not sure that Mr. Purviance, bearer of the letter, will go to Rome. He is of a respectable commercial family and the young gentleman will be grateful for any civilities Concanen may show him.

Archivum Generale Ordinis Praedicatorum, Series 13, Volume 03150 (through the courtesy of Rev. Hugh Fenning, O.P.).

118. TO CARDINAL MICHELE DI PIETRO, Baltimore, 17 June 1807

Carroll finally brought himself to compose and send a letter recommending candidates for the new sees he had suggested the previous year (see No. 111).

In December[1] Carroll had sent the cardinal a letter promising further information soon, especially on the priests designated for the new dioceses to be cut off from Baltimore. "But when the time came for this designation to be made, I was so torn by identifying those names I would submit that I have been unable up to this present day to supply this supplement to my former letter." For Boston there are two priests outstanding in virtue and knowledge, both French, fourteen years in exile, [Francis] Anthony Matignon, about 50, a doctor of the Sorbonne and professor of the College of Navarre, and John Cheverus, pastor in the diocese of Le Mans, about 36. Matignon would be preferred for his virtues, learning, diligence, "and care in the remarkable building up of the Church, and conspicuous prudence in directing men of diverse character," but he is so op-

---

[1]*Actually 22 November. Carroll probably referred to his third letterbook for this letter, to which he had assigned no date.*

posed to being a bishop that, if offered, he would immediately return to Europe. Moreover, his strength and eyesight are bad so that he should be spared the burden. He therefore recommends Cheverus, of good health and tireless zeal, an eloquent preacher, able to draw to himself Catholic and non-Catholic alike and to dispel prejudices against the Church. Matignon regards him as a son. Carroll also proposes that Cheverus be placed over the diocese of New York, since he can think of no one there fit for the bishopric, and recommends that it not be established as a diocese or else be placed under Cheverus. For Philadelphia he had originally thought of three priests [Carr, Egan, and Gallitzin], but now suggests only one, Michael Egan, a Franciscan near 50, of good health "and great strength of soul." He was "learned, humble, and modest . . . maintaining earnestly the spirit of his religious life in every respect." In a letter to Concanen he had mentioned Demetrius Augustine Gallitzin, of a princely family in Russia, about 30. His mother now lives in a monastery in Westphalia.[1] "From the beginning of his priesthood he has labored in the care of souls, and with great strength of spirit, for both the unlearned and the learned. Almost 300 miles from here he chose a place to live and has drawn many Catholic families, and he nourishes them with unending service. Especially trained in sacred and secular learning, he

---

[1] *Carroll had forgotten that he himself had written Gallitzin of his mother's death (No. 107), a fact he also mentioned in the original draft of his letter to Rome of 22 November 1806 (No. 111).*

seems quite fitted to lead the Church of Philadelphia. But on account of various things that have happened in the past, I think it unwise for him to be appointed bishop. In spite of what he has accomplished, he is too harsh in his zeal and not patient enough with those he counsels; he is not suitable or safe enough to be chosen." For the see in Kentucky, whether in Frankfort or Bardstown, he proposes four priests: Benedict Flaget, Stephen Badin, Charles Nerinckx [crossed out], and Thomas Wilson. Flaget and Badin are from France, the first a Sulpician. Wilson is an English Dominican, whose headquarters is in Flanders. He came with companions into the diocese and began a college for young men. The first, Rev. Mr. Flaget, is now employed here in the flourishing college of St. Mary's near the Seminary of St. Sulpice. For many years he was stationed at Vincennes, where he "exercised a benevolence toward all that led to the promotion of piety," but was called back to the seminary. He is at least 40. Rev. Mr. Badin, "founder and father" of all the churches in Kentucky, for a number of years worked alone in that immense vineyard with undiminished vigor. It would seem the episcopal dignity was due him, so learned and a writer of books, but his way of acting displeases many, who say he is too harsh in the tribunal of penance so that many confess only once a year or never unless another priest visits the area. He has defended himself so often against the complaints made about these things that Carroll has not dared to judge ill regardless of what was said about him. Moreover, something of jealousy prevents cooperation with the other priests, especially the Dominicans. Carroll has little to say about Wilson except to mention his great zeal and the esteem he enjoys among the people. He has not been in the country long enough for Carroll to make a perfect judgment. [There are two lines difficult to read in which Carroll says more of Badin and Nerinckx.] He excuses himself from offering a third [?] candidate. As for Louisiana he dares suggest no one. Among the natives of this country there seems none to whom a task so difficult can be confided. And it would be extremely difficult for a bishop of French, Spanish, or English background to exercise leadership in the turbulent state of Louisiana. They have asked Carroll to administer it temporarily even if it be very burdensome, and he is willing to do so until other provisions can be made. Meanwhile he has appointed Rev. Mr. John Baptist Olivier,[1] who once worked in this diocese, to act as vicar general with wide powers. All outside New Orleans acknowledge his authority, but in the city a Capuchin, Antonius de Sedella [see No. 120], has many followers. While they recognize Carroll's authority, they openly resist that of the vicar general he has appointed. Carroll sets himself the task of bringing things back to normal, which he hopes will be soon.

APF, Atti (America Settentrionale), 145: 110r-12r; Letterbook 3, pp. 79-83 (see *JCP*, 3: 27-28).

---

[1]*Rev. John Baptist Olivier had served at Cahokia in the Illinois Country from 1799 until 1803, when he went to New Orleans to become chaplain for the Ursuline nuns.*

119. TO REV. LOUIS SIBOURD, July 1807

Carroll sent this letter of appointment to the new pastor of St. Peter's Church in New York.[1]

> Since it is evident that the recipient has all the requisite virtues for the care of souls, Carroll commits to his care the pastorate of the Roman Catholics of New York and the rectorship of St. Peter's Church. He concedes full authority for him to govern there in matters of divine worship, the sacraments, Christian doctrine, and sodalities approved by the Church, all conducive to the sanctity of the faithful.

Letterbook 3, pp. 83-84 (see *JCP*, 3: 29).

120. TO REV. ANTONIO DE SEDELLA, O.F.M.Cap,[2] n.p., 14 March 1808

Carroll wrote to this troublesome Capuchin in an attempt to bring order to the city of New Orleans.

> From indisputable documents Carroll has known for some time that when his vicar general, Rev. Mr. John Olivier, wanted in accordance with his office to make a canonical visitation of the cathedral parish of St. Louis he was denied entrance. Later Sedella agreed, as if it depended on his own will, for Olivier

---

[1]*Beginning "By the Grace of God and the Apostolic See . . . ," this was apparently the standard form Carroll used in the appointment of pastors. See JCP, 2: 533, for an identical letter of appointment to Rev. Adam Britt.*

[2]*Spanish-born Antonio de Sedella, O.F.M.Cap. (1748-1829), known as Père Antoine to his French parishioners, had also defied the authority of Olivier's predecessor.*

to say Mass but exclusively for the parish. In denying such lawful authority, Sedella was committing an intolerable act of presumption. [What follows Carroll crossed out. He threatens excommunication for any further such treatment of his vicar general. Any prohibition of the vicar general's entrance into the church to say Mass on Sundays or feastdays will bring a decree of interdict. No Eucharist may be reserved in the tabernacle, only hosts in the sacristy for the sick. Any priest who ignores the interdict will automatically incur excommunication, with the ban to be reserved to the Holy Father. The letter concludes with a solemn decree putting all this into effect.][1]

Letterbook 3, pp. 85-86.

121. TO REV. SIMON FELIX GALLAGHER, Baltimore, 18 March 1808

Carroll wrote to Gallagher concerning Catholic children at the orphanage and other matters.

Carroll pleads his incessant occupations at the writing desk or other matters for the long delay in writing Gallagher, especially now that affairs in Charleston bring more satisfaction than heretofore. He rejoices at the happy reunion of the Lynah family with Gallagher,

---

[1]*There is no evidence that this letter was ever sent. John Gilmary Shea made no "transcript" of it. Sedella continued to refuse any other priest entrance into the cathedral. Because of Sedella Bishop DuBourg (appointed bishop of Louisiana and the Two Floridas in 1815) located the seat of his diocese at the city of St. Louis. That Carroll handled the situation in Louisiana poorly is argued by Charles Edwards O'Neill, "'A Quarter Marked by Sundry Peculiarities': New Orleans, Lay Trustees, and Père Antoine," Catholic Historical Review 76 (1990): 235-77.*

which will strengthen the Catholic part of the family and perhaps lead to the conversion of the good old doctor [Edward Lynah's father]. Carroll has no objection to Gallagher's taking his turn at the chapel of the orphanage as he had done before, when he effectually excluded any idea of communication *in sacris cum Acatholicis*. But he asks Gallagher to try to get permission for Catholic orphans to attend their own church on Sundays and feastdays and be catechized in Catholic doctrine. Plain remonstrance and simple explanations of Catholic obligations have the best effect on directors of public institutions. The Sunday afternoon services must be borne with but the Catholic children should be cautioned against joining the prayers of heretical teachers. Carroll asks Gallagher to try to avoid litigation between the vestry and Samuel Corbett, who, though overofficious during the time of troubles, had not used church property for his own advantage. After having kept "the excellent Miss [Melanie] Marsan" and her sister so long in suspense, Carroll makes amends.[1] He also sends best wishes for the health and happiness of the Lynah family, not forgetting that amiable boy, James 3rd [son of Edward]. Rev. [John] Tessier, a professor of theology, concurs that Gallagher may take his turn at the orphans' chapel.

APF, America Centrale, 5: 141r-42r.

---

[1] *Exiled from Saint Domingue, the Marsans had lived for a time in Baltimore before moving to Charleston.*

122. TO MAJOR RICHARD NOBLE, n.p., 5 May 1808

Carroll wrote to Major Noble of Brownsville, Pennsylvania, of a marriage dispensation.

> In consequence of a letter from Rev. [Stephen] Badin, who was happy to make the acquaintance of Major Noble and his family [on his way back to Kentucky], Carroll advises the major that under extraordinary circumstances such as his the revalidation of his marriage may be done privately. Since the closest priest, at Greensburg, Mr. [Peter] Helbron, is a German with an imperfect command of English, the major and his wife might do better to go to Frederick, Maryland, or Carlisle or York or, Carroll's preference, Hanover, Pennsylvania. To whichever priest Carroll will send instructions.

Letterbook 3, p. 87.

123. TO REV. PETER HELBRON, n.p., 6 June 1808

Carroll sent the form of a dispensation to Rev. Mr. Helbron apparently to validate the marriage of Major Noble and his wife (No. 122).

> The bishop grants N. and N. dispensation from the impediment of affinity in the first collateral degree so that their marriage may be legitimized by a Roman Catholic priest.

Letterbook 3, p. 88.

124. TO REV. ROBERT MOLYNEUX, S.J., Baltimore, 1 July 1808

Carroll wrote Molyneux about the falling off of students at George-town College and the prospects for New York.

The shortest way for Carroll to get Mr. Rossiter's request to Molyneux is to send his letter[1] and request immediate attention. Carroll avails himself of the occasion to write about New York. A cause of the diminution of scholars at Georgetown and their flocking to Baltimore is that the priests of Philadelphia, New York, and Boston are flattered by the civilities of the superiors of St. Mary's College. Is it possible to spare for New York one of the Fenwicks [Benedict or Enoch]? Though it would upset the plan adopted for them, will the Society not be compensated by the footing obtained for it in that flourishing city? There will be a fine opportunity soon to effect this.[2]

MPA, box 57.5, folder 11, no. 203P3.

125. TO MADAM GENEVIEVE ELIZABETH SALADIN, Baltimore, 21 July 1808

From 1793 Carroll evidenced a special concern for this former Visitation nun (see JCP, 2: 101-2 and No. 110).

Madam Saladin would see by the enclosed that Carroll had tried a year ago to inform her of

---

[1]*Carroll's letter is written at the end of Rossiter's to him, which asks Carroll to request Molyneux to authorize the sale of land to a trustee of St. Mary's, Philadelphia.*
[2]*Carroll does not indicate what the opportunity will be.*

the success of her request [for a dispensation]. When her letter of 18 January arrived, the government had imposed a strict embargo on all shipping. Carroll was not sure why there had been a relaxation in favor of the ship by which he was sending this package, which would give her peace of soul, "the greatest good in this life," and fresh assurances of the interest he has always taken in her. Enclosed was a copy of the rescript in which the pope authorizes Carroll to absolve her through a priest delegated by himself so that she may live in the world, wearing secular but modest dress, observing the vow of chastity and of poverty as it can be kept in the world under the rules of strict frugality, but making provision for illness that might occur in old age. Any surplus she might acquire should be devoted to works of charity and piety. To preserve in her heart a perpetual memory of her former obligations she is ordered to wear under her outer clothing some sign of her [former] religious habit. Carroll has appointed as subdelegate any priest named by the archbishop of Santiago de Cuba or his vicar general, who would lift the censures and impose a penance suitable to her situation. To obviate any difficulties Carroll encloses a letter to the archbishop, which he leaves to Madam Saladin's decision to submit or not.

Letterbook 3, pp. 89-90.

126. TO REV. SIMON FELIX GALLAGHER, Baltimore, 7 August 1808

Carroll wrote Gallagher of fairly normal affairs in Charleston.

Mr. Beeston informed Carroll that Mr. Green [?] will call tomorrow for the holy oils for Gallagher, which reminded Carroll that he had not yet answered his letter of 28 May. He should have an assistant for his correspondence, but it would have to be a priest because of the nature of the correspondence, and Carroll can not reconcile himself to employing one when so many Catholics solicit in vain for a priest. Gallagher can in any event best judge justly and mercifully with regard to poor Mr. Corbett, but Carroll hoped he had not appropriated for him the fund for the organ, to which object the public generally contributes more readily than any other. Carroll asks that Gallagher deliver the enclosed to Miss Marsan, whom with her sister Carroll continues to recommend to Gallagher's paternal care. Enclosed also is a printed circular concerning contributions for the "great work" of the cathedral, very light for Gallagher's parishioners. In a P.S. Carroll presumes that Mr. [Bernard] Dornin, bookseller of New York, has sent him a catalogue. Carroll especially recommends *The Spirit of Religious Controversy.* He asks Gallagher to forward some of the circulars to Rev. [Anthony] Carles [in Savannah].

APF, America Centrale, 5: 616rv.

127. TO REV. SIMON FELIX GALLAGHER, Baltimore, 23 August 1808

Carroll followed quickly his last to Gallagher (No. 126) with another suggesting a change.

Since his last letter by Mr. Green Carroll received Gallagher's of 29 July and informed Mr. [Dominic] Jordan's daughter of its contents. Mr. [Robert] Purviance, the lawyer, can not recover the money due him from Mrs. [Susanna Egan] McDonnald because of a clashing claim. Gallagher's opinion regarding Corbett was adopted because suggested by charity. Tell the excellent Misses Marsan that he has not forgotten them. Mr. [Louis] Sibourd is tired of the pastoral charge of New York because of his difficulty in giving satisfaction in English sermons. Rev. Matthew O'Brien is now out of employment, so a great preacher is needed there. Carroll mentions this not to seduce Gallagher from Charleston, which would be in an uproar for losing him, but if his health demands a more northerly climate he knows Sibourd desires milder winters and a change could be accommodated. He will not even mention this to Mr. Sibourd till he receives Gallagher's answer.

APF, America Centrale, 5: 618r-19r.

128. TO THE TRUSTEES OF THE SEVERAL CATHOLIC CHURCHES IN PHILADELPHIA, Baltimore, 20 October 1808

Carroll urged the sometimes troublesome trustees of Philadelphia to provide a proper maintenance for their new bishop.

Upon receiving news of the erection of the see of Philadelphia and the appointment of Dr. [Michael] Egan to that see, Carroll thought it "indispensably necessary" to make provision for the initial expenses of installation and for his permanent support. Upon reflection it appeared necessary to address to the trustees directly a particular recommendation, a solid assurance that he be above the danger of straitened circumstances or fluctuations of public opinion. Carroll places the greatest trust in the zeal of the trustees to provide an income suitable and honorable to his station.[1] "This is perhaps the last act of that pastoral care which it has long been my duty to exercise in behalf of my dear children in your State[;] my conscience reproaches me often, and ever will reproach me, for many omissions and errors in the execution of that awful ministry." Carroll prays that the remaining days of his life "may be employed in repairing the evils, which can yet be remedied." Though his former connections will soon be dissolved, "still my heart is and always will be united with you."

John Gilmary Shea, *Life and Times of the Most Rev. John Carroll*,

---

[1] *A resolution was passed 1 November for the three churches of Philadelphia to provide annual quotas: St. Mary's $400, Holy Trinity $200, and St. Augustine's $200.*

Bishop and First Archbishop of Baltimore (New York: John G. Shea, 1888), pp. 637-38; APF, America Centrale. 6: 663r-64r, an Italian translation.

129. TO REV. WILLIAM PASQUET, Baltimore, 14 December 1808.

Carroll penned this extract of a letter to Rev. William Pasquet concerning the management of Bohemia, an estate in Cecil County awarded Carroll by the Corporation of the Clergy in 1806.

> Pasquet should have the mill with Barney [a slave] at £100 for the year 1809, paying all expenses for the mill during that term and restoring it the same as before. Mr. Corbaley [?] has replaced the lost or damaged articles. Carroll is thus freed from expenses for Barney. Pasquet should see that Corbaley makes good the deficiencies as promised. Carroll will send a line to Mr. Cradock [?] to pay the taxes. If Dr. Scanlan [?] and others who owe for the hire of negroes do not pay a reasonable amount at the end of the year, Pasquet should look for other masters. If they pay, the money will remain with Pasquet as part of the $200 due him.

Letterbook 3, p. 91.

130. TO MR. JOHN PEEMANS, Baltimore, 2 February 1809

Carroll addressed this letter to a benefactor of the American missions at Louvain and good friend of Rev. Charles Nerinckx of Kentucky.

Carroll received three days ago Peemans' long expected letter of 3 June 1808 to Revs. [William] Beschter and [Charles] Wouters, which not being sealed he presumed was for his reading. They, together with Revs. [Charles] Nerinckx, [John] Henry, and [Francis] Malevé,[1] were constantly busy in the most important services for the salvation of souls. Though a letter from Mr. Badin concerning the illness of Nerinckx occasioned Peemans grave concern, Carroll is happy to report that he was entirely recovered. Carroll sent by way of New York a heavy package of Nerinckx's letters for Brabant addressed to N____. Though he rejoiced at the erection of the diocese of Kentucky and the nomination of Mr. Flaget to fill it, a man destined to unite all differences of opinion there, Nerinckx was upset by his own nomination to the prefecture apostolic of the diocese of Louisiana and says "he will abscond in a Trappist cell rather than to accept the dignity." But nothing is yet decided or will be until the very uncertain arrival of Bishop Concanen of New York, who carries the briefs concerning changes in the government of that western portion of the church. Mr. Nerinckx, of Peemans' diocese of Mechlin [Mechelen], a

---

[1]*All from Belgium, Henry and Malevé had been sent over as Jesuits by the Russian general.*

most zealous missionary, is nominated vicar apostolic of Louisiana.

Camillus P. Maes, *The Life of Rev. Charles Nerinckx* (Cincinnati: Robert Clarke & Co., 1880), pp. 193-94.

131. TO MRS. ELIZABETH ANN SETON,[1] n.p., 24 March [1809]

Carroll wrote to the widow Elizabeth Seton concerning the pronunciation of her first vows.

Carroll sends the formulary for vows to be taken tomorrow. If it needs alteration, it is to be made with the advice of her director [DuBourg]. A blank is left for her name and for the word *poverty* if it is to be inserted. Carroll has doubts as to whether and how far she can keep that vow in her present circumstances.

AMSV.

---

[1]*Elizabeth Ann Bayley Seton (1774-1821), a convert and widow with five children, had, under the aegis of Rev. Louis William DuBourg, drawn other women to her in Baltimore in 1808 and 1809 who were interested in being religious sisters. In June 1809 they would move to Emmitsburg, Maryland, where the Sisters of Charity of St. Joseph's was established. The traditional date of foundation is 31 July 1809. For the year above given see Annabelle M. Melville, Elizabeth Bayley Seton, 1774-1821 (New York: Charles Scribner's, 1951), pp. 190, 239, and 428n.80.*

132. TO MESSRS. THOMAS WRIGHT AND COMPANY, n.p., 14 April 1809

Carroll wrote of the Du Moulin account and other matters.

Enclosed is Mr. James Du Moulin's bill for £60 in Carroll's favor dated 13 April and directed to be placed to Carroll's credit. In Wright's last the account's balance in Carroll's favor was £35.16.2 since which Carroll drew in Mr. [William] Tunstall's [?] favor £23.2. In the course of the next month Strickland will pay to Carroll's credit at least £55.16.4. Last Christmas and the mid-summer dividends on £400 in the 5% stock will be £18 and the balance remaining of the £12.14.2 with Du Moulin's bill will amount to £146.10.6. On this Carroll drew today in favor of Tiernan and Company at sixty days for £158 and had delivered this bill before discovering that he had overdrawn by miscalculating on the stock. But that stock being in Wrights' hands Carroll relied on the bankers' honoring the draft.

Letterbook 3, p. 91.

133. TO MR. ARCHIBALD LEE, Baltimore, 20 April 1809

This letter to "dear Archy," son of Thomas Sim Lee,[1] was written at a time a stricter enforcement of the embargo on all American shipping was enacted.

Carroll wishes Archy well on his voyage. He encloses a letter from the Spanish consul in Baltimore[2] to one of the best houses in Cadiz and another from Robert Barry to Mr. Gould of Madeira, a brother of Mrs. Barry formerly of Baltimore.[3] But Carroll thinks his destination may have to be changed in light of news he had received from Washington that morning. He would probably go directly to England, if that could be done. Mr. Bernabeau says he could take tobacco to Cadiz, but it could not be sold to any but the government; it could be deposited in the King's warehouse without duty and could be reshipped free. Carroll signs "Your affectionate Godfather" and pays his respects to Mr. and Mrs. Ringgold.[4]

HLC/MHS.

---

[1]*Archibald Lee (1781-1839) of Montgomery County, Maryland, oldest surviving son of Thomas Sim Lee, never married.*

[2]*Juan Bautista Bernabeu, the Spanish consul for Maryland, was a friend of Carroll.*

[3]*Robert Barry was a nephew of James Barry, friend of Carroll and husband of Joanna (Gould) Barry. Robert was then the acting consul in Baltimore for Portugal.*

[4]*Archibald's sister, Mary Christian, married Tench Ringgold of Maryland and Louisiana.*

134. TO MESSRS. THOMAS WRIGHT AND COMPANY, Baltimore, 17 May 1809

Another letter of Carroll to his London bankers.

About ten days ago Carroll heard from Strickland who said that instead of paying to Wright and Company the annual sum that passes through his hands he intends to use it to discharge a debt of one of Carroll's "clerical brethren" for books ordered by him, of which Carroll had no knowledge. This would have been all right if Carroll had received timely notice to prevent him from sending the bill of 14 April [No. 132]. Carroll was alarmed for its fate, but no authority was needed from him for Wright and Company to hold any of his property under their control until their claims are satisfied.

Letterbook 3, p. 91.

135. TO REV. SIMON FELIX GALLAGHER, Baltimore, 30 May 1809

Carroll wrote Gallagher of another possible change.

Gallagher's letters of 15 February and 29 April acknowledged. Carroll's only apology for not writing sooner is the effects of age upon his nervous system that produce such an apathy as to render writing most painful. Gallagher's letters have often been placed on his desk with the resolve of answering them immediately but afterwards filed for a more propitious occasion. This makes the assistance of a secretary all the more necessary, but he is still reluctant to deprive congregations of the service of a priest. It would give Carroll great pleasure to see Gallagher at Baltimore and have Rev. [Louis] Sibourd spend the summer in Charleston. No weather is too warm for him. He is under the care of an oculist, however, and is thinking of returning to France for the benefit of his eyes, so Carroll has but faint hopes of his going to Charleston. When Rev. [Patrick] Kelly went with Carroll's letter of introduction, Gallagher sensed correctly that he was unsuited for Charleston and knew that Mr. Sibourd would not have lived with him. Kelly returned to Baltimore a fortnight ago from St. Augustine. Carroll felt no displeasure for Gallagher's having declined New York. Carroll rejoiced in fact that he was not lost to his diocese. But what would Gallagher think of the pastorship of the city of Washington if Rev. [William] Matthews thought of going elsewhere? He would be glad to see him in the national capital if a worthy successor could be found for Charleston. Dr. Carr of Philadelphia and Dr. [Matthew] O'Brien formerly of New York are now at Mr. DuBourg's college, and Carroll might consider sending the latter to Charleston for a few months to give Gallagher some relief. Mr. Beeston presents his respects and will send the holy oils by Captain Hall [?]. Present Carroll's respects to the families of Messrs. Lynah Sr. and Jr. and tell Miss Marsan he will write soon. The long detention of Bishop Concanen of New York in Italy with the official documents entrusted to him brings everything to a standstill. In a P.S. Carroll says Mr. Sibourd will be in Baltimore next week, and they may confer on his going to Charleston.

APF, America Centrale, 5: 147r-48r.

136. TO MR. JAMES EARLE JR. of Easton, Maryland, Baltimore, 15 June 1809

Carroll wrote to this Carroll descendant concerning legacies controlled by Anthony Carroll, S.J.[1]

Mr. Brice [?] had sent Carroll Earle's letter of the 7th inquiring if he had an answer concerning Anthony Carroll, who had spent a few months in Maryland and Pennsylvania in 1774-1775, a nephew and heir of James Carroll. Dominic, a nephew but not a brother of Anthony, had numerous heirs, but Anthony was unable to discover who they were in order to distribute the small sum to which each would be entitled before his death [Anthony was murdered in 1790]. Carroll had mentioned the legacy to Anthony in London in 1790, but he was unable at the time to supply

---

[1] *In 1729 James Carroll, then the principal representative of the Carrolls of Maryland (after the death of Charles Carroll I), drew a will in which he awarded from his vast estates in Maryland various legacies to his many relatives and to the Jesuits. His nephew Anthony Carroll became the surviving executor. This will deserves a study in itself as a basis of the falling out among the Carrolls and a revival of anti-Catholic sentiment in Maryland, especially on the part of one of the executors, Dr. Charles Carroll of Annapolis (exact relationship uncertain).*

satisfactory information. Carroll had written Earle's father. When he returns to Baltimore [after an imminent trip] in about six weeks he will attend to the matter. Carroll knows nothing of the estate in England falling to Dominic's heirs.

Letterbook 3, p. 92 (see *JCP*, 3: 88).

137. CERTIFICATE CONCERNING JAMES WHITFIELD, Baltimore, 14 August 1809

Carroll copied and certified a dimissorial letter of Bishop William Gibson, vicar apostolic of the Northern District of England, for the ordination of James Whitfield.

Carroll certifies that the foregoing copy entirely conforms to the original, which [copy] he retains lest it [the original] perish *per mare aut in via* [by sea or on the way].[1]

AAB, 23A-V-2 (Whitfield Papers).

---

[1]*Carroll, at the request of Rev. Ambrose Maréchal, had obtained this dimissorial from Bishop Gibson through his friend Charles Plowden, who was unable, it would seem, to send it himself to Maréchal because of the war with France. See JCP, 3: 82. At Maréchal's prompting Whitfield would come to Baltimore in 1817 and succeed him as fourth archbishop of Baltimore in 1828.*

138. NOTATIONS FOR REV. CHARLES NERINCKX, [15 September 1809]

On the margin Carroll responded to several questions posed by Ner-inckx in a letter of 15 September 1809.[1]

> To the question of whether Elias Newton, who had applied for a dispensation to marry a widow closely related to him but was then married by a Protestant minister, could, if he repented or became gravely ill, be granted that dispensation, Carroll answers "No." As to whether in the diocese of Louisiana the Council of Trent is to be promulgated or local custom followed, Carroll answers "I do not know." As to whether those who eat freely on fast days can be dispensed by the pope, the bishop, or any other, Carroll answers "No" in each case. He ignores an inquiry for a definition of parish and parochial rights. As to the question of paying or delaying debts, avoiding usury, etc., Carroll answers "Let him judge for himself."

AAB, 8A-W-6.

---

[1] JCP, 3: 105, says that Carroll's "comment" on this letter concerned Nerinckx's "transmigration to Louisiana or the Illinois." He does not mention these questions and Carroll's responses.

139. TO MOTHER ELIZABETH ANN SETON, n.p., 9 November 1809

Carroll wrote to Mother Seton about the direction of the Sisters of Charity and other matters.

Carroll tells "My Dear Madam and Honored Mother" that he has just received her letter of 2 November via Mr. DuBourg. He had received some days ago a letter from Bishop Concanen, dated Florence 1809, the one to which he presumes Mother Seton refers. After the choice made by "yourselves" of living under the protection of the priests of St. Sulpice, Carroll surrenders as much as a bishop can "your" government into their hands. If Mr. Nagot or the council of the seminary see fit to restore DuBourg to the place he had filled, Carroll concurs though he sees "formidable objections." Her motives for wanting him back are edifying and worthy of her humility, "as well as your sentiments of submission on another subject, concerning which the gentlemen of the Seminary are even more earnest, than when I left them, before my journey."[1] Since his return Carroll has received a letter from "our admirable friend, Mrs. B."[2] of 15 August from Cork. She was distressed at not hearing from friends in Madeira that the remains of her daughter Ann were sent to America, where she would go when she heard. She remembers Mother Seton with "warmest affec-

---

[1]*For the best account of DuBourg's resignation as spiritual director and Mother Seton's reaction to it see Melville,* DuBourg, *1: 189-203.*

[2]*Joanna (Gould) Barry, widow of James Barry, had known Elizabeth in New York.*

tion." Carroll wishes Mother Seton had told him that William[1] had recovered and that Sister Cecilia[2] was well. Tell Kitty Mullen[3] that he had tried in vain to meet her sister and tell "our good Rose"[4] that her mother, sisters, her "lovely boy Charles," and brother George are all well. Harriet's[5] husband arrived two days ago. A letter of 9 June from Leghorn speaks of the Messrs. Filicchi[6] without any mention of sickness. Carroll supposes that Mother Seton has heard of the death of Mr. John Seton's wife[7] in Alexandria, the result of her jumping from a gig pulled by runaway horses. Miss de Neuville,[8] now Mrs. Lirizee [?], came some days ago to pay Carroll a visit but was unable to go on to Emmitsburg. Carroll can not "reflect with patience" upon the prospect of a winter in their "open and inconvenient" house, since the new one, as DuBourg told him, would not be ready until the next year. In a P.S. Carroll says Louise Caton[9] was out of pa-

---

[1] *William Seton (1796-1868), Elizabeth's oldest son.*

[2] *Cecilia Seton (1791-1810), Elizabeth's sister-in-law, joined her in Baltimore in 1809.*

[3] *Catherine Mullen joined the community in June 1809.*

[4] *Rose Landry White, a widow, joined the community in June 1809. Carroll united Rosetta Landry to Joseph White Jr. on 14 February 1799. See Appendix 1.*

[5] *This Harriet can not be identified. She can not be Mother Seton's sister-in-law Harriet Seton, who, though affianced, never married.*

[6] *Antonio and Filippo Filicchi, merchants of Leghorn, Italy, had brought Elizabeth in contact with the Catholic Church.*

[7] *Mary Wise had married John Curson Seton, Elizabeth's brother-in-law, in 1799.*

[8] *Melville, DuBourg, 1: 207-8, identifies "Miss de Neuville" as the Baroness Hyde de Neuville, wife of Jean-Guillaume Hyde de Neuville, French minister to the United States 1816-1821. She was a benefactor of the Daughters of Charity in France. There was apparently some confusion in Carroll's mind as to her marital status in 1809.*

[9] *Louisa Caton (1791-1874), daughter of Richard Caton and Mary Carroll, the daughter of Charles Carroll of Carrollton. See No. 148.*

tience with Mother Seton for not writing. He is sure her encouragement was good for Louise and her sisters.

AMSV.

140. TO MOTHER ELIZABETH ANN SETON, Baltimore, 28 December 1809

Carroll had more than one occasion to console Mother Seton on the death of a relative or child.

Already saddened by the death of his "very dear companion,"[1] Carroll asked that Mr. Weis[2] defer the sad news he had brought until after the Christmas Mass, but the latter insisted. Carroll was happy that he did so because he could then remember Cecilia [Mother Seton's sister-in-law] in the Mass. It was an event for which even the letter of "our beloved Barton"[3] had not prepared him. Divine Providence would lead Mother Seton to perfection through the road of suffering, and Carroll hopes that she will always walk in the way of the cross with resignation and much spiritual profit. It was a dispensation of mercy that Cecilia had followed her to St. Joseph's Valley [the motherhouse], a reflection that must have

---

[1]*Rev. Francis Beeston, rector of St. Peter's Procathedral, died unexpectedly on 20 December 1809. See JCP, 3: 108-10, for Carroll's tribute to him.*

[2]*George Weis, who had built the house in which Elizabeth Seton lived in Baltimore, became her close friend. He was also contractor for the minor seminary of Mount St. Mary's in Emmitsburg.*

[3]*Edward Barton of Boston entered St. Mary's College and then the seminary and was one of DuBourg's favorite students.*

given Mother Seton great consolation. Carroll has ever since remembered Cecilia and the "most lamented Mr. Burton" [?] in his devotions. He knows all that will be felt for Burton by Rose [White] and Kitty [Mullen], to whom, with her remaining sister, her dear girls, and all the Sisters he begs a most affectionate remembrance. There is no late news from Mrs. Barry, whose niece[1] is full of veneration for Mother Seton.

AMSV.

141. TO THE EDITOR OF THE *FEDERAL GAZETTE*,[2] 23 February 1810

As "A.B." Carroll submitted a letter to the editor of this Baltimore newspaper for publication in response to a letter published 22 February from "A Methodist Episcopalian."

Was it to dampen the patriotic ardor of celebrating Washington's birthday that "A Methodist Episcopalian" chose this day "to proscribe as impious, one of those public entertainments in which neither religion nor reason discover any moral deformity?" Or was it to insult the memory of the dead, the amiable and charitable Rev. Dr. [George] Roberts, who had gone with respectable friends to see the

---

[1] *Perhaps the Miss Gould whom Carroll frequently mentioned in his correspondence with the Barrys.*
[2] *Its full title was* Federal Gazette and Baltimore Daily Advertiser.

circus, which [Methodist Episcopal] clergyman the "Methodist Episcopalian" pretends to defend against the charge. The latter in his system of morality views going to the circus as grievous an offence as going to the theater, "the chapel of Satan." The writer [Carroll] pretends not to a knowledge of the canons of the Methodist Episcopal Church of Maryland, but knows well enough the good sense of its members to be convinced of their contempt of the "wretched sophistry" that identifies the unimpassioned spectacle of the circus with horse racing, intemperance, extravagance, etc. "Let the 'Methodist Episcopalian' beware of turning his eyes on a pasture, into which high spirited horses are turned fresh from the stable, lest he should behold a more vivid resemblance of a horse race than any exhibited at the circus, and thereby fall under the censure of the canon [against horse racing]."

AAB, 11-J-5.

142. TO REV. JAMES MAXWELL, Baltimore, 30 May 1810

Carroll wrote the pastor of Ste. Genevieve [Missouri] concerning complaints against his conduct.

Carroll has received repeated remonstrances against Maxwell's conduct as pastor of Ste. Genevieve. Lately a petition of forty-three persons states that he spends days and nights at cards, gambles for large sums, attends balls, gives dances at his house, and the like. Carroll would normally request an examination by the vicar general of Louisiana, Rev. John Baptist Olivier, but age and distance makes this impractical. He will appoint Mr. [Stephen] Badin to conduct the investigation.[1]

Letterbook 3, pp. 93-94 (see *JCP*, 3: 117).

143. TO MESSRS. THOMAS WRIGHT AND COMPANY, n.p., 23 June 1810

Another letter from Carroll to his bankers in London.

On their way are bills of exchange, one dated yesterday for £9.11.2 at twenty days sight drawn for James Du Moulin, who talks of making himself a more ample allowance, and with it an acknowledgment of Mr. [William] Tunstall for £15. Carroll also draws upon Wright today £66.13.4 in favor of James Earle Jr. [see No. 136] at sixty days and £15 in favor of Luke Tiernan at thirty days. A duplicate was sent 28 July 1810 "with second [set] of exchange."

Letterbook 3, p. 94.

---

[1]*Maxwell resigned rather than submit to an examination by Badin, claiming that the source of the complaints was one of Badin's former parishioners, Joseph Fenwick, who wished Maxwell replaced by Badin (see AAB, 5-J-1).*

144. TO MOTHER ELIZABETH ANN SETON, Washington, 11 September 1810

In this letter Carroll wrote Mother Seton about several matters in an almost business-like manner.

Carroll has been in the neighborhood of Washington for more than five weeks to little purpose. He expects to return to Baltimore the 13th with the bishop elect of Kentucky,[1] who has told Carroll of his visit to Mother Seton's community. Mr. David[2] is going with him to Kentucky, which must necessitate some change in the government of St. Joseph's. She will hear from Carroll on how this will affect her "interesting family." David Barry, Mrs. Barry's nephew, had written on 18 June that he had visited her in Cork and found her health and spirits so bad that he doubted she would be able to carry out her wish to return to America in August. Carroll is sending this letter by his nephew Mr. Brent and his wife.[3] Though he does not want to intrude upon the life of the sisters, the wife is not a Catholic and Carroll hopes their good example will influence her to become one. Mother Seton, her community, and her dear boys and girls know how much Carroll wishes for their happiness, the perseverance in virtue of the

---

[1] *Benedict Joseph Flaget, S.S., would be ordained bishop by Carroll at St. Patrick's in Baltimore on 4 November 1810.*

[2] *John Baptist Mary David, S.S., had replaced DuBourg as spiritual director of the sisters. He would later become coadjutor bishop of Flaget.*

[3] *This was probably William Brent, youngest son of Robert and Ann (Carroll) Brent, and his first wife, Catherine Walker Johnson.*

former and "a daily improvement of the latter."
In a postscript Carroll reports that Mrs. Brent is
not going to Emmitsburg.

AMSV.

145. TO MR. W. B. JACKSON, Baltimore, 25 September 1810

Carroll wrote to this Bladensburg businessman about a bank loan.

Messrs. Gilmor[1] have sent Jackson's letter of
15 September to him. He understands Jackson's proposal to be that he would continue
his loan for bank interest. Though it does not
amount to much, Carroll hopes that 7% will
be agreeable and gives his bond accordingly.

Letterbook 3, p. 94.

146. TO MESSRS. THOMAS WRIGHT AND COMPANY, Baltimore, 31 October 1810

Another letter to Carroll's London bankers.

Carroll repeats the information in his last letter
dated 23 June (No. 143). Rev. [Robert] Plowden
of Bristol sent notice of having paid Messrs.
Wright on 9 March £32.19 for Carroll's credit,
which with balance on Du Moulin and the dividend on the 5% stock authorized Carroll's draft
for £100 in favor of Campbell and Ritchie [?].
Should his credit be not that much, the securi-

---

[1]*Robert Gilmor (1742-1822) was a wealthy Baltimore merchant.*

ty for repayment is in Wrights' hands. In a P.S. Wrights' last was received 19 February 1810.

Letterbook 3, p. 95.

147. TO MESSRS. THOMAS WRIGHT AND COMPANY, Baltimore, 23 February 1811

Another letter of Carroll to his London bankers.

Carroll's last of 31 October was followed by Wrights' of 16 November telling him they had placed to his credit £50 for Mr. William Tunstall, "he being urgent for payment" despite the unfavorable rate of exchange. Yesterday Carroll drew £50 for Tunstall. Wrights' last had shown a balance in his account of £146.1.11, but interest on 5% stock since accruing and perhaps other payments must have made his credit equal to the bill in favor of Tunstall.

Letterbook 3, p. 96.

148. TO THE CARDINAL PATRIARCH OF LISBON[1], n.p., [between 23 February 1811 and 12 February 1812]

Carroll wrote the patriarch of Lisbon on behalf of Marianne Patterson.

Although Carroll does not know whether the cardinal remains in his see in the midst of the

---

[1]*Carroll was obviously unaware that there was no cardinal patriarch of Lisbon at that time. Antonio José de Castro had been presented to the Holy See by Prince Joseph, regent of Portugal, in 1809 for the patriarchal see, but he was never confirmed because of the detention of Pius VII by Napoleon and the occupation of Portugal by French troops.*

turmoil of war or has gone to Brazil, he still
dares to write to ask his protection for "one of
my most dear relatives," Mrs. Mary Patterson,[1]
who for the sake of health is ordered to take a
sea voyage in the company of her husband,
Mr. Robert Patterson. Carroll commends her
to the "eminent Patriarch" so that some
Catholic influence may be injected into this
mixed marriage.

Letterbook 3, pp. 97-98.

149. TO BISHOP LEONARD NEALE, Baltimore, 6 March 1811

*In this extract Carroll told Bishop Neale how best to deal with a
scandalous priest.*

Tell Mr. [James] Van Huffel to cease every exercise of his order and the ministry until the
scandal given by the undue use of them [?]
shall be repaired in the following manner. He
shall go to Bishop Egan of Philadelphia as superior of his order[2] and submit to any penance
enjoined by him and convince him he was living in conformity to his vows. This is the
mode recommended by the Council of Trent.

Letterbook 3, p. 97 (see *JCP*, 3: 146).

---

[1]*Marianne Caton (1788-1853), daughter of Richard Caton and Mary Carroll, was a
cousin of John Carroll through the Darnalls. After the death of Robert Patterson, her first
husband, in 1822, she married Richard Wellesley, the Marquess Wellesley, in 1825.
Robert was brother of the ill-fated Betsy Patterson, sister-in-law of the Emperor Napoleon.
The Marquess Wellesley was brother of Arthur Wellesley, the first Duke of Wellington, who
defeated Napoleon at Waterloo in 1815.*
[2]*Bishop Michael Egan was a Franciscan.*

150. TO REV. WILLIAM PASQUET, Baltimore, 2 August 1811

On a letter from Pasquet dated 23 July 1811 Carroll penned his response.

> If after the inquiry Pasquet intended to make into the character of Mr. [George] Fillingham he found him acceptable, Pasquet can bargain with him on his terms [for the mill]. If Fillingham is unacceptable, Carroll would prefer the mill continue under Barney's management. [See No. 129.] Listen to Barney [a slave] and don't compel him into service if he has good reasons for wanting otherwise. If no one else will give $70 for him, Carroll will try to find him employment.

AAB, 6-D-10.

151. NOTATION FOR SISTER STE. MARIE OLIVIER, [2 August 1811]

On a letter from Sister Ste. Marie Olivier of New Orleans dated 2 August 1811 Carroll listed the points he covered in his response.

> "Condoleance."[1] Ladies from France.[2] French clergy [indecipherable][3] - DuBourg.[4] S. Emelie

---

[1]*Sister Ste. Marie had written of "the sorrows we have experienced of all kinds [unspecified]."*

[2]*Ursuline sisters from France who had brought with them a new rule.*

[3]*Perhaps the clergy to whom the writer asks to be remembered, otherwise not clear.*

[4]*Rev. Louis William DuBourg, S.S., had just returned to Baltimore from Martinique, where he had gone for reasons of health. He had befriended the Ursulines during their stay in Baltimore before their going on to New Orleans.*

Jourdan.[1] S. La [?] Sabloniere.[2] Funds[3] - Miss
Padrelles [?] - Mullanphy.[4]

AAB, 6-C-3.

152. NOTATION ON THE CONFRATERNITY OF CHARITY, [September ?] 1811

Along with the rules of the Daughters of Charity Rev. John Dubois[5] received and translated the rules of the Confraternity of Charity composed also by St. Vincent de Paul, both of which Carroll reviewed.

On "Rules of the Confraternity (Association) of Charity," Carroll writes: "Confraternity is a word improperly applied to an association of ladies alone. *Sisterhood* would be a more proper word, if it were not now appropriated to religious communities of pious women."

AAB, 11A-G-1.

---

[1]*Sister Emélie de Ste. Françoise Jourdan (see No. 155) had been allowed to spend a year in the country for health's sake but, according to the writer, spent most of her time in the city with bad companions.*

[2]*Sister Stanislas Sabloniere, one of the bad companions, had moved to Philadelphia.*

[3]*A great deal of this letter is taken up with the sale of property and investments, about which the writer asks Carroll's advice.*

[4]*Neither Miss Pradelles nor [John ?] Mullanphy can be found in the legible part of this letter.*

[5]*Dubois replaced Rev. John Baptist David as spiritual director of the sisters.*

153. TO MOTHER ELIZABETH ANN SETON, Baltimore, 11
September 1811

[This letter is published in *The John Carroll Papers* (3: 155-57) but as from a copy, whose source is not indicated, in the Archives of St. Joseph's Central House, Emmitsburg, Maryland (ASJCH). The original is in the Archives of the Sisters of Charity of Mount St. Vincent-on-Hudson (AMSV). The *JCP* version has over a hundred inaccuracies in transcription, most of them minor, for example, the omission of thirty-six commas. There are, however, three inaccuracies of substance rather than style. On page 156, line 4, "misap[rahens]ion [*sic*]" should read "impression." On the same page at the end of line 6, the omission of "to and." On page 157, line 21, "Mr. Js Barry" should read "Mrs. Ja. Barry" (Mrs. Joanna Barry). It should be noted that, in spite of Carroll's prediction that it would be at least a century before the sisters would be able to take up the care of the sick, just two years after Mother Seton's death in 1821, her sisters assumed charge of the Baltimore Infirmary, later the University Hospital.]

154. TO REV. SIMON FELIX GALLAGHER, Baltimore, 15 September 1811

Carroll wrote Gallagher on the new rules of the vestry of Charleston that excluded the pastor from its meetings.

Carroll cannot account for his inexcusable delay in answering Gallagher's several letters on the invasion of pastoral authority and violation of ecclesiastical discipline. When first told of them Carroll perhaps held the vestry's efforts in too much contempt and felt sure of Gallagher's ability to completely defeat the machinations of the innovators, having in his possession the documents that could prove the falsehood of their allegations. But after Gallagher informed him a second time of their disorderly, or "*disorganizing* pretenses," Carroll knew he should have taken action earlier and will now do so. He hopes that the accompanying declaration on the limitation of the power of the laity in the administration of church affairs will confirm Gallagher's authority.[1] Carroll is grieved and almost indignant at the base ingratitude of the members of his flock who attempt to exclude Gallagher from a seat on the vestry, since his presence and counsels lend greater respectability than all the others together, to say nothing of the right of his sacred office. Carroll must go to a meeting that begins at Georgetown tomorrow. Tell Miss Marsan he will write before his return

---

[1]*Carroll's declaration has not been found.*

and hopes that she and her beloved sisters are in good health. In a P.S. Carroll asks that Gallagher have a copy made of the enclosed for he had not the time to transcribe and keep one for himself.

APF, America Centrale, 5: 151rv.

155. NOTATION CONCERNING SISTER EMÉLIE DE STE. FRANÇOISE JOURDAN, [1 October 1811]

On a long letter from Sister Emélie de Ste. Françoise Jourdan dated New Orleans, 1 October 1811, Carroll wrote the following:

"Mme. Jourdan. N.O. Oct. 1 1811. Interesting and requiring new consideration."[1]

AAB, 4-I-9.

156. TO MOTHER ELIZABETH ANN SETON, n.p., 18 November 1811

Carroll sent his sympathies for the continued suffering in Mother Seton's family and for the death of Joanna Barry.

Carroll did not receive Mother Seton's letter of the 3rd until the 14th and was "exceedingly sorry" to hear of her dear Anina's[2] and William's continued suffering as well as her

---

[1]*In this, her fourth letter to Carroll, Sister Emélie speaks of her reluctance to go back to the convent and a harsh superior (see No. 151).*
[2]*Anna Maria (Anina) Seton (1795-1812) was Elizabeth's oldest child and William the next.*

own crippled arm. Mrs. Barry of Gay Street,[1] to whom Carroll continues to forward Mother Seton's letters, said her account of William was more alarming than that sent to himself. A copy of the will of their deceased friend[2] will not be made public. Her heart was larger than her fortune. She has left Mother Seton $500 and whichever of her daughters—she could not remember which—was the favorite of her deceased daughter Anne a grand piano and her music. Carroll has received a "most edifying" letter from Rose [White]. Her mother, whom he had seen that evening, is in good health.

AMSV.

157. TO REV. FRANCIS MALEVÉ, S.J., Baltimore, 2 December 1811

Carroll wrote to the pastor of Frederick concerning the congregations he was to serve.

Carroll received Malevé's of 29 November and is pleased to note an improvement in his English. He thought he had written him when he decided to place Mr. [Matthew] Ryan at Hagerstown. "*Inter nos*" Carroll is fearful Ryan will not give complete satisfaction to the congregations he is to serve, but knowing him to be a good and zealous priest Carroll decided to

---

[1]*The wife of Robert Barry, nephew of Joanna Barry, who had offered the Setons hospitality when they first came to Baltimore.*
[2]*Joanna Barry died 18 October 1811. See JCP, 3: 124-25, for Carroll's obituary, probably to a Washington newspaper through his nephew Robert Brent, but misdated by JCP.*

give him a trial during the winter. One of his motives was concern for Malevé. The field he had embraced was so immense that he could not serve the whole of it during that inclement season without great danger to his health. He knows well Ryan's temper and the difficulty he would have sharing the duties at Hagerstown, so he asks Malevé not to meddle there nor with its missions, namely, one at Conocheague in Maryland about 14 miles from Hagerstown, Martinsburg and Winchester in Virginia, and in the summer season Bath, near which Ryan owns a small tract of land. As to the missions up the Potomac, namely, Cumberland, the South Branch [of the Potomac], and Hardy County [now West Virginia], Malevé may use his discretion, but he is sure he will want to keep a love for the faith alive by an occasional visit. If he finds it difficult to attend the whole circuit, he may divide those stations with Mr. Ryan, each choosing the most convenient. It would give Carroll particular pleasure if he could sometimes visit "my dear child in Christ," Mrs. Marshall [?]. Carroll is told she has a number of children. Several years ago he offered to board one of her daughters at the Ladies school [Visitation Academy] at Georgetown, but she was not sent. Mr. Ryan should not object to his going once more to Martinsburg. Whatever Carroll may have said of the most distant congregations, Malevé knows what is best for them. If he ever goes to Old Town, he should not forget Mrs. Young [?]. Carroll is happy with the progress made on the chapel of Barnstown,

Seneca, and authorizes Malevé to bless it under the title of our Blessed Immaculate Lady.
Neither has Carroll heard from Mr. Peemans
since the return of the bishop of Kentucky.

MPA, box 20, folder 13, no. 59T3.

158. TO MOTHER ELIZABETH ANN SETON, Baltimore, 20 January 1812

Carroll wrote in anticipation of the imminent death of Mother Seton's oldest child.

While Anna Maria's condition fills with sorrow the hearts of Mother Seton and her
friends, they have occasion to bless God for
the daughter's singular resignation and the
mother's fortitude. "May the Prince of Peace
continue to calm the emotions of your soul."
Mother Seton's friend [probably Mrs. Robert
Barry] and her family are well, but he has not
seen them since receiving Mother Seton's letter, because Sunday was too bad a day for
them to come to church. Carroll himself has
great antipathy to leaving his warm chamber,
having just begun his 76th year. The weather
may have also laid up Mother Seton, her family, and the sisters. None of the Caton family
are in town except Mrs. Patterson[1] and Louisa.
The latter talks much of her dear Mrs. Seton
but often forgets the Mother's salutary counsels and examples. "Oh! deducing and deceit-
ful world! How happy for you and your

---

[1]*Mary or Marianne Caton was wife of Robert Patterson. See No. 148.*

blessed companions to be removed from its contagious breath!" Now that the constitutions have received the approbation of the community, Mr. Dubois informs Carroll that the election of its officers would be made immediately, and no doubt in a spirit of charity and humility. Though he fears he will omit some, Carroll asks Mother Seton to tell Juliana White and her sister Miss Wiseman, Anny Cox, Anne Nelson, and dear little Mary Harper[1] that he loves them tenderly, as well as her own sweet girls. Tell dear Anna that "viewing her almost as the happy inhabitant of a better world," he feels for her "an awful respect." In a P.S. Carroll says his other commissions will be given to Dr. Rose [?].

AMSV.

159. TO REV. AMBROSE MARÉCHAL, Baltimore, 12 February 1812

Carroll wrote to Maréchal in France concerning his recommendation of Louis William DuBourg for the bishopric of Louisiana.

Maréchal has been told that Carroll intends to recommend Maréchal's friend the president of St. Mary's College for New Orleans. No one is warranted to say so. Some of his friends wish to draw the secret from Carroll. To Maréchal he freely confesses that he has often thought

---

[1]*Daughter of Robert Goodloe Harper and Catherine Carroll.*

of doing so, but difficulties gave him pause:
the belief the college would sink if he were tak-
en away and the need to extricate it from debt.
Carroll still wavers. To Maréchal alone and to
their friend the rector of the Point[1] Carroll
confides. If this reaches Maréchal before he
embarks,[2] he should supply the information
to those who must be informed. Born in Saint
Domingue of lawfully married parents, ordained, "possessed of eminent talents," age
45, of sound faith and morals, etc., DuBourg
is highly recommended for his zeal. Because
Louisiana has been long without a bishop,
there has been disorder of every kind among
clergy and laity. Firm and active and fluent in
three languages, DuBourg is a fit person to restore order and discipline. "I am sensible this
is an informal mode of nomination: but in
these times, forms must be dispensed with for
the sake of doing substantial good."

Letterbook 3, pp. 100-1 (see *JCP*, 3: 175-76).

160. TO MESSRS. THOMAS WRIGHT AND COMPANY, n.p., 8 March 1812

Another of Carroll's letters to his London bankers.

Wrights' of 1 January showed a balance of 18
shillings and one pence due by Carroll. He

---

[1]*Antoine Garnier, S.S., had been pastor of St Patrick's at Fells Point, the second church of Baltimore, before being recalled to France in 1803.*
[2]*Recalled to France in 1803, Maréchal decided to return to Baltimore in 1812 when the Society of St. Sulpice was temporarily suppressed in 1811.*

was surprised not to find himself credited 1810 or 1811 for the payment of Mr. [William] Strickland. Carroll has written him, hoping he will place one of the yearly annuities to his credit exclusive of that which will fall due in May or June. Carroll will give the notice desired to Mr. Edward Fenwick. If Messrs. Wright hold the evidence or certificates of the £800 at 8%, they are asked to tell Carroll of the measures he must take to have it transferred.

Letterbook 3, p. 101.

161. TO MOTHER ELIZABETH ANN SETON, n.p., 10 March 1812

Carroll wrote again on the health of Mother Seton's oldest.

Their "valuable and amiable friend," Mr. Bruté,[1] brings Carroll the news that Anina is still alive, and Bruté is almost persuaded that through a "miraculous interposition" she will recover. Carroll would rely on his and the prayers of "heavenly Mr. Nagot."[2] But when Bruté read him Mother Seton's lines, Carroll's hopes sank, and he cautions her against a "delusive expectation" that her daughter will recover in spite of new symptoms that had raised the confidence of Mr. Dubois. Carroll wants Mother Seton to tell the sisters how in-

---

[1] *Simon Gabriel Bruté de Rémur, S.S. (1779-1839), a teacher at Mount St. Mary's Seminary, would later become the bishop of Vincennes.*
[2] *The saintly Francis Nagot, former Sulpician superior, whose death was expected momentarily for a number of years, lived until 9 April 1816.*

terested he is in their happiness. If he had the time he would inquire of Margaret George[1] how she and her mother are doing since they moved to Emmitsburg. He has received an affectionate letter from Anne Nelson, which he will acknowledge with best wishes to her and her sister Charlotte. Poor Nancy Lefevre has heard of her mother's death from Mrs. Howard,[2] who has engaged her as her housekeeper. Nancy shares Mother Seton's sorrows.

AMSV

162. TO REV. FRANCIS IGNATIUS NEALE, S.J., Baltimore, 11 April 1812

This letter can no longer be found, but a card concerning it carries the following notation:

"Faculties of Diocese" and "Contains a little note from P.[Fr.] E[noch]. Fenwick"

MPA, card catalogue.

163. TO MESSRS. THOMAS WRIGHT AND COMPANY, n.p., 28 October 1812

Another letter of Carroll to his London bankers.

Wrights' of 15 May and duplicate show that Carroll has credit for £168.16.11. In addition

---

[1]*A Baltimore widow who entered the community on 2 February 1812.*
[2]*Probably Mrs. John Eager Howard.*

to this Carroll now encloses in duplicate an exchange of [James] Du Moulin drawn 15 August for £100 in Carroll's favor. He also draws on Mr. Charles Ghequiere.[1] The reason for his inquiry about the £400 at 5% was that he might know how to transfer it from England if it should ever prove advantageous to sell it and invest in stock in the United States but wishes it to remain as it is now.

Letterbook 3, p. 101.

164. TO REV. JOHN ANTHONY GRASSI, S.J., Baltimore, 11 November 1812

Carroll wrote to Grassi, president of Georgetown College, about the future of two able priests.

This will be delivered to Grassi by Rev. Mr. [Peter] Lavadiere or Rev. Mr. [Joseph] Harent. The latter, after living about twenty years in Baltimore and Conewago and leading a life more like a priest than a layman, decided finally to be a priest. After studying divinity at the seminary, he was ordained last summer. He agreed to assist Rev. [Leonard] Edelen [S.J.] at Newtown, who with his and Rev. [Notley] Young's assistance can perform the necessary services in neighboring congregations without overloading Mr. Edelen. Carroll had been told of Mr. Lavadiere's coming some two years ago by Mr. Peemans of Louvain and Mr. Saive [?],

---

[1] *German-born Charles Ghequiere (1758-1818), a wealthy Catholic merchant of Baltimore.*

the Jesuits' two principal benefactors in Belgium. He wishes to join the Jesuits. Grassi will further that object. But Carroll learned from a letter of Rev. Benedict Fenwick to his brother Enoch that Mr. Kohlmann had invited him to be president of the Literary Institution [in New York]. It would be a most unwise measure Carroll believed for a novice of the Society and a stranger just arrived to be so. If Kohlmann wishes someone else to be president than himself, surely Mr. Benedict Fenwick is preferable to anyone. If either Georgetown College or the Literary Institution is to be discontinued, it must be the latter in justice to parents who expect competent teachers. Friends of the institution should be informed of the Society's inability to find such if this decision has to be made. Tell little Matthew [Deagle] that the accounts of his behavior and application [at Georgetown] give much pleasure to his excellent mother. Harent will not be able to deliver this till next week. Lavadiere has now told Carroll that he made his novitiate some years ago but never made vows. In a postscript Carroll says that he has just received Grassi's letter concerning Mr. [Peter] Epinette [S.J.]. His only reason for forbidding him to preach at the college is his imperfect command of English. Carroll knows French and Italian better than Epinette knows English, but he would never attempt to preach in either, in or out of the time of the sitting of Congress. If Epinette insists on leaving the college, Grassi may do as he pleases. Epinette is needed more at St. Thomas [Manor], where poor Mr. Pile[1] can do nothing and Fr. John Fenwick[2] is overburdened.

MPA, box 57.5, folder 1, no. 203B2.

165. TO MARGARET [?], n.p., [1813?]

To an unidentified laywoman or religious sister Carroll wrote of correspondence and a journey.

The weather is too bad to see "my good Margaret" but he reads [?] to her Mr. [Enoch ?] Fenwick's letters, his own for Georgetown [Visitation convent ?] and Mount Carmel, and Mr. F. to Louisa Jones (Sister Gonzaga), which will give Margaret the pleasure of seeing the [illegible] of that community if she has time. The archbishop wishes her a happy journey, though the present weather gives no great promise of it.

AAB, 9-U-1.

---

[1]*Henry Pile (1743-1813), a former Jesuit, did not reenter the Society of Jesus but apparently lived at St. Thomas Manor.*

[2]*Rev. John Ceslas Fenwick, O.P. (c1759-1815), uncle of Bishop Edward Fenwick and the first American to become a Dominican, taught abroad before returning to Maryland about 1800, where he lived and died at St. Thomas Manor.*

166. TO MR. THOMAS SIM LEE, Baltimore, 18 January 1813

A proposal (not described) by Lee posed a dilemma for Carroll since it would seem to run contrary to the interests of the Corporation of the Clergy.

Lee's letter of the 14th has remained unanswered for two [four?] days to allow Carroll time to consider if it is possible to reconcile his proposal with the duty he owes to the Corporation, since the $1200 annual interest would absorb all its means of ever paying the capital. But Carroll's views may be different from that of "my Brethren" [the Jesuits]. Mr. Francis Neale [fiscal agent] may have sounded their opinion and discovered means of payment, of which Carroll was unaware. If so, he would advise Neale to call the trustees together, though it would probably not be in Carroll's power to meet them. Lee is aware of his desire to do everything in his power to serve him. Carroll has learned that Mrs. Ringgold, Lee's "most excellent daughter," is in a critical state and asks that Lee assure her of his deep concern for her sufferings, which she knows how to render "the source of abundant rewards in another life." He pays his respects also to Mrs. Horsey and Mrs. William Lee and their husbands[1] and gives his love to Archy and John.[2] Carroll regretted the shortness of Archy's visit, "the moreso, because I found in

---

[1]*Lee's youngest daughter Elizabeth married Outerbridge Horsey (1777-1875), U.S. Senator from Delaware from 1810 to 1821. Lee's son William married Mary Holliday.*

[2]*Lee's son John (1788-1871), educated at Harvard, would be a U.S. Congressman 1823-1825.*

him treasures of intelligence, and especially relative to interests, which I have much at heart."

HLC/MHS.

167. TO BISHOP MICHAEL FRANCIS EGAN, O.F.M., n.p., [January/February 1813]

Only the last nine lines of this extract appear in JCP, 3: 210. In it Carroll spoke of a conference he had with Rev. William Vincent Harold, O.P., one of the pastors of St. Mary's Church in Philadelphia.

Carroll answers Bishop Egan's letter of the 24th and 25th at once. The day after Mr. Harold arrived [in Baltimore] they had a long conference about his grievances with the trustees, about the insolence of the sexton and clerk of St. Mary's towards the priests there and of his "dilapidation of the provisions of the house." Harold accuses the sexton-clerk of being the cause of the present disagreement and complains of the bishop's keeping such a man in his confidence and employment and of the bishop's saying from the altar that peace was made between "us," which Harold takes to include the priests and Egan. Harold knew nothing until then of Egan's having come to an understanding with the trustees and concludes he has no protection for his character in this country and is resolved to leave after March. He would not hear of another situation. Though Carroll would regret the loss of his talents to the country, he feels he cannot insist. They parted with a promise to continue the conference, but it has not taken place. Egan knows better than Carroll the fitness of Mr. Harold Sr.[1] for Pittsburgh. Harold questions whether Egan has any charge . . . [the rest as in *JCP*, 3: 210].

AAB, 11-M-3 (inside letter of Egan to Carroll).

168. CERTIFICATE FOR REV. STEPHEN THEODORE BADIN, Baltimore, 17 February 1813

Carroll certified as to the accuracy of an appeal by Rev. Stephen Badin and gave his endorsement.[2]

Carroll certifies that Badin's statement is correct and "only expresses very inadequately his great services in the cause of civilisation, morality, and religion" and that he is entitled not only to public encouragement but, as Carroll "is not afraid of adding," to public gratitude.

AAB, 1-J-12.

---

[1] *James Harold, uncle to William Vincent Harold and co-pastor of St. Mary's, to whom Bishop Egan proposed a transfer to Pittsburgh.*

[2] *Badin asked for contributions for buildings in Lexington and Louisville and in Shelby County, where a hurricane [tornado ?] unroofed a building. Bishop Neale also concurs, and a list of contributors in Maryland follows that includes Robert Brent and Charles Carroll of Bellevue.*

169. TO REV. WILLIAM VINCENT HAROLD, O.P., n.p., 18 March 1813

Carroll wrote to Harold after the conference mentioned in No. 167.

If the business of recovering [?] will permit Harold's going abroad, Carroll wants to converse with him as soon as possible. His friends are anxious for Harold's return, but Carroll can not respond on the subject of their missive[1] without an explanation of Harold's present dispositions. Carroll feels the utmost anxiety for Harold's continuance in America, even at Philadelphia in preference to any other place, the hope of which will involve sacrifices [on Harold's or Carroll's part ?].

Letterbook 3, p. 105.

170. TO MESSRS. LUKE TIERNAN AND JOHN WALSH, n.p., 6 July 1813

Carroll wrote Messrs. Tiernan and Walsh regarding their proposal to establish a Dominican parish in Baltimore for the Revs. William Vincent Harold and John Ryan.

When it was first proposed to build another church, Carroll had no objections other than its threat to progress on [the construction of] the cathedral. Carroll had only the verbal guarantee of the trustees at the time he signed the bond [?]. Tiernan and Walsh were confident it did not

---

[1] *A petition sent by a committee of parishioners of St. Mary's, Philadelphia, in Harold's favor (AAB, 11-D-15).*

threaten the progress of the cathedral. Carroll said then and now repeats that if the majority of the other trustees[1] agree he would consent to the building of a church in Baltimore for the Dominicans. It would not have parochial privileges until Carroll or his successor saw fit. This would not deprive the Dominicans of respectability or means of subsistence. Emoluments at St. Peter's [Procathedral] had no bearing on Carroll's decision. If the pastor [of the new church] should ever want, it would be the result of his own "remissiveness in duty," in which case he would not deserve public favor, or "from a spirit of turbulence & resistance to regular authority." Whenever Tiernan and Walsh and the other trustees can meet and discuss the effects of the building of another church on that of the cathedral, Carroll would give his fullest sanction subject to the above limitations.

Letterbook 3, pp. 105-6.

171. NOTATION CONCERNING REV. THOMAS MONNELLY, [between 6 July 1813 and 31 March 1814]

Carroll recorded information from others on the derelictions of Rev. Thomas Monnelly of St. Joseph's Congregation on the Eastern Shore.

Information from Mr. Councell [?] as to Monnelly's drinking and swearing and from Mr. Callahan [?] as to his transportation of timber from public to private use.

Letterbook 3, p. 106.

---

[1]*Tiernan and Walsh were trustees of the cathedral congregation.*

172. TO BISHOP FRANCIS MOYLAN, Baltimore, 28 December 1813

Carroll wrote the bishop of Cork regarding misrepresentations made by Rev. John Ryan, O.P., in England and Ireland.

Bishop Moylan has by this time seen Rev. Mr. Ryan.[1] On his coming to Baltimore, his talents and temper so impressed Carroll and the congregation there that they hoped he would, with the permission of his superiors in Ireland, remain with them. But since his return to Europe he has caused Carroll more displeasure than he can express. Carroll quotes a letter from London lately received.[2] The writer [Charles Plowden] had met two Irish priests just returned from America, Ryan and Harold, who freely gave an unfavorable account of the writer's friends in Maryland, saying that they held estates formerly owned by the Jesuits with a great number of slaves, that they trafficked in that kind, and that religion suffered greatly in consequence of their being planters. The two admitted that the Jesuits' slaves were more mildly treated than those of laymen but the very idea disgusted the slaves and others, and the archbishop himself was a great slaveholder. Carroll wishes that a more favorable account of the progress of the true religion could be given, but it would be an act of ingratitude to God and an injustice to the zeal-

---

[1]*John Ryan, O.P., joined his friend William Vincent Harold, O.P., in Philadelphia, where differences with Bishop Egan (see Nos. 167 and 169) induced them to return temporarily to Ireland and England.*
[2]*See JCP, 3: 246-47.*

ous efforts of "my Rev: Brethren" not to say that great and wonderful has been the increase of faith and piety in many parts of the United States, and if it has not been even greater the chief impediments have been a want of laborers and the pernicious example of some employed in the ministry. It is true the Jesuits, the only clergy before the Revolution, employed slaves on their estates, as all clergy, secular and regular, still do in every country in America. That enthusiasm for emancipation now so fashionable in England "had not yet furnished a field for so much declamation and hypocrisy." But it is a wicked calumny to say the clergy here ever trafficked in slaves. The retailers of that calumny should have added that the clergy, willing to respond to such unjust prejudices, "were actually employing their endeavours to give liberty gradually, to all the coloured generation belonging to their estates." As to the personal charge against him Carroll assured Bishop Moylan that before he was twenty-six he had renounced all his paternal inheritance in slaves, which had devolved on him from his father's will, and since then has not owned one. So much for the accuracy of the two Irish priests. When they left, Carroll had been sorry, particularly for the loss of Mr. Harold, whose talents and zeal were of the first order.

APF, Congregazione particolare, Anglia, 146: 533rv (a copy of Carroll's letter in a letter of Ryan to another).

173. NOTATION FOR REV. WILLIAM PASQUET, [18 January 1814]

Carroll penned a notation on a letter of Rev. William Pasquet dated 18 January 1814 concerning slaves at Bohemia.

> Carroll says to note the contents about Rachel but particularly Phyllis [whom Pasquet had hired out], Joe, and Jacob.

AAB, 6-E-5.

174. TO REV. SIMON FELIX GALLAGHER, Baltimore, 15 February 1814

Carroll wrote Gallagher concerning an apology and once again the possibility of a change.

> From the postscript Carroll now realizes Gallagher's last letter was written back in October, the postscript itself telling Carroll that Rev. [Joseph] Clorivière had acknowledged that he had wronged Gallagher and apologized.[1] For Carroll also he had corrected his misstatement regarding Gallagher not only to remove the latter's uneasiness but to give also a pledge of guarding himself from the effects of a zeal not always tempered by patient inquiry and consideration. "Such is the genius of his country." The young woman Joanna [blank] who came a

---

[1] *Clorivière had quoted a letter of Rev. John Tessier as saying that Carroll disapproved of the need to get permission from the vestry to bury anyone allowed by Gallagher.*

few days ago from Charleston to enter the Sisters of the Order of La Trappe was much disappointed at seeing their manner of living and unstable situation. There was no likelihood of a permanent settlement in Baltimore, since the leader had departed leaving five or six poor, uneducated women, who but for the charity of Mr. Moranvillé[1] might have starved. After one day Joanna proceeded to New York with the intention of joining the Ursulines from Cork. She had told Carroll that Gallagher was often indisposed, a matter of concern to Carroll since he sees Gallagher as a bulwark of religion in Charleston. The priests of New York plan a quarterly or monthly of a historical and apologetical character, and Carroll hoped that Gallagher could contribute an occasional article from his store of knowledge. He well remembered Gallagher's telling him of a defense of the church he had done. Would Gallagher send this to Mr. Kohlmann[2] and to Mr. Benedict Fenwick, who will be the chief conductor of the magazine? If Gallagher could be spared from Charleston, how delighted Carroll would be to have him as the head of this undertaking. He would be in a healthier climate and less fatiguing situation. Carroll has learned that the good Mrs. [James] Lynah died lately and extends his condolences to her son [Edward].

APF, America-Canada, 2: 202r-203r.

---

[1]*John Moranvillé was pastor of St. Patrick's Church in Baltimore.*
[2]*Anthony Kohlmann, S.J., had been appointed by Carroll administrator of the diocese of New York.*

175. TO REV. SIMON FELIX GALLAGHER, Baltimore, 19 March 1814

This letter was a follow-up to No. 174.

Gallagher's of 8 March requests further information on Joanna [blank], who was unsuccessful in her application to the Ursulines near New York, perhaps because she had no recommendation. Her traveling companion, Mr. [Francis] Vespre [S.J.], during the course of the journey became convinced she was unsuited for the religious life and probably communicated his opinion to Mr. Kohlmann. She returned to Baltimore, where Mr. Moranvillé placed her with a pious family until he could judge the propriety of her joining the house of the Sisters of La Trappe, where she would have to suffer hardships to which she was not accustomed. Another singular person who calls herself Mrs. Madgett claims acquaintance with Gallagher. Carroll remembers a priest who came several years ago to Philadelphia with an introduction from the British secretary of state to Mr. [Robert] Lyston, at that time minister of England to the United States. Carroll conferred often with Mr. Lyston about him. Carroll understood that he went to [South ?] Carolina with respectable persons of that state to introduce the culture of the vine, since which nothing more was heard of him until this woman arrived, who says he was murdered. She is quite insane when she talks about herself and the persecutions she suffers and is penniless. Charitable persons offer temporary relief, but the hospital for lunatics would be the best place for her. Can Gallagher send any information about her? Carroll will tell Messrs. Kohlmann and [Benedict] Fenwick of New York they can expect a contribution from Gallagher for their periodical, for which no prospectus has yet been published. After Easter he will direct Mr. [Enoch] Fenwick of Baltimore to send Gallagher the holy oils by Mr. Clorivière's friend.

APF, America-Canada, 2: 204r-205r.

176. TO REV. WILLIAM PASQUET, n.p., 5/6 May 1814

Carroll penned an extract of a letter to Pasquet concerning slaves at Bohemia.

Carroll can not decide about James's family. At times Pasquet proposed selling them to make good [the Corporation's] claim on him. At other times he would have nothing to do with such a settlement. Carroll is of the opinion that Pasquet and Mr. [Francis] Neale [the agent] should work it out between them. He is surprised that nothing has yet been done about old Jack after Pasquet's telling him that the bargain had been concluded for $130 or $120 and that Jack was gone to the neighborhood of Nottingham. Carroll would be much dissatisfied if the old man was turned out without any security for a home or his last year's wages. How was he to reconcile Pasquet's two reports?

Letterbook 3, p. 107.

177. NOTATION ON SLAVES AT BOHEMIA, [29 May 1814]

On a letter of 29 May 1814 unrelated to the notation Carroll re-marked again on the slaves at Bohemia (see Nos. 173 and 176).

> Fanny and her family wish to be sold. Carroll offers his opinion [not given] and lists the members of the family [see Appendix 3].

AAB, 11-N-2.

178. TO REV. ENOCH FENWICK, S.J., Washington, 15 June [1814]

Carroll informed the rector of St. Peter's Procathedral in Baltimore of current events and future plans.

> On his return from Georgetown [College] Carroll received Fenwick's of 13 June. Mr. Bitouzey did not meet "us" probably because of the rain and whether he will join "us" today is uncertain.[1] The letter that Fenwick suspected was from the nuncio in Brasil [?] might have reliable news of the pope. Carroll has no doubt about the pope's restoration and in his leisure moments is preparing a pastoral about it that will be printed when he returns home next week.[2] It will contain directions for a *Te Deum* and other expressions of thanksgiving and should not be preceded by other public demonstrations but Fenwick should prepare the performers for that festivity. Carroll has

[1] *See* JCP, 3: 273.
[2] *The pastoral appeared under the date 17 July 1814 (JCP, 3: 279-83).*

just celebrated Mass for poor Columbus [?]
and to obtain every blessing for the "superex-
cellent Betsy Rusk" [?]. If she is still alive, tell
her she is often in Carroll's thoughts. Carroll
hopes that Peggy Read's [?] symptoms are not
serious. Mr. Godefroy[1] may have told Fenwick
of his proposal for a grand festival for the revolution [?] in "the Cathedral" after some
preparations ingeniously devised by him, but
Carroll can not reconcile himself to "the idea
of this motley fitting up" of that venerable
building. Tomorrow he will send him an answer. Carroll asks Fenwick to remember him
to "good Mr. Mertz,"[2] Dr. Gallagher, and "our
other R^d Brethren."

MPA, box 58, folder 25, no. 204Z20.

179. TO [ARCHBISHOP GIOVANNI BATTISTA QUARAN-
TOTTI ?],[3] n.p., 12 July 1814

*Under the above date Carroll indicated in his letterbook what he
had written the "Secretary of the Propaganda."*[4]

Carroll says he wrote a short letter to the Secretary of the Propaganda having had only a

---

[1]*Maximilian Godefroy (c1806-1824), a noted architect, had designed the chapel at St.
Mary's Seminary, the first Gothic revival church in America, as well as the Unitarian
Church of Baltimore.*

[2]*Rev. John Mertz replaced Rev. Frederic Cesarius Reuter at St. John's German church in
Baltimore.*

[3]*It is not certain to whom Carroll wrote. Archbishop Quarantotti was secretary of the
Propaganda from 1808 to 1816 but was also pro-prefect (acting prefect) from 1809 to 20
May 1814.*

[4]*JCP, 3: 279, citing a letter of 17 July 1815 (JCP, 3: 344), says a letter of July 1814
to Cardinal Michele di Pietro (prefect until May 1814) was not found.*

half hour's previous notice of the opportunity to do so. The letter contained simply an expression of the general joy felt by Catholics in the United States for the liberation of the pope[1] and an assurance that he would shortly forward a statement "of all material events" about ecclesiastical matters during the long suspension of correspondence and "other things for which provision was now to be made."

Letterbook 3, p. 107.

180. TO REV. JOHN ANTHONY GRASSI, S.J., Baltimore, 27 September 1814

Carroll wrote the Jesuit provincial concerning a proposed change.

Having no expectation of going soon to Washington or Georgetown, Carroll thinks proper to inform Grassi by mail that he can not for a moment think of sending Mr. [James] Raymond [S.J.] to St. Thomas Manor or Newtown. He has given his reasons to the Right Rev. Bishop of Gortyna.[2]

MPA, box 52, folder 13, no. 204N19.

---

[1]*Pius VII had been held captive by Napoleon Bonaparte from 1809 until the latter's abdication on 11 April 1814.*
[2]*For the reasons given Bishop Neale see* JCP, *3: 296.*

181. TO HIS SUFFRAGAN BISHOPS,[1] n.p., [October/ November 1814]

After consulting his coadjutor, his suffragan bishops, and others, Carroll reported their conclusions.

The bishops and priests consulted feel it their duty to seek a suitable candidate for the bishopric of Philadelphia not only in that vacant diocese but also in other dioceses. The first choices are Messrs. David of the diocese of Bardstown and DuBourg, administrator of the diocese of Louisiana. The first was named by all consulted and the second by Messrs. Gallitzin and Hurley[2] of the diocese of Philadelphia. The only objection to David, "eminent in prudence, constancy, ecclesiastical learning, piety, zeal for instruction," is the difficulty in taking him from "the good Bishop of Bardstown." The talents of DuBourg are known, but it may be doubted that it is proper to nominate someone outside the ecclesiastical province [of Baltimore] in an office directly under the Holy See. Gallitzin has lived for so long so far distant that Carroll can not speak with confidence of his present dispositions. His sacrfices and his theological learning are considerable, but he has incurred a great load of debt "rashly though for excellent and charitable purposes." Hurley is talented but in

---

[1]*The suffragan bishops were John Cheverus and Benedict Flaget, but Carroll probably sent this letter also to his coadjutor, Leonard Neale.*

[2]*Michael Hurley, O.S.A. (1778-1837), born probably in Pennsylvania, enjoyed great popularity in Philadelphia.*

need of "leisure for improvement." He might be a useful prelate later.

American Catholic Historical Researches 10 (1893): 185-86.[1]

182. TO REV. JOSEPH PETER PICOT DE CLORIVIERE,[2]
Baltimore, 3 November 1814

Sadly Carroll granted Clorivière the exeat *he requested.*

Carroll has received Clorivière's painful letter of 27 October announcing his departure for France sooner than expected. Many advantages to the congregation of Charleston enjoyed through his zeal will be lost. Dr. Gallagher's age and infirmity will not allow him to supply the deficiency. But Carroll will not withhold his consent. On the other half sheet is his *exeat* written with a heavy heart. May God reward him for his services, and protect him on his voyage and for the rest of his days. Mr. [Enoch] Fenwick presents his respect and joins Carroll in congratulating Dr. Gallagher on his safe return. Mr. Mertz does the same. The amiable Mr. Maréchal wants only the recovery of his former strength for a perfect reestablishment. The enclosed [not found] is for Clorivière's venerated uncle.

---

[1]*This letter is given in full also in Guilday,* Carroll, *pp. 677-78, who cites* Researches *as his source but gives the wrong pages.*

[2]*On the unusual career of Clorivière (1768-1826) see Guilday,* Carroll, *pp. 742-43. Also see Anna Wells Rutledge, "A French Priest, Painter and Architect in the United States: Joseph Pierre Picot de Limoëlan de Clorivière," in* Gazette Des Beaux-Arts *33 (March 1948): 159-76.*

[*Exeat:*] Not wishing to delay Clorivière any longer or resist his valid arguments for revisiting his native land so that he may give the same efforts for the good of souls there he has given in this diocese, and not without singular sorrow, Carroll grants permission to leave his diocese for France. Furthermore Carroll testifies that, as far as he knows, Clorivière is free from all censure and canonical impediment so that he may celebrate Mass and conduct all the customary ministries of the priesthood with the permission of his superiors.

APF, America Centrale, 5: 149r-50r.

183. TO CARDINAL LORENZO LITTA, 7 January 1815

Carroll wrote to the prefect of the Congregation of the Propaganda Fide regarding dispenations and filling sees.

[This letter in the Propaganda Fide archives is represented by two different documents in *JCP*: 3: 301-3 and 3: 344-46. The first deals with marriage dispensations that Carroll wants approved by the pope and the second with filling the vacant sees of New York, Philadelphia, and New Orleans.]

APF, Congregazioni Generali, 917: 306r-7v, 314r, 316rv.

184. TO REV. SIMON FELIX GALLAGHER, Baltimore, 20 February 1815

Carroll wrote Gallagher of an irregular burial and other matters.

Carroll was not able to answer Gallagher's letter of 4 February until today. It describes a most melancholy occurrence, but Gallagher has the faculties to relieve the sick person of the censure incurred by him and in case of his death to admit him to a Christian burial. The eleventh of his faculties gives him power to absolve in all [such] cases. If death does not follow, there is no cause for refusing Christian burial [?]. With regard to the other parties, though they fall under the general censure of excommunication pronounced by the Council of Trent, they need not be denounced publicly and be shunned. Carroll wishes Gallagher had not done so and asks him to tell the parties and all concerned that the prohibition of associating with the culprits no longer subsists. Carroll was pleased that Gallagher's letter contained no complaint about his health, but it would have been more welcome had it mentioned something about Gallagher's intention of associating Rev. [Robert] Browne with him since he alone would not be able to fill all the duties of his station now that Mr. Clorivière had departed. Gallagher's old friend Dr. Matthew O'Brien, who had grown tired of the unproductiveness of the vicinity of Salem, is now in Baltimore uncertain of his future course. Carroll's good companion Mr.

[Enoch] Fenwick, the marvelous and honest Mr. Mertz, the gentlemen of the Seminary, and Mr. Moranvillé are well. Tell Dr. Lynah his letter will be answered soon. Carroll often sees his dear boy, who is daily more dear to him and gives general satisfaction. In a P.S. Carroll tells Gallagher that since his departure he has had the misfortune to lose his sister [Mary] Young, whom he recommends to Gallagher's prayers.

APF, America Centrale, 5: 20r-21r.

185. NOTATION ON SLAVES AT BOHEMIA, [May 1815]

Carroll made the following notation in the Bohemia ledger probably during a visit to Bohemia in May 1815.

Carroll estimates the price of Fanny and her family if sold for a given term of years [for price and term of years see Appendix 3]: Fanny age 48, Regis 19, Jacob 15, Bill 13, Dick 7, John 4, Lucy 3, Nancy 20 and infant, Polly 17 and infant, Lucy about 18 months, Barney 53, Joe 45, Dick 32, Phyllis about 36, Maria 16, Price 14, James 12, Tom 7, and twin boys about a year old.

AAB, Bohemia Plantation Book, 1790-1815, pp. 34-35.

186. TO MOTHER ELIZABETH ANN SETON, Baltimore, 7 May 1815

In this letter Carroll made an unusual proposal to Mother Seton.

Returning from the Eastern Shore [Bohemia] on the eve of the Ascension, Carroll found a letter from Charlotte [Nelson] expressing "her determination to cultivate, as much as your present regulation allows, that confidence and communication with you, whom she loves so dearly." Her separation was the source of her depression. In a few days he expects to receive and send $25 for the present quarterly payment [for Charlotte ?]. Carroll then proposes to Mother Seton and Dubois that they receive the wife of Mr. Robert Oliver[1] as a boarder, at the behest of the Caton and Harper families, in an attempt to cure a mental derangement, wherein she suspects attempts to poison her by those around her. Mr. Oliver is willing to pay a thousand or more dollars a year. Mrs. Oliver is a sister of the late Mrs. Craig of Philadelphia, whom Mother Seton probably knew[2] and who had corresponded with Mr. Babad[3] on religious subjects. Carroll was surprised by a visit of Sisters Fanny and Juliet,[4] whose departure must have grieved Mother Se-

---

[1]*Robert Oliver (c1757-1834), a Presbyterian, was a wealthy merchant of Baltimore.*

[2]*The Craigs had intermarried with the Bayleys of New York.*

[3]*Pierre Babad [Babade], S.S., had been confessor and spiritual adviser of Mother Seton, a bone of contention between her and DuBourg.*

[4]*Fanny Jordan and Julia Shirk entered the community on 29 June 1810 under the influence of Rev. John Baptist David, S.S. Their presence in Baltimore at this time can not be explained.*

ton. Carroll's growing weakness of mind and body, though his health is good, reminds him of the need to have the prayers of her community and her pupils. Susan, the bearer of the letter,[1] "appears so ripe for heaven." He is solicitous for Mother Seton's dear William and Rev. Mr. Bruté since "the late calamitous news."[2]

AMSV.

187. TO MOTHER ELIZABETH ANN SETON, n.p., [Summer 1815 ?]

This letter dealt mostly with Carroll's concern for the plight of the Nelson sisters, former boarders at Mother Seton's school.

Carroll missed the opportunity of sending Mother Seton a letter by Mr. Grover [?] but does so now through Mrs. Roach, who, having recently lost her husband, was free to be near her daughter, one of Mother Seton's students. Henrietta Brown, who had just paid him a visit, was much improved in health and mind. She said that Becky[3] was again suffering her former pains so that Mother Seton needs again all her faith and resignation "to bear so many shocks and trials." Tell Rose [White] and Kitty [Mullen] that the violent heats prevent him from writing them. Carroll has received affec-

---

[1]*Probably Susan Clossy, who entered the community 24 May 1809 and died 6 May 1823.*
[2]*The escape of Napoleon from Elba.*
[3]*Rebecca Seton (1802-1816) was Elizabeth's youngest child.*

tionate letters from Charlotte and Anne [Nelson],[1] whose peculiar situation gives him many uneasy moments. He is unable to follow Mother Seton's suggestion to find a family in Baltimore who would take them in for a few weeks without his revealing the reason. Carroll proposes that the girls go to a place like Hanover or York, Pennsylvania, to stay a few days with their mother, who Carroll understood from Mother Seton had reformed in part. Their example, prayers, and entreaties might effect a solid conversion. The mother might then find "creditable subsistence" far from Philadelphia, and the girls might then return with alacrity to St. Joseph's until they could find their place in life. His solicitude for them prompted such schemes rather than that he remain insensible to their happiness. Because of the heat he could write no one but Mother Seton. Their friend on Gay Street [Mrs. Robert Barry] is well and sends her respects.

AMSV.

---

[1]*Their name was really Smith. They had been sent from Philadelphia to Baltimore by Bishop Egan to avoid the influence of a bad family. See Melville, Seton, p. 360n.59 (see also Nos. 161 and 186).*

188. TO MOTHER ELIZABETH ANN SETON, n.p., 12 July 1815

In this letter Carroll wrote to Mother Seton about her son William and other matters.

> Carroll has just received two long letters from Mr. Bruté, dated 31 May, Bordeaux, telling him he had committed William, in perfect health, to a family traveling to Marseilles, from which place he could easily reach Leghorn. As soon as he can get the letters transcribed, he will forward them to Mr. Dubois. That morning Anne [Nelson] surprised him by a visit, and Charlotte would send Mother Seton a further account of what was judged proper in their regard. On no account should they go with their mother if she settles elsewhere. They will remain in Baltimore some days. Louisa Caton, before she left for Canada with her two married sisters and father, left some bank notes with Carroll to be sent to Mother Seton. Carroll is so enervated by the heat that he can only assure her beloved sisters of his unvaried attachment to them, although there were some he thought of more frequently as having known them in Baltimore.

AMSV.

189. TO MR. CHARLES GRIMKE COSSLETT, Baltimore, 27 July 1815

Carroll wrote to this prominent layman of Charleston, South Carolina, concerning the return of Rev. Joseph Clorivière.

Carroll acknowledges Cosslett's interesting letter of 21 June. Mr. Clorivière has written twice about his return, explaining why he had not left England in May or June as he once intended. Carroll intends to restore him to Charleston to perfect the work so well begun[1] and is pleased to learn from Cosslett that an arrangement is being made to place him in a more eligible situation, which Carroll hopes will be a separate habitation. He has not had the pleasure of a personal acquaintance of Rev. [Robert] Browne, but the good reports in his favor induced Carroll to yield to Dr. Gallagher's request that Browne divide his time between Charleston and Augusta so that Gallagher might make a long voyage for the benefit of the church of Charleston. Instead he has gone to New York. Carroll rejoices that Browne gives satisfaction, but he has received from Augusta a gentle rebuke for having consented to the removal after the exertions there to build a church. Browne will probably be restored to Augusta when Gallagher returns or Clorivière arrives. Carroll asks Cosslett to announce his intentions regarding Clorivière to his friends and to pay his respects to Cosslett's venerable mother, who will be happy at the news.

APF, America Centrale, 5: 153rv.

---

[1] *Some members of the vestry resented Carroll's informing others, but not the vestry itself, of his plans to restore Clorivière. This letter was also printed in J. P. De Clorivière,* Further Documents showing the Cause of the Distressed State of the Roman Catholic Congregation in the City of Charleston *(Charleston, 1818), pp. 4-5.*

190. TO MR. AND MRS. J. W. DATTY, Baltimore, 27 July 1815

Carroll wrote of the return of Clorivière (see No. 189) also to the Dattys, former exiles from Saint Domingue.[1]

It gives Carroll pleasure to answer their undated letter by assuring them of his determination to reappoint their excellent friend Mr. Clorivière to his station in Charleston upon his return, which from his last letter Carroll does not expect to be before the last of September, when Clorivière would meet them with redoubled zeal.

APF, America Centrale, 5: 22r.

191. TO MESSRS. THOMAS WRIGHT AND COMPANY, n.p., 9 August 1815

Carroll sent a short notice to his London bankers.

Carroll has today drawn on Messrs. Wright for £130 in favor of Mr. Charles Ghequiere [see No. 163].

Letterbook 3, p. 109.

---

[1] *J. W. Datty resigned from the vestry in early 1816.*

PORTFOLIO III: LATER YEARS

Left 1. Leonard Neale. Like Carroll Maryland-born and probably elected bishop (1794), Carroll's coadjutor would be, in 1800, the first of four Carroll raised to the episcopacy. In the background of this oil is the academy of the Visitation Sisters, of whom Neale was the American founder. (Archbishops of Baltimore Collection)

Below 2. Cathedral of the Assumption. This photograph was taken in 1906 for the centenniel of Carroll's laying of the cornerstone of this magnficent edifice designed by Benjamin H. Latrobe, architect of the Capitol in Washington. It was not completed until 1821. (Archives of the Archdiocese of Baltimore)

3. Louis William Valentine DuBourg. A talented Sulpician, founder of St. Mary's College, first director of Mother Seton's Sisters of Charity, DuBourg was in 1812 chosen by Carroll administrator of the diocese of Louisiana and the Two Floridas. (Mount St. Mary's College, Emmitsburg, Maryland)

4. Richard Louis Concanen. When Carroll was unable to name anyone to fill the proposed bishopric of New York, the Holy See chose this Dominican, who had spent most of his adult life in Rome and had been Carroll's agent there since 1806. He died, however, at Naples, in 1810, while awaiting clearance to sail. (Shea, *Life,* opposite p. 624)

5. John Louis Lefebvre de Cheverus. When Francis Matignon refused the proposed bishopric of Boston, Carroll chose Matignon's friend Cheverus, who had labored with him in Boston since 1796 with great success. Though Carroll disliked travel, he would twice visit Cheverus in Boston. (Shea, *History of the Catholic Church in the United States*, vol. 3, opposite p. 112)

6. Benedict Joseph Flaget. This zealous Sulpician had served as a missionary to Vincennes, taught at Georgetown College, attempted to found a college in Havana, and was teaching in the Baltimore seminary when chosen by Carroll to be bishop of Bardstown, Kentucky. (Archives of the Archdiocese of Louisville)

7. Ambrose Maréchal. Though esteemed by Carroll, Maréchal was recalled to France in 1803, but during a temporary suppression of the Society of St. Sulpice he returned to Baltimore in 1812. There he would succeed Leonard Neale as archbishop. (Archbishops of Baltimore Collection)

8. Luke Tiernan. Irish-born Tiernan became a prosperous merchant of Baltimore. He often served as Carroll's intermediary in his British negotiations. A trustee of the cathedral congregation for forty-three years, he played a leading role in the funding of the new cathedral. (Riordan, *Cathedal Records*, p. 63)

Baltre Aug 28th 1815

My dear Madame

155

If my absence from home during part of the

last month, and that insuperable antipathy to the labours
of the desk, which age has produced, might not be offered as
some apology for my delay of answering the favour of my
dear Annette, ever since it was received about the 12th
of August, I should be at a loss to offer any motive for sol:
liciting your indulgence — You indeed had a right to
expect consolation from me after the loss of your dearest Sis:
ter; tho that event affected me, so much, that every word
of consolation written to you, would have wrung my own
soul with sadness for the departure of that friend so inter:
esting and amiable. If any thing within my power remained
to be done, by which she could be benefited, that I have
not failed to do and recommend to others. My sollicitude
for her, whilst she was living, is now transferred, dear An:
nette, to you; and it has been a great comfort to me to
know, that you continue to merit so much the favours of the respec:

9. Carroll's last letter. In a hand not markedly different from that of the earlier
years, Carroll wrote this letter of sympathy, the last letter that has been preserved.
(University of Notre Dame Archives)

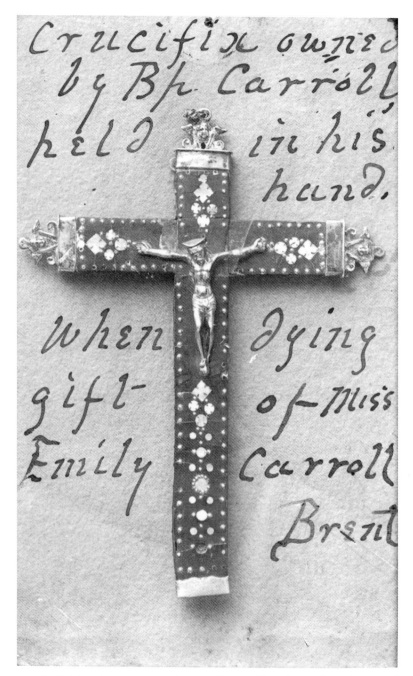

Crucifix owned by Bp. Carroll held in his hand.

when dying gift Emily of Miss Carroll Brent

10. Crucifix held at death. A crucifix Carroll is said by Shea to have brought from Rome in 1773 was, as a Brent relative here relates, in his hands at the time of his death. (University of Notre Dame Archives)

192. TO MESSRS. THOMAS WRIGHT AND COMPANY, n.p., 10 August 1815

This is a follow-up to No. 191 to Carroll's London bankers.

Carroll sends a duplicate of 9 August via a Liverpool packet from Alexandria, Virginia, and explains how he will pay the £130. Enclosed is Du Moulin's bill of 7 August for £156 made payable to Wrights' by Carroll's endorsement. More than two years of the annuity formerly paid through Mr. Strickland and now probably through Mr. Tristam[1] have created a credit for Carroll of more than £107. Add to this the interest which has accrued for upwards of two years on £400 5% navy stock and the bankers will find Carroll's credit with them sufficient to answer the present draft. He had taken the liberty of forwarding £12 to Mr. Clorivière 28 July then and perhaps still in London without notice to the bankers. Their Mr. Selby will receive a separate letter concerning Mr. James Du Moulin [No. 193].

Letterbook 3, p. 109.

---

[1]*Joseph Tristam, S.J., succeeded William Strickland as financial agent for the English Jesuits.*

193. TO MR. W[?]. T. SELBY, Baltimore, 10 August 1815

Carroll wrote to Mr. Selby, a partner of Messrs. Wright and Company and an acquaintance, concerning James Du Moulin (see Appendix 6).

> A letter from Captain A[ndrew]. Du Moulin, which Carroll will answer in a few days, requests him to send his brother to England, at which Carroll is "rejoiced," though it will be difficult to do so unless a person "endowed with firmness and humanity" can be found to accompany him. Otherwise Carroll almost despairs of his consenting to go, "tho [because ?] he lives thro his own act so unconformably here." He has already raised many objections. However, preparations are begun to fit him out and inquiries made for a ship captain to whom Carroll would be willing to entrust him. Please communicate this to his brother with Carroll's compliments.

Letterbook 3, p. 110.

194. NOTATION ON SLAVES AT BOHEMIA, 19 September 1815

Carroll noted the terms by which certain slaves at Bohemia were to be manumitted.

> Dick, if he serves faithfully for eight years, to be free, in the meantime to be carefully maintained. Joe, if he serves faithfully for six years, to be free.

AAB, Bohemia Plantation Book, 1790-1815, p. 35.

195. TO REV. NICHOLAS ZOCCHI, n.p., 21 September 1815

Carroll wrote to Zocchi about the difficulty of granting a dispensation in the absence of a response from Rome.

There is still no answer from Rome in Edward Fowler's case. Carroll's last from Rome was dated 11 March. Though he had sent duplicate copies in October, none had reached their destination. It seems to Carroll that a strong case can be made for a bishop so remote, whose communications with Rome had been so long intercepted, of exercising the extraordinary power to which resort must sometimes be had. Edward Fowler and Rebecca Durbin have been separated for six months to satisfy for their past scandal, into which Carroll asks Zocchi to make inquiries, and if they have duly complied by leading virtuous lives he grants them a dispensation "to make valid the marriage once invalidly contracted because of the impediment of kinship in the first degree, arising from [il]licit relations with the sister of the same Rebecca, now deceased" [all of this in Latin]. Before revalidation Zocchi will, if satisfied with their dispositions, absolve them from the censures incurred. The ceremony should be private in the presence of a few friends.

Letterbook 3, pp. 110-11 (see *JCP*, 3: 359-60).

196. TO MRS. ANNETTE M. TALVANDE,[1] Baltimore, 28 October 1815

This letter of sympathy to one of the Marsan sisters is the last that Carroll wrote before he died that is preserved.

His absence from home during part of last month and "that insuperable antipathy to the labours of the desk" is Carroll's apology for the delay in answering the letter of "my dear Annette" received 12 August. The death of her dear sister Melanie affected him so much that every word of consolation "would have wrung my own soul with sadness." His solicitude for Melanie is now transferred to Annette. He is happy she now has a husband, to whom and her other sister he offers respects. Her friend Mr. Clorivière was probably now on the ocean. In Carroll's letters to him he always insists on his viewing Charleston as the future theater of his zeal.[2] In a P.S. Carroll says that "the ladies, who are pleased to take charge of this [letter ?]," appear to have great affection for Annette and are worthy of her friendship.

APF, America Centrale, 5: 155rv.

---

[1]*The Charleston* Times *of 6 January 1812 reported that Thursday evening last [2 January] Mr. Andrew Talvande, merchant, was married to Miss Ann Marsan by Rev. Dr. O'Belan [possibly Matthew O'Brien].*
[2]*Clorivière returned to Charleston on 27 November 1815.*

197. NOTATION CONCERNING SEMINARIANS AT GEORGETOWN COLLEGE, [date uncertain]

For the benefit of the Directors of Georgetown College Carroll penned his observations on an oath to be taken by ecclesiastical students there.

Carroll proposes: 1) to delete the word *voveo* [I vow] supposing it was not the intention of the Directors to require a vow but an oath of the young ecclesiastics, by which they, in return for services done them, promise their benefactors some future services; 2) the words *expleto studiorum curriculo* [the course of studies having been completed] to comprehend the whole course of their education, since Carroll is informed it was not the meaning of the Directors to invest the president with the power of retaining them in the service of the college after they have gone through their Divinity [Theology], for which reason he suggests to the Directors the change above made *completo philosophiae cursu* [the philosophy course having been completed]; 3) Carroll wishes them to consider also whether three years of prefectship be not adequate to six years teaching. The former is a less honorable and more fatiguing duty. Besides which the habit of teaching will beget almost of necessity a habit of study but six years prefectship will almost infallibly cause a disuse and consequently disgust of application.

MPA, Box 19, folder 6, no. 56Z1$\frac{1}{2}$

APPENDICES

APPENDIX 1

THE PASTORAL MINISTRY OF JOHN CARROLL

The part of Carroll's life that is almost entirely ignored by biographers and historians alike is that devoted to parochial activities. In addition to his episcopal responsibilities he also carried out normal parish duties, helping the rector of St. Peter's congregation, sharing with him the administration of the sacraments. These contributions are amply demonstrated in the sacramental records of St. Peter's Procathedral.

The officiating minister at particular ceremonies was not always indicated in the parish registers, in fact, never so during the rectorship of Rev. Charles Sewall, who served in that capacity from 1782 until 1793. Beginning with the rectorship of Rev. Francis Beeston in the spring of 1793 the officiating minister was always recorded for marriages and often for baptisms but not for funerals. Beeston's successor in 1810, Rev. Enoch Fenwick, S.J., continued the practice. Carroll developed a strong bond with both Beeston and Fenwick largely as a result, there can be little doubt, of the concern they shared for the spiritual well-being of the parishioners of St. Peter's.

Undoubtedly from the time of his arrival at the rectory of St. Peter's in 1786 (he was back and forth between Rock

Creek and Baltimore that year) Carroll assisted the rector in the administration of the sacraments, not so much, perhaps, because the latter was overburdened as because Carroll himself wanted to make the parochial care of souls, the *cura animarum*, a greater reality in his life, and to have a closer and more frequent contact with his spiritual children. On the average Carroll performed about a fourth of the marriages every year, sometimes less, sometimes more, and it may be assumed he performed about the same percentage of baptisms and funerals. A number of the baptisms are in his hand.

The number of marriages are known because Carroll recorded them himself or because the rector unfailingly designated the one who performed the marriage. Other local or visiting priests also administered the sacrament of marriage but none with the frequency of Carroll.

A number of reasons prompt the inclusion of the marriages Carroll performed as the principal contribution of this appendix. The first, already mentioned, is that since all are known they are the best gauge of the extent to which he performed all the sacraments. Secondly, they tell us whether Carroll tended to favor one class in society rather than another. Although Carroll did perform the nuptials for the most important members of the congregation, he seems not otherwise to have made any distinction as to the social or ethnic backgrounds of the other couples he united in matrimony. He united, in fact, slaves or free persons of color as often as any other. Thirdly, the names will offer some indication of the truly cosmopolitan mix of the cathedral congregation, of whose ethnic composition no study has ever been made. And fourthly, the names may prove of interest to the growing number of genealogists.

1793

August 15.	James Stewart and Margaret Britt
August 25.	John Brady and Mary McFee
September 18.	Robert Campbell and Catherine Rarity
November 16.	John Baptist Alexis Mary Deseze, son of Alexis Deseze, attorney general of the Council of Cape Français, and Mary Louisa Fortunata Buron, daughter of Julien Buron and Mary Danilles De Ville Franche
December 1.	Jacob Burnell and Mary Thompson
December 1.	Henry Bener and Elizabeth Heimlin
December 2.	John L'Englê and Susanna Guilmain
December 21.	Samuel, negro, and Appolonia, free mulatto

1794

March 14.	Mr. La Treyte and Marie Deshilds
July 15.	Simon Burns and Mary Knowlan
July 18.	Alexander Valcourt and Margaret Gold
July 27.	Frederic Mery and Eva Rosenbyke
August 25.	Joseph Yves Bizouand and Margaret Reine Paterson (of St. Domingo)
August 31.	Edward Cramer and Mary Britt
September 4.	Joachim Crossillant and Charlotte Round
September 8.	Patrick Flaherty and Catharine Conner
September 8.	Neal Daugherty and Mary Green
November 8.	Richard Gore and Ally Sandilland
November 10.	William Coghan and Catharine Kirk
November 27.	Jacques Simon Soulot de Beaulieu and Catharine Mary Elizabeth Haij

1795

April 16.	Frederick William Dannenberg and Dorothy Koenig
April 17.	Paul Bartholomy Heineman Livingston and Letitia Smith
April 20.	John Hooke and Sophia Honko

April 23.	William Reeves and Abigail Grate
April 23.	William Hagerty and Jenny Barrett
November 12.	Patrick Clougherty and Honor Faherty
November 22.	Patrick Van Bibber and Mary Young
December 16.	David Williamson and Julia de Mullet
December 17.	Anthony Gilles Landrieve Desbondes and Mary Clare Le Gardeur Tilly

1796

January 17.	James Hannan and Eliza Thomas
March 30.	Robert Casey and Elizabeth Davies
May 26.	John Liddle and Catharine Foy
August 26.	John James Joseph Miniere and Jane Mary Anne Mattheus
August 27.	John Renaud and Ariana Finegan
September 8.	James Hudson and Joanna Macnamara
September 11.	William Dorney and Elizabeth Green
September 17.	Robert Charles Le Grand Boislandry and Louisa Frances Buscaille
September 18.	Cornelius Gormly and Mary O'Brien
September 25.	John Blair and Catharine Cronan
September 25.	John Dorney and Jane Blaney
October 1.	Edward Sweeny and Elizabeth Blatchford
October 2.	Daniel Carrick and Bridget Flaherty
October 2.	Alexander Martin and Mary Gipson
October 9.	Michael Bentley and Eleanor Caton, both natives of Ireland
October 13.	Thomas Lee Jr., son of Thomas Sim Lee [former governor], and Eleanor Cromwell [grandparents of Governor John Lee Carroll]
December 27.	Michael Rossinot and Mary Rose Pallerin

1797

March 12.	Dennis Norton and Margaret Murphy
April 16.	Anthony Butler, free negro, and Ruth Middleton, free mulatto

September 5.   Peter Peduzi and Sally Shaw
September 18. John McDermott and Catharine Joyce
September 19. Paul Placide and Louisa Duvenois
December 5.   Henry McDermott and Esmy Jordan
December 17. John Frederic Ebbeeke and Catharine Fry
December 24. George, negro slave of Archibald Campbell, and Jane Reed, free negro
December 27. Livy Hamilton of Charles County and Abigail Barry

1798
February 20. William Dwyer, widower, and Elizabeth Casey, widow
February 20. Peter Lemoine and Elizabeth Monge
April 21.   John Dizabeau and Magdalen Holmes
September 23. Arnold Livers and Polly Stansbury, both of Frederick County
October 6.   Stephen Bradbury and Margaret Colgan
October 9.   Felix O'Neale and Rose Morgan
November 4.   William Foose and Martha Merit
November 4.   John Breidenbaugh and Anne Morgan
November 5.   Philip Myers and Hannah Henley
November 11. Bennett Green and Anne Jones
November 25. John Brown and Mary Rosensteel
December 15. James Lalor and Anne O'Neale
December 18. Jack and Sukey, slaves of Col. John E[ager]. Howard
December 20. Michael Sandford and Martha Lucy, widow
December 20. James Heyden and Elizabeth Nussear

1799
January 2.   Marcellin Gonet and Louise Catharine Pallon
January 8.   Matthew, slave of Mr. Purviance, and Juliet, slave of Mr. Caton
February 14. Joseph White Jr. and Rosetta Landry [Rose White, companion of Mother Seton]

February 18.	James Irvin and Mary Steiger
July 11.	Thomas Dempsey, widower, and Eleanor Hogi, widow
July 16.	Charles Adonis and Elizabeth Lachenal, free mulattos of St. Domingo
July 27.	Henry Say and Mary Deal
August 12.	John Stephen Nicolle and May Glace
August 25.	John Let and Mary Monnier, widow
September 7.	James Escavaille and Mary Hargrove
October 7.	Antony Caijol and Modeste Tardieu
November 28.	Charles Gouvernet and Margaret Wells
November 30.	Alexius, servant of Bishop Carroll, and Henrietta, free mulatto
December 3.	Herman Ficke, native of Germany, and Ann Cain
December 11.	Laurence Goudain and Sophia Maria Magdalen Desobry
December 28.	Henry Mullan and Susan O'Brien

1800

March 6.	Capt. Joseph Jenny and Mary Conway
April 24.	Bartholomew Grache and Mary Ann Richards
May 8.	Clement Green and Rebecca Todd
July 1.	Edmund Frahar and Kitty Dillon
July 1.	James Buckley and Mary Leary
November 20.	Walter C. Hayes and Maria Barbara Wonder
November 24.	Thomas Henry and Monica Carter, free negroes
November 27.	Daniel McMeal and Catharine Dalton, widow
December 1.	_____ Ferri and Catharine Truman, natives of Naples

1801

January 27.	Awbreay Jones, widower, and Margaret Doran
February 12.	Thomas Combs and Ann Bahon

April 7.	Michael Costigan and Mary Walter
May 7.	At Annapolis. Robert Goodloe Harper and Catharine Carroll [daughter of Charles Carroll of Carrollton]
May 19.	Barney Hagerty and Margaret Braniff
June 11.	Joseph Hailey and Ann Connelly
June 11.	John Deshon and Elizabeth Rey
July 23.	Daniel Connell and Mary Roberts
August 13.	Joseph Watts, Protestant, "he having first promised to allow his wife to educate their children in the Catholic faith," and Margaret David
August 25.	Joseph Herbert and Eleanor Jenkins
November 10.	Patric [sic] Kelly and Bridget ô Connor [Carroll often rendered "O'" as "ô" in his correspondence]
November 15.	William Hunter and Ann Hunter
November 19.	Peter Davis, widower, and Esther Philippe, widow
November 28.	Cornelius and Prudence, mulatto slaves of Walter Dorsey, Esq., with written permission
November 28.	William Bleakley and Eleanor Phelan
December 27.	Robert Miller and Elizabeth Butler

1802

March 1.	Michael Lyons and Mary Russell
April 7.	Patrick McGiverin and Ann Martin
April 10.	John, slave of Pat. Deagan, and Priscilla, slave of Mr. Le Duc
April 18.	Ben, slave of Eliza Neale, and Catharine, free negro
April 19.	Gerard, slave of Richard Caton, and Violet, slave of Phineas Bond
April 22.	Gabriel and Mary, free negroes from St. Domingo
April 23.	William Morgan, Protestant, and Mary Connor, "with promise"

April 26.	Samuel Cromwell, free negro, and Rachel Lance, free mulatto
No day and month.	Thomas Paisley and Mary Wilde
August 4.	John Baptist Henry La Bruere and Armande Victoire Vastinel, widow Bertrand
November 16.	William Hopwood and Mary Anne Walther
November 18.	George Duprat and Jainey Angeli, free negroes of St. Domingo
November 21.	William Disney, Protestant, and Mary Moran, no promise

1803

January 6.	Patrick McCarty and Mary Roney
May 29.	John Fennell and Mary Jordan
June 7.	Philip Staelet and Catharine Overhoff, Lutheran
June 7.	James Bond and Margaret Stewart
June 9.	Richard L. Head and Margaret Stichter, widow
June 12.	Owen Duffy and Mary Kelly, widow
August 25.	John James Reubell and Esther Pascault, Jerome Bonaparte, "adjutant general in the service of the French Republic," a witness
December 18.	Jacob Nussear and Elizabeth Verley, widow
December 24.	"With license I this day joined in holy matrimony according to the rites of the Holy Catholic Church, Jerome Bonaparte, Br. of the First Consul of France, and Elizabeth Paterson, daughter of Wm. Paterson Esq. of the city of Baltimore, and _____, his wife" [Dorothy Spear]
December 31.	John Peterson and Elizabeth German

1804

January 6.	Jean L'leville, native of Bengal, and Justine, free negro woman

February 7.	John Strickney and Mary Ann Grache
February 13.	Peter McDonough and Cecily Toole
April 12.	Dennis White and Rebecca Herrick
June 7.	Thomas Connelly and Mary Weeks
October 21.	Manus Grant and Jane Caldwell
December 22.	Isaac Baxter and Lydia Burgess

1805

February 3.	Paul Maddegan and Bridget Campbell
February 5.	William Lemon and Ally Burns
February 6.	Daniel Brand and Mary White
February 6.	Dominque and Antoinette, from St. Domingo
March 9.	William Laht and Elizabeth Switzer
April 25.	Nicholas Burke and Sarah White
October 8.	Josias Jenkins and Elizabeth Hillen
November 2.	Oliver Pollock and Winifred Ann Deedy
November 4.	Jacob Kintz and Harriot Hudson
November 4.	Jacob Ottensen, of Denmark, and Desirée Bourges, native of Bordeaux

1806

January 9.	Michael Jenkins and Anna Worthington
January 23.	Thomas C. Jenkins and Elizabeth Gold
February 15.	John Owings and Margaret McAllister
February 16.	Jacob Nussear and Sylvanna Crous
April 8.	John White and Sarah Bahon
April 19.	John Marsh and Catharine Madden
May 1.	Robert Patterson Esq. and Mary Ann Caton, daughter of Richard Caton of Brookland Wood, Baltimore County [married 2nd Richard Wellesley, Marquess Wellesley]
May 19.	Charles Benson and Ann Eve Barney, widow
July 7.	Bennet Busey and Elizabeth Slade
August 3.	Arthur Rice and Elizabeth Connell

October 18.	William and Lucy, slaves of Mr. Richard Caton
October 20.	James, slave of Robert Goodloe Harper, and Margaret Stevenson, free mulatto
October 21.	John Neale and Susanna Cissell
November 30.	Daniel Hendrickson and Mary O'Connor, widow
December 16.	Stephen White and Juliet Martin

1807

January 22.	John Gray and Sophia Gold
February 1.	Peter Cox and Margaret Minchin
February 5.	John Henry Lancaster, of Charles County, and Juliet Trenton
April 18.	Lob, slave of Charles Carroll Jr., and Betty, slave of John Eager Howard
April 29.	William Burke and Mary Powers
July 19.	Daniel Donnelly and Margaret Hyde
July 21.	Joseph Gold and Harriot Landre
November 10.	Frances Younker and Elizabeth Rosen
December 24.	Edward and Milly, slaves of Robert Patterson

1808

February 4.	Jean Louis, dit La Rose, and Marie Magdelaine, dit Zeline, free French negroes
March 10.	Christopher Armat and Mary C. Hunter
July 7.	Henry Irvin and Sarah Mackie, widow
July 26.	James Devine and Jane Keys
August 7.	Henry McDonnell and Helen Dempsey
October 22.	Enoch, slave of Rob. N. Carnan, and Cecily, slave of Richard Caton
October 28.	Maurice Kidney and Eleana McCrosson

1809

March 2.	William Grey and Catharine McSherry
June 8.	Hugh Gallagher and Grace McCormick

August 28.   John Williams and Elizabeth Green
September 13.   Alexander Mary Brulé and Mary Teresa
                 Baroteaux
September 14.   John Lewis Pharon and Eugenia Boisson
September 17.   Henry Jenkins and Ann Harrion
October 2.   William Lee and Mary Lee Holliday
November 7.   Thomas H. Fairbairn and Maria Eliza Henry
November 9.   Vincent Augustin Mayre and Margaret
                 Louisa Judith Nina Reynaud de Chateaudun
November 26.   Philip and Polly, slaves of Richard Caton
November 27.   Charles Doizé and Louisa Magdalen Rosel-
                 la de la Rue
November 28.   John Hunter and Martha Hillen
December 18.   Francis Matthews and Catharine Walsh,
                 widow

1810
January 15.   Terence Kelly and Eleanor Crosby, widow
February 5.   Andrew Izuandi, born Bilbao, and Anne
                 Paterson, widow
March 5.   Thomas Meredith and Maria Spalding
May 8.   Francis M. Wells and Margaret Fisher
July 11.   Andrew Quigley and Margaret Bevins
July 21.   John Purel and Emilia Chevoilleau, widow
                 Jonca
July 29.   Robert Billups, non-Catholic, and Louisa
                 Wynn
October 18.   William Walter and Margaret Boyd
November 18.   John M. McGuire and Catherine Connell

1811
January 5.   William and Becky, slaves of Mr. Charles
                 Carroll Jr.
March 21.   George Clark and Ann Susanna Cobb
April 23.   Matthew Bennet and Harriot Kerret

July 2.   At Green Hill, Prince George's County, Robert Leroy Livingston of the State of New York [a U.S. Congressman] and Ann Maria Diggs [witnessed by fourteen Brent, Carroll, Fitzpatrick, Lee, Sewall, and Young relatives]

September 30. James Conrad and Margaret Connelly

October 1.   Peter Grain and Anne Eliza Higgenbotham

November 28.   James C. McGaurin and Elizabeth Fox

December 16.   William Carroll of Montgomery County [Carroll's greatnephew] and Henrietta Maria Williamson

1812

April 17.   Richard Jackson of Virginia and Jane Donaldson

1813

March 11.   John L. Scott and Rosanna Connell

July 4.   Thomas Peacock and Eleanor McGlellan, both born in Ireland

July 19.   Philip, slave of Charles Carroll of Carrollton, and Charity Joice, a free black woman

August 4.   Don Juan Joseph Bernabeu, son of Don Juan Baptista [Bautista] Bernabeu, Consul of His Catholic Majesty Ferdinand 7th for the state of Maryland, and Ellen Moale, daughter of late John Moale Esq. of Baltimore

November 25.   Philip Wederstrand and Helen Smith

1814

January 4.   Robert Young Brent of Washington City [Carroll's greatnephew] and Eliza Lydia Carrere of Baltimore

February 1.   David Williamson and Rebecca Tiernan

April 11.   James W. Mitchell and Ann Maria Price

April 20.	Daniel Sunderland and Elizabeth Williams, widow
May 10.	Felix Jenkins and Martha Coskery
May 11.	Cornelius McDonald and Rachel White
June 30.	William Ford, widower, and Margaret Porter, widow
July 17.	Thomas Griffith and Anne Murray
July 21.	Henry Bragger, native of Rotterdam, and Anne Preuderville, widow
July 24.	Francis McLaughlin and Anne Haley, widow
August 1.	William Walker and Mary Costigan
September 8.	Patrick Tiernan and Ann Susanna Clarke, widow
November __.	James McDonald and Grace McHenry

1815

February 7.	John Flaherty and Catherine Behner
February 16.	Charles F. Pochon and Harriot Phillips
August 15.	Adrian Posey and Margaret Byrne, widow
August 22.	Martin Fenwick and Ann Louisa Ghequiere
August 29.	Charles Keenan and Elizabeth Greene

APPENDIX 2

JOHN CARROLL'S ORDINATIONS

Until 19 May 1812 Carroll recorded all the ordinations he performed, including tonsure and all the orders, in his own hand.[1] Then and thereafter they were inscribed by Rev. John Mary Tessier, S.S., rector of St. Mary's Seminary, who continued to record the ordinations during the short tenure of Archbishop Leonard Neale. When Ambrose Maréchal became archbishop in 1817 he returned to Carroll's practice of writing out his ordinations himself.

With the exception of the ordination of Leonard Neale to the episcopacy on 7 December 1800 (p. 29), which was inscribed in Latin, Carroll recorded all ordinations in English until 12 March 1808, but thereafter in Latin.

Carroll performed most of the ordinations himself. The exceptions were the tonsures conferred by Bishop Leonard Neale in 1802 on six seminarians (p. 31) and the ordination of four of them to the priesthood in 1808 (p. 34),[2] including Benedict Leonard Fenwick, future bishop of Boston.

With but a few exceptions Carroll apparently performed all the rites of ordination in St. Peter's Procathedral (which he always called St. Peter's Church). Exceptions were the tonsures he conferred in 1798 on four seminarians in the chapel of Georgetown College (p. 28) and three ordinations performed in the chapel of St. Mary's Seminary. Two of these are worthy of note. In 1802 and 1803 he raised to the priesthood John Peter Monnereau (p. 30) and George Mary

---

[1]The "Register of Ordinations" is in the Sulpician Archives of Baltimore (SAB). Page numbers that follow are from this register. Carroll may have originally intended to use this ledger for a chronicle of events for his episcopacy (see No. 6), but the chronicle was not continued.

[2]Since all of these students at Georgetown entered the Society of Jesus soon after it was revivied in the United States in 1805, it may well be that plans were being laid this early (1802) for its restoration. The next year (1803) Carroll and Neale made their first overtures to the general of the Jesuits in Russia (see No. 83).

Florimond de Taillevis de Perigny (pp. 32-33). Both had done their theological studies elsewhere, had come from French colonies, Monnereau from Martinique and Perigny from Saint Domingue, and had waited a number of years before deciding to seek ordination to the priesthood.[1] And on 4 November 1810 he raised to the episcopacy Benedict Joseph Flaget at St. Patrick's Church, Fells Point.

In addition to Neale's, Carroll also recorded his ordination to the episcopacy of Michael Egan, O.F.M., to the bishopric of Philadelphia on 28 October 1810 (p. 38) and of John Cheverus to the bishopric of Boston on 1 November 1810 (p. 39), but surprisingly not Benedict Joseph Flaget to the bishopric of Bardstown, perhaps because it was not performed at St. Peter's. He also recorded the bestowal of the pallium on himself by Bishop Neale on 18 August 1811 (p. 41).

The amount of information Carroll supplied on the candidates over time was uneven. The earliest entries were quite extensive, as those quoted below will show.

Before beginning his record of ordinations Carroll transcribed (p. 22) Bishop Charles Walmesley's certificate (in Latin) of his own ordination to the episcopacy. Translated, it reads:

> Herein we testify that the Rev. John Carroll priest, elected to the bishopric of Baltimore, after the reading of the Apostolic Letters from St. Mary Major, under the seal of the Fisherman dated November 6, 1789, and after the taking of the prescribed oath by the elect according to the Pontifical, was consecrated by us in the episcopate on August 15, 1790, the day of the Assumption of the Blessed Virgin Mary, in the chapel of Lullworth [Lulworth] Castle in Dorsetshire, England, assisted by Rev. Charles Plowden and Rev. James Porter, priests.

---

[1] *On Perigny see p. 222, n. 4.*

It was signed by Charles Walmesley, "Bishop of Ramaten and Vicar Apostolic," and witnessed by Charles Plowden, assisting priest; James Porter, assisting priest; Charles Forrester, priest and missionary apostolic; and Thomas Stanley, priest.

Carroll then records (pp. 23-24) his first four rites of ordination, all performed on 22 September 1792:

> The first ordination in this diocese was held at Baltimore in St. Peter's Church on Saturday Sepr 22^d 1792, being ember week: on which day one subdeacon was ordained; two clerks received the minor orders; and one other received the first tonsure and minor orders likewise; viz:
>
> 1. Stephen Theodore Badin was ordained Subdeacon, having first exhibited the certificate of his birth, legitimacy, & baptism on the 17th day of July 1768, in the parish of St. Paul's at Orleans in France; item a certificate of the Bishop of Orleans testifying, that he had conferred the first tonsure on the said Badin, April 11th 1789; and another certificate of having conferred on him the four minor orders, Novr 16 1791: and finally, dimissorials from the said Bishop of Orleans, calling himself Bishop of the department of Loiret, empowering the Bishop of Baltimore to ordain Stephen Theodore Badin, Subdeacon, Deacon, & Priest, dispensing him at the same time from keeping the interstices; or being obliged to produce a clerical title.
>
> 2. John Thomas Michael Edward Pierron de Mondesir promoted to the four minor orders, having first exhibited his certificate of birth, legitimacy & baptism, March 8th 1770 in the Parish of St. Hilaire, of Nogent le Rotrou, Diocese of Chartres in France; item the certificate of [John B. Joseph de Lubersac in another hand] the bishop of Chartres, that he had conferred the clerical tonsure on the said Mondesir, June

10th, 1786; & letters dimissorial of the said Bishop, dated March 5th 1791, to the Archbishop of Paris, or any other Bishop appointed by him; and finally dimissorials from the Archbishop aforesaid directed to the Bishop of Baltimore &c, dated March 24- 1791. 3. Peter Joseph Perineau, promoted to the four minor orders, having first exhibited a certificate of birth, legitimacy and baptism, July 30- 1771, in the parish of Montreal, diocese of Quebec in Canada; item, dimissorials addressed to any Catholic Bishop, for ordaining him to priesthood inclusively, from [John Francis Hubert in another hand] the Bishop of Almira, Coadjutor of Quebeck [*sic*]; and a certificate of the Vicar General of the Archbishop of Paris, that the said Perineau received the clerical tonsure, May 24th, 1788. 4. John Floyd; promoted to the clerical tonsure, and the four minor orders; he was born in the Middle district of England, & presented dimissorials dated May 20- 1791- from the Bishop of Acon [Thomas Talbot in another hand], Vicar Apostolical in said district.

Entries thereafter, as observed, are not as informative. The fifth person to receive orders from Carroll (p. 25) was Prince Demetrius Gallitzin:

Fourth [*sic*] ordination, held at the same place [St. Peter's], Sep. 13th 1794- Demetrius Augustine Gallitzin, lawful son of Prince Demetrius Gallitzin, & Amelia [Amalia], Countess of Schmettau [blank] his wife, known since his residence in America by the name of Augustine Smith, born Decr 22^d in the year 1770 - received the clerical tonsure and four minor orders.

On 21 November 1794 (p. 26) Carroll recorded Gallitzin's ordination as subdeacon "on the title of his patrimony, & the subsidiary title of obligation to serve the Church in this Diocese." He also observed that since his father was a Russian prince when the ordinand was born in the Hague "no dimissorials were requisite, as was agreed by the best Divines, who were consulted on this occasion."

An interesting entry that indicates the variety of nations from which his clergy were drawn was dated 5 July 1806 (p. 33).

> Francis Roloff, of the Diocess of Vienna in Austria, &c now domiliciated in that of Balt^re; Peter Shaefer [Schaeffer], native of the Diocese of Fulda in Germany, having legitimate dimissorials; Dennis Lewis Cottineau, of Nantes in Brittany, having legitimate dimissorials; John Gallagher, of the Diocess of Londonderry in Ireland, but now domiciliated in that of Balt^re; James Hector Nicholas Joubert of the Diocess of Saintes, but now domiciliated in that of Baltimore; and John Hickey of the Diocess of Baltimore, were admitted to the ecclesiastical tonsure.

The place was presumably St. Peter's since the next entry indicates that on the same day "William ô Bryan" [William F. X. O'Bryan/O'Brien of Charles County] of the Diocese of Baltimore received minor orders "in the Church of S. Peter."

From 1800 on Carroll performed ordination rites about four times a year, two years only once but one year seven times and another six. His last was on 2 October 1815, when he conferred the four minor orders on Honoratus Xaupi and Martin Joseph Kerney and the priesthood on Roger Mary Joseph Lawrence Smith (p. 45).

APPENDIX 3

JOHN CARROLL'S SLAVES

On 12 December 1813 Carroll wrote to his friend Charles Plowden, "We [the Corporation of the Clergy] in Maryland have certainly some slaves on our estates, but I individually hold not a single one: the servts. who wait on me, are one lent to me by my sister, & one free person hired by me."[1] A modest household for an archbishop to be sure, but the question of Carroll's ownership of slaves is a little more complex than Carroll makes it out to be in this claim to Plowden.

John Carroll was always a bit testy on the question of slavery. Even before he was named bishop, a wandering Irish priest named Patrick Smyth published a work that accused the Maryland Jesuits of having, among other things, profited from the traffic in slaves, whom they mistreated cruelly. This was, according to Carroll, "his most atrocious charge." Carroll wrote a long and heated rebuttal of Smyth's charges, insisting, among other things, that the Jesuits' slaves were treated with greater mildness than those of others. He was dissuaded by Archbishop John Troy of Dublin from publishing it.[2]

Carroll, it would appear, always had a slave at his disposal in Baltimore, and it seems doubtful that this slave was simply on loan from a member of his family. Alexius, or Alexis, is mentioned in his letter of 1 November 1804 to his nephew Daniel (see No. 95). Alexius was owned by Carroll as early as 30 November 1799, when Carroll joined in marriage Alexius, "servant of the bishop," to Henrietta, a free mulatto (see Appendix 1). On 21 July 1806 Carroll wrote to

---

[1]JCP, 3: 247. *This is one of the few occasions that Carroll used the word "slave." Mostly he wrote "servants" or "negroes."*

[2]*Guilday,* Carroll, *pp. 309-21.*

his friend James Barry, "Let Mrs. Barry know, that I parted with my drunken servt. Alexis to this gentleman [William Stenson], who was not deterred by my account of Alexis." He added, "So much for this depraved young man who has banished from himself happiness & comfort."[1]

Carroll apparently had another slave in his employ during Alexius's stay. On 10 August 1800 Elizabeth, "slave of Bishop Carroll," witnessed the baptism of the "natural daughter" of another slave.[2] When Carroll drew his will on 22 November 1815, he bequeathed to his nephew Daniel Brent "my black servant Charles" with the instructions that he be manumitted within twelve months of Carroll's decease so that he might settle in or near his friends in Washington and that he be given fifty dollars "in testimony of his faithful services."[3]

Although he tried, unsuccessfully, to distance himself from the affairs of the Corporation of the Clergy, Carroll was eventually involved in its decisions concerning the slaves it owned. "The sale of a few unnecessary Negroes," he advised Rev. Francis Neale, the corporation's fiscal agent, "three or four, and stock, would replace the money" that was needed for the general fund.[4]

As proprietor of Bohemia Plantation in Cecil County Carroll was the master of some two dozen slaves. Though they belonged to the Corporation of the Clergy, Carroll was allowed to dispose of them as he saw fit. Carroll was awarded this property by the Corporation in 1806 in lieu of the $800 that had been paid him annually from the general fund. On 14 December 1808 he wrote William Pasquet, the priest who managed the estate for him and ministered to its congregation, that if those who owed for the hire of its slaves did not pay a reasonable amount, Pasquet was to find

---

[1] JCP, 2: 521.
[2] *St. Peter's Baptismal Register, 1782-1801.*
[3] JCP, 3: 371.
[4] *Ibid.,* 2: 497.

other masters for them (see No. 129).

On 5/6 May 1814 Carroll complained to Pasquet of a letter just received from him that treated mostly the disposition of slaves (see No. 176). Pasquet had written that a buyer was interested in a daughter of a slave named James, but James's wife wanted her daughters to be sold for a term of years and wanted to go with them. Pasquet told her he would have to get Carroll's consent. "She has so many children, and she has not done breeding," Pasquet explained. James also wanted his wife and children sold for a term of years but wanted himself to remain with Pasquet. The affairs of another, "Old Jack," were still not settled. Although Pasquet had wanted from $120 to $130 for him, he asked Carroll if $100 would be acceptable. Jack's son wanted to buy his father's freedom.[1]

Carroll was annoyed at Pasquet's indecision on James's family. He would leave the decision to Pasquet in consultation with Rev. Francis Neale, fiscal agent of the corporation. "I shall be most dissatisfied," he added, "if the old man [Jack] has been turned out of doors, without having any security for a home or your obtaining the money for him" (see No. 176).

In the spring of 1815 Carroll went to Bohemia to investigate affairs there, including the status of the slaves, whose future disposition he wished to determine. In the plantation ledger he listed the names of Fanny, age 48, and her nine children, two of whom had infants, and of Phillis, 36, and her six children. Molly also had a son; her husband Harry was willing to buy them both in the spring of 1816 for $150. And there was Barney, 53, Joe, 45, and Dick, 32, but no mention of James (Fanny's husband) or Old Jack.

Fanny's three oldest boys were estimated to be worth $350 each if sold for a term of twelve years. The next two, if they served until age 24, were valued at $120 and $60 re-

---

[1] *AAB, 6-E-9, Pasquet to Carroll, Bohemia, 2 May 1814.*

spectively. The two oldest girls with infants, if they served for ten and twelve years respectively and their infants till age 24, were worth $200 each; the next girl, if she served eleven years, $150. No value was placed on an 18-month-old daughter. Only Fanny's children were so evaluated. Barney was to be manumitted after four years if it could be done legally. Later (19 September 1815) Carroll made provision for the manumission of Joe after six years and Dick after eight.[1]

On 15 July 1815 Carroll sent Pasquet a rather harsh letter dismissing him for having failed to serve properly the needs of his congregation. But he ended, "Give all comfort in yr. power to James's wife."[2]

On 3 October 1815 Carroll wrote Francis Neale: "You have been informed already, that all has been done there [Bohemia], which depended on me: but Jem's [James's] family are not disposed of; the purchasers for a term of years could be had; and in my own estimation I had settled that term, and its correspondent price." It was necessary, Carroll added, to have Neale's concurrence on the terms. But Carroll was "surprised and mortified" to learn that "in direct contradiction to the humane decision of the Corporation, sales of Negroes for life have been made and are making from the estate of the White-marsh."[3]

A few months before, Carroll had told Archbishop Troy that the members of the corporation, "anxious to suppress censure," had begun some years ago and were still in the process of gradually emancipating the older slaves on their estates. "To proceed at once to make it a general measure, would not be either humanity towards the Individuals, nor

---

[1]AAB, *Bohemia Plantation Book, 1790-1815, pp. 34-35. See Nos. 173, 177, 185, 194.*
[2]JCP, *3: 343-44.*
[3]*Ibid., 3: 361.*

doing justice to the trust, under which the estates have been transmitted and received."[1]

This and Carroll's insistence to Plowden mentioned at the beginning of this Appendix that he owned no slaves was occasioned by statements that a Dominican named John Ryan, who had served in Philadelphia, had lately circulated in London and in Ireland. To Bishop Francis Moylan of Cork Carroll wrote that Ryan's statements had "caused me more displeasure than I can express." Ryan had said that the Jesuit planters had trafficked in slaves and "that the Archbp. himself was a great slaveholder." The "retailers" of that "most wicked calumny" should have mentioned, Carroll insisted, as he had to Archbishop Troy, that the clergy were now gradually freeing their slaves. Carroll repeated that, since he had renounced his paternal inheritance at age twenty-six, he had not owned a single slave (see No. 172).

That the slaves of other plantations of the Corporation thought of Carroll as their master is indicated in a letter of Rev. Thomas Monnelly of St. Joseph's on the Eastern Shore to Archbishop Neale some three months after Carroll's death. "The Negroes here," he said in a postscript, "thought themselves free at Doct^r Carroll's Death and Consequently went off and w^d not work for two months."[2]

---

[1]*Ibid.*, 3: 313. *Undated but internal evidence indicates it was written in the late spring of 1815. In 1838 the Maryland Jesuits still had 272 slaves. These they sold that year to a planter in Louisiana. Blacks in southern Maryland told an agent of the Maryland Colonization Society that they now put no more trust in priests than in kidnappers. See Robert Emmett Curran, "'Splendid Poverty': Jesuit Slaveholding in Maryland, 1805-1838," in Randall M. Miller and Jon L. Wakelyn, eds.,* Catholics in the Old South: Essays on Church and Culture *(Macon, Ga.: Mercer University Press, 1983), pp. 125-46.*

[2]*AAB, 12A-J-6, Monnelly to Neale, St. Joseph's, 4 March 1816.*

APPENDIX 4

SOCIETIES FOUNDED BY JOHN CARROLL

John Carroll may perhaps be accounted the most civic-minded member of the American hierarchy. He may perhaps be accounted the most civic-minded citizen of Maryland in his day. He was, for example, on the boards and chosen president of boards of several institutions of higher learning. As early as 1783, the year after it was founded, he joined the board of visitors of Washington College, Chestertown, Maryland, from which he received an honorary degree in 1785 (see *JCP*, 1: 193). In 1785, the year it was incorporated, his name headed the list of canvassers (those chosen to solicit subscriptions) for St. John's College, Annapolis, and in 1789 was elected to the board.[1] In 1803 he was elected president of the board of trustees of Baltimore College. In 1812 he was named provost of the University of Maryland, a position he declined because of age.

More important as indicative of his sense of concern for civic betterment were the many learned and humanitarian societies in whose foundation he played a prominent, if not leading, role. In 1795 he was the principal founder of the Library Company of Baltimore, of which more will follow. About the same time he founded the Baltimore Benevolent Society, of which more will also be said. In 1800 Carroll was one of the founders and later president of the Maryland Society for Promoting Useful Knowledge, from which he gracefully withdrew in 1805 for reasons not clear.[2] In 1801 or earlier he organized the Female Humane Association Charity School, which will likewise receive special attention. Out of it came also the Humane Impartial Society for

---

[1] *Tench Francis Tilghman, "The Founding of St. John's College, 1784-1789,"* Maryland Historical Magazine, 44 *(1949): 75-92.*
[2] *See* JCP, 2: 472-73.

indigent women incorporated in 1811. In 1802 he was a founder of the Baltimore General Dispensary.[1]

Carroll's compulsion to promote the betterment of the urban community of which he was a respected and influential member created a bond with the clergy of other denominations also engaged in humanitarian projects. Active associates in the Library Company of Baltimore were the leading Episcopal and Presbyterian ministers of the city as were also Lutheran, Methodist, United Brethren, and Episcopal ministers in the Female Humane Association.[2] These friendships reinforced Carroll's ecumenical bent.

Of all of his civic projects the Library Company of Baltimore was his favorite.[3] Being the founder, he was given by the board carte blanche in determining its policies, procedures, and acquisitions. He obviously chose the secretary, Rev. Francis Beeston, rector of the procathedral. He also chose the librarian, for the first few months John Edward Mondésir, a talented seminarian, and then George Perigny, an exile from Saint Dominque but a doctor of the Sorbonne.[4] Perigny would be ordained by Carroll in 1803 (see Appendix 2) and would remain librarian for as long as Carroll was president of the board, which was until January 1815, when Carroll resigned the presidency.

---

[1] *On 23 June 1812 Carroll, writing from Easton, Md., empowered Rev. Enoch Fenwick, rector of St. Peter's Procathedral, "to vote in my behalf in favour of Dr. John Connor; as one of the Physicians of the Baltre. Dispensary, and for such other Candidates for said offices, as you may approve" (JCP, 3: 184).*

[2] *See Spalding,* Premier See, *pp. 59-60.*

[3] *See Stuart C. Sherman, "The Library Company of Baltimore, 1795-1854,"* Maryland Historical Magazine, *39 (1944): 6-24; J. Thomas Scharf,* History of Baltimore City and County *(reprint, Baltimore: Regional Publishing Co., 1971), pp. 658-59; and Patrick W. Browne, ed. and trans.,* Beginnings of the Catholic Church in the United States, Being Etat de l'Eglise Catholique ou Diocèse des Etats-Unis de l'Amérique Septentrionale, par Jean Dilhet *(Washington, D.C.: Salve Regina Press, 1922), pp. 61-62.*

[4] *In the ordination record Carroll noted that Perigny had associated himself with the diocese of Blois in France, for which diocese he had apparently studied for the priesthood. It is Dilhet who says he was a doctor of the Sorbonne (Browne,* Beginnings, *p. 52). He may have made his studies for the priesthood there. He was able to present Carroll with certificates of all orders except that of priest but was unable to say where he should apply for a dimissorial. In the ordination record Carroll wrote that he had lived in Baltimore for nine years. As a priest he served as chaplain for the Carroll family at Doughoregan Manor.*

Organized in late December 1795, the Library Company drew up a constitution and bylaws early the following year. It was not incorporated, however, until 20 January 1798. At that time it published *A Catalogue of the Books, &c. Belonging to the Library Company of Baltimore; to Which are Prefixed the Act for the Incorporation of the Company, Their Bye-Laws, and an Alphabetical List of Members.*[1] By then the library contained over 3,000 volumes and counted 278 members. Though the greatest number of volumes were under the categories of theology and history, readership ran more to fiction and poetry.

According to the constitutions an initial share in the company cost $20 and $4 every year thereafter. A general meeting was held annually, at which twelve directors were elected (mostly reelected). In elections to the board or of new members to the company white (for) and black (against) balls were used. The board chose the other offices, including the president (pro forma in the case of Carroll as well as Perigny as librarian). The board met monthly to approve expenditures and elect new members, which required a quorum of eight, and to transact other business, such as the approval of acquisitions. According to the bylaws the librarian attended the library Monday, Wednesday, and Friday from ten to one o'clock (later every day but Saturday and Sunday). A folio volume could be taken out for six weeks, a quarto for five weeks, and one octavo, two duodecimos, or four pamphlets for two weeks. Non-members had to pay fees and give security.

By 1796 the Baltimore Benevolent Society had been established "under the Patronage of the Bishop of Baltimore, and the Rector of St. Peter's Church Baltimore." In that year was published *Rules and Orders to be Observed by the Baltimore*

---

[1]*Printed by John Hayes, Baltimore, 1798. A copy with the stamp "Ex Bibliotheca Domus Archiepiscopalis Baltimorae" can be found in the Special Collection of the library of the Catholic University of America. The archiepiscopal library in Baltimore was donated to the university by Archbishop Michael J. Curley.*

Benevolent Society, in Order to Raise a Fund for the Mutual Relief of the Members Thereof, in Case of Sickness or Infirmity; and for Any Other Charitable Purposes, to Which, the Members of Said Society May Hereafter Agree.[1] This pamphlet of 15 pages contains 31 articles describing the organization and procedures of the society and the responsibilities and benefits of its members. The first article indicated that it was for the benefit of Roman Catholics residing in or near Baltimore.

General meetings of the officers and the twelve members of the committee were held every three months. Monthly meetings were held in town and at Fells Point on different days for the purpose of collecting dues. Application for benefits were made to the committee but granted at collections meetings. No one was admitted who was over forty-five. A member paid one dollar to enter, a half dollar every month for the first six months, and a quarter of a dollar every month thereafter. Those in arrears were fined.

Benefits for the sick ranged from one to four dollars a week depending on the degree of illness. They were visited weekly. When a member died, the society paid all funeral expenses "in as frugal a manner as possible," and a sum was given his widow or children "at the discretion of the Society." Interesting is Article X:

> If one member shall be guilty of striking another, at the meetings of the Society; he shall be fined one dollar: - if guilty of giving abusive language and disturbing the good order of the meeting; or of being intoxicated; one eighth of a dollar. If guilty of swearing, irreligious and immoral discourse or unchaste expressions; one sixteenth of a dollar. If the presiding Officer calls for silence, or order, and it be not attended to; he shall be empowered to impose a fine of one sixteenth of a dollar, on all such as shall transgress in that point.

---

[1] *Printed by Samuel Sower, Baltimore, 1796.*

The last article (XXXI) states that the society shall not be dissolved and a dividend made of the fund without the consent of five-sixths of the members. There is no record as to when this may have occurred.[1]

The longevity of the next society to be considered, which spawned several others, is well attested. In 1798 a number of charitable ladies of Baltimore began to care for the needs of indigent women in winter and soon those of poor girls also.[2] For the latter they began a school. Probably in 1801 Carroll organized a group of men to assume charge of the temporalities of the school. On 31 December 1801 the Female Humane Charity School was incorporated. In 1803 it published *A Brief Account of the Female Humane Association Charity School, of the City of Baltimore* that described the association's work.[3] That same year Mr. Robert Sinclair deeded land to the trustees of the association (see Appendix 5). The first four of the nine trustees named were clergymen: Rt. Rev. John Carroll, Rev. William Otterbein (United Brethren), Rev. J. Daniel Kurtz (Lutheran), and Rev. George Roberts (Methodist Episcopal).

In 1807 it published *A Brief Statement of the Proceedings and Present Condition of the Female Humane Association Charity School* that boasted its ongoing achievements.[4] It now had 27 pupils. Some 111 had been clothed, educated, and often boarded since the beginning of the association. It had been so well supported that a larger building had been purchased.

---

[1] *This society received no mention in Carroll's correspondence, which suggests that it was short-lived. Such Catholic beneficial societies were not prominent until the later coming of immigrants in large numbers.*

[2] *Joseph M. Finotti,* Bibliographia Catholica Americana: A List of Works Written by Catholic Authors, and Published in the United States *(New York: The Catholic Publication House, 1872), p. 22.*

[3] *This 23-page pamphlet work is listed by Finotti (p. 22), but he omits the word "Association" in the title. Its printer was Warner & Hanna, Baltimore. "A Catholic institution in its origin," adds Finotti, "it made no distinction of creeds." A copy of this pamphlet can be found at the Maryland Historical Society.*

[4] *It was printed by Geo. Dobbin and Murphy of Baltimore. A copy of this eight-page "Statement" can be found in the Special Collection of the library of the Catholic University of America and was probably a part of the archiepiscopal library donated by Archbishop Curley.*

Nine lady managers, out of seventeen in all, presently conducted the school. One was Mrs. Rose White, undoubtedly the future superior general of the Sisters of Charity of St. Joseph's of Emmitsburg. The Right Rev. Bishop Carroll headed the list of five trustees who signed the statement.[1]

On 31 December 1808 the school was incorporated as the Orphaline Charity School. Archbishop Carroll, Rev. Daniel Kurtz, and now Rev. James Inglis, an Episcopal minister, headed the list of incorporators. In 1827 the name would be changed to the Baltimore Female Orphan Asylum, and in 1850 to the Baltimore Orphan Asylum; boys were now admitted.[2] By then, however, Catholics played no part in its administration.

An outgrowth of Female Humane Association Charity School was the Humane Impartial Society. Several of the women involved with the charity school returned to the work of caring for indigent women. This effort was organized at a meeting of the trustees of the charity school in Bishop Carroll's residence on 7 January 1802. It was incorporated 27 December 1811. In 1850 it became an aged women's home, by which time it also had no Catholic connections. In 1802 the trustees of the Female Humane Association Charity School also began a school for boys, but it was never incorporated.[3]

In Carroll's lifetime Catholics played a prominent role in these societies; Charles Carroll of Carrollton and George Digges of Warburton were perhaps the most often recorded as active members or benefactors. Gradually thereafter the names of Catholics disappeared from the lists. With the coming of Catholic immigrants in large numbers they disappeared altogether.

---

[1]*Carroll was the only Catholic to sign. Of the seventeen lady managers only three, or possibly four, can be identified as Catholics.*
[2]*Scharf,* History, *p. 594.*
[3]*Ibid., p. 595.*

JOHN CARROLL LANDHOLDER[1]

Corporation sole was a concept alien to John Carroll. Ownership of church property, he believed, should be vested in the parochial congregation, not in the bishop. When this was not possible, as in the District of Columbia, it should be held by an ecclesiastic other than himself (as at St. Patrick's in the city of Washington). Lay ownership of private chapels that served neighboring Catholics, a common arrangement in the colonial era, was also acceptable to him. Even when the trustees of a parochial congregation betrayed the trust confided in them, Carroll was never tempted to assume ownership as the easiest way to eliminate discord and confusion.[2]

But Carroll was not categorically opposed to assuming the ownership of real property for church use. On 24 December 1799 the proprietors of the Boston Theater sold a lot at the end of Franklin Square in Boston to Bishop Carroll of Baltimore and Rev. Francis Matignon of Boston for the erection of Holy Cross Church.[3] The idea of including Carroll in the deed may not have originated with Carroll but with Matignon and others concerned with the project in Boston. On 26 October 1801 Daniel Carroll of Duddington for one dollar deeded Bishop Carroll square 698 in the city of Washington for the purpose of building a church.[4] On 1 February 1803 William Thornton Alexander and Lucy his

---

[1]*Research in the AAB and land records for Baltimore County for this appendix was done by Father Paul Thomas.*

[2]*Despite contrary claims Carroll never repudiated the trustee arrangement he had encouraged from the beginning. See Spalding,* Premier See, *pp. 75-76, 496-97n.38, and Patrick W. Carey,* People, Priests, and Prelates: Ecclesiastical Democracy and the Tensions of Trusteeism *(Notre Dame, Ind.: University of Notre Dame Press, 1987), pp. 220-21.*

[3]*Lord, Sexton, and Harrington,* Archdiocese of Boston, *1: 556-57; Annabelle M. Melville,* Jean Lefebvre de Cheverus, 1768-1836 *(Milwaukee: Bruce, 1958), p. 90.*

[4]*AAB, 11A-K-2/1. On this location St. Peter's Church would be dedicated in 1821.*

wife of King George's County, Virginia, deeded Carroll a parcel of land in Alexandria, Virginia, at Washington and Church streets for the church in that town.[1] Carroll would allow lay owners of land on which their private chapels were built to deed the land and building to himself. On 5 July 1802, for example, Thomas Attwood Digges of Warburton, Prince George's County, Maryland, for one dollar and a prayer book, "of which the said Thomas standeth in need," deeded in trust to Carroll for the benefit of the congregation of Piscataway and its vicinity the chapel built by his father and put in good repair by the donor together with "two acres of Wood Land."[2]

In the Archives of the Archdiocese of Baltimore are a few deeds or other conveyances that will also be found in the list of land transactions in Baltimore County that follow. One, however, is worthy of note here. On 4 April 1806 Charles Carroll of Carrollton signed to John Carroll a deed of confirmation for lot 156 at Charles and Saratoga streets.[3] This adjoined lot 157 to the west that had been deeded by Carroll's father to the Jesuit superior in 1764 for the purpose of building a church, St. Peter's.[4]

The Baltimore County land records show Bishop or Archbishop John Carroll involved in forty-three or more land transactions. Not all, however, were for church purposes. In fact, most were not. Almost a fourth were trust deeds negotiated as favors to others, acts of charity in reality that obligated Carroll to see to the well-being of the grantor or the grantor's family without any apparent benefit to himself or the church. An even greater number were leases, negotiated mostly in 1801, when Carroll decided, evidently for investment purposes, to become a landlord by

---

[1] *MPA, box 38, folder 9.*

[2] *AAB, 11A-L-1.*

[3] *AAB, Cathedral Deeds.*

[4] *See Riordan,* Cathedral Records, *p. 48, for a diagram of these two lots. Lot 156 was intended as a cemetery.*

leasing or subleasing at least nineteen lots on tracts of land he had acquired from Col. John Eager Howard and the Sulpicians. The following entries in the Baltimore County land records, which included the city of Baltimore, show Carroll acting in the capacity of owner, trustee, landlord, and proprietor, handling deeds, trust deeds, leases, assignments, and mortgages.

(1) 16 September 1791. John Leypold and Frederick Grammer deed to Rev. Dr. John Carroll for £850 part of a tract in Baltimore County called Chatsworth beginning at the fourth boundary stone of Lunn's Lot (WG#GG: 485).[1]

(2) 21 October 1791. Rev. Dr. John Carroll to Rev. Francis Charles Nagot, [S.S.], for £850 the tract sold by Leypold and Grammer to Carroll [see No. (1)] (WG#GG: 487).[2]

(3) 5 June 1794. Arabella Young, widow, to Rev. [Dr.] John Carroll, in anticipation of a second marriage, a trust deed for lands in Baltimore, Philadelphia, and Anne Arundel County, Maryland, plus slaves and personalty, so that she may continue to enjoy their sole use after her marriage (WG#OO: 366).[3]

(4) 7 March 1795. Frederick Kinsell to [Rev. Dr.] John Carroll, as trustee of William, John, and Hannah Young, children of deceased William Young, a mortgage of ground on the west side of Howard Street (WG#RR: 142).

---

[1]*This citation, as also for the other conveyances that follow, indicates the liber (volume) and the first folio page (of one or more) for the land records of Baltimore County. For the location of Chatsworth and Lunn's Lott see map on p. 111 in Riordan, Cathedral Records. The metes and bounds of this and the other tracts in the following deeds and leases are usually described.*

[2]*For this transaction see Christopher J. Kauffman,* Tradition and Transformation in Catholic Culture: The Priests of Saint Sulpice in the United States from 1791 to the Present *(New York: Macmillan, 1988), p. 42. The Sulpicians had brought £2,400 with them to purchase land and begin the seminary.*

[3]*The intended husband was Patrick Goulding, to whom she was married 7 June 1794 at St. Peter's Procathedral. In WG#65: 229 (1800) Arabella Goulding and Carroll as trustee release one of her mortgages.*

(5) 7 April 1796. Catherine Walsh, widow, to Rt. Rev. John Carroll, a trust deed for lot 119 in Fells Point at Fells Street and Market Square for the sole use of said Catherine should she remarry (WW#VV: 355).[1]

(6) 16 April 1798. Michael O'Conner and Catherine his wife, formerly Catherine Walsh [see No. (5)], to Rt. Rev. John Carroll a trust deed for shares in and loans to the Bank of Maryland [totalling $2,400] formerly held in the name as Catherine Shaw [?] for her sole use (WG#54: 345).[2]

(7) 1 February 1799. John O'Donnell of Baltimore County Esquire and William Bell of Philadelphia, merchant, lease to Rt. Rev. John Carroll, as attorney for the [trustees of the] Roman Catholic Church of Baltimore, lot 596 on the west side of Apple Alley [now Bethel Street] near Wilks Street [now Eastern Avenue] for a yearly rent of £15 (WG#57: 393).[3]

(8) 21 October 1799. John Eager Howard to Rt. Rev. John Carroll, a 99-year lease of one acre and 73 square perches [on Lunn's Lot] bordering a tract called Chatsworth and next to [north of] a lot sold by Howard to Rev. Francis Charles Nagot [who later sold it to Carroll; see No. (11) below] for a yearly rent of £5.16.6 in half Johannes [Portuguese gold coin] at £3 each and Mexican dollars at 7 shillings and 6 pence each (WG#60: 32).[4]

---

[1]*And AAB, 11A-P-1. On 9 April 1787 Edward Walsh, a native of Ireland, married Catherine Conway in St. Peter's Church. He died 7 April 1795, age 28, and was buried from the same church.*

[2]*And AAB, 11A-O-2. On 18 February 1798 Catherine Walsh, widow, married Michael O'Conner in St. Peter's Procathedral, "both of Fells Point."*

[3]*This was apparently for St. Patrick's Church, Fells Point, which was dedicated by Carroll in 1797. John O'Donnell (1749-1805), a Presbyterian, was one of the wealthiest men in Baltimore.*

[4]*John Eager Howard (1752-1827), from whom was also purchased the land where the Cathedral of the Assumption would be built, was a Revolutionary War hero, former governor of and U.S. senator from Maryland. Though he was not a Catholic, his daughter Sophia, wife of William George Read, and a grandson named for him were. His equestrian statue adorns Mount Vernon Place north of the cathedral.*

(9)   29 October 1799.   Richard Whelan to Rt. Rev. John Carroll as trustee for Catherine O'Conner [see Nos. (5) and (6)], a trust deed of lot 166 in Fells Point (WG#60: 95).

(10)   28 July 1800.   Jacob Nussear Junior to Bishop Carroll, a trust deed of one half of rents from various parcels of ground for his wife Elizabeth and children (WG#63: 245).[1]

(11)   3 June 1801.   Rev. Francis Charles Nagot, [S.S.], to Rt. Rev. John Carroll, for $600, ground on [north of] Franklin Street [to the east of Eutaw Street extended], part of Lunn's Lot, sold by John Eager Howard to Nagot on 30 March 1793 (WG#67: 281).[2]

(12)   20 August 1801.   Bishop John Carroll to Anthony Livers, lease of lot 1, part of Lunn's Lot "at the north east intersection of Eutaw Street Continued and a street lately laid out by John E. Howard called New [later Franklin] Street" for a yearly rent of $85.50 (WG#68: 414).[3]

(13)   20 August 1801.   Bishop John Carroll to Adam Alten, lease of lot 8 on the east side of Eutaw Street extended for a yearly rent of $24 (WG#69: 141).[4]

(14)   20 August 1801.   Bishop John Carroll to Adam Sisenop, drayman, lease of lot 15 on the east side of Eutaw Street extended for a yearly rent of $20 (WG#69: 188).

(15)   20 August 1801.   Bishop John Carroll to Peter Whelan, lease of lot 5 on the east side of Eutaw Street extended for a yearly rent of $20 (WG#69: 430).

---

[1]And AAB, 11A-O-1. See Appendix 1, where a Jacob Nussear married Elizabeth Verley on 18 December 1803 and Sylvanna Crous on 16 February 1806. This could have been either Jacob Nussear Senior or Junior.

[2]Lunn's Lot, a crescent-shaped tract running from the (now) intersection of Biddle and Calvert streets to the Patapsco River below Federal Hill, was laid out for Edward Lunn in 1672. In 1688 Lunn sold this tract to George Eager Jr., and it passed by inheritance to his grandson John Eager Howard, son of Cornelius Howard and a daughter of George Eager Jr. See map in Riordan, Cathedral Records, p. 111.

[3]This is the lot purchased from Nagot. See No. (11). Anthony Livers (1734-1820) was a grocer who lived on Franklin Street from 1799 until his death.

[4]This and the leases that follow were apparently subleases of the tract that John Eager Howard leased to Carroll for 99 years in 1799. See No. (8). In these subleases Carroll usually designates himself as "John Carroll Bishop of the Catholic Church" or "John Carroll Roman Catholic Bishop of Baltimore."

(16) 20 August 1801. Bishop John Carroll to George McKinzie, lease of lot 16 on the east side of Eutaw Street extended for a yearly rent of $20 (WG#71: 47).

(17) 20 August 1801. Bishop John Carroll to John Brachen/ Bracken/Brackin, cooper and drayman, lease of lot 9 on the east side of Eutaw Street extended for a yearly rent of $24 (WG#71: 55).[1]

(18) 20 August 1801. Bishop John Carroll to John Clogharty, drayman, lease of lot 6 on the east side of Eutaw Street extended for a yearly rent of $20 (WG#72: 8).

(19) 20 August 1801. Bishop John Carroll to George Kintz, carpenter, lease of lot 2 on the east side of Eutaw Street extended for a yearly rent of $19.20 (WG#72: 18).

(20) 20 August 1801. Bishop John Carroll to Roger McLean, lease of lot 4 on the east side of Eutaw Street extended for a yearly rent of $20 (WG#72: 38).

(21) 20 August 1801. Bishop John Carroll to Alexander Thompson, carpenter, lease of lot 7 on the east side of Eutaw Street extended for a yearly rent of $20 (WG#72: 109).

(22) 20 August 1801. Bishop John Carroll to James Kirby, carpenter, lease of lot 12 on the east side of Eutaw Street extended for a yearly rent of $20 (WG#72: 236).

(23) 20 August 1801. Bishop John Carroll to James Kirby, carpenter, lease of lot 13 on the east side of Eutaw Street extended for a yearly rent of $20 (WG#72: 238).

(24) 20 August 1801. Bishop John Carroll to Edward Sanders, lease of lot 10 on the east side of Eutaw Street extended for a yearly rent of $17.67 (WG#72: 349).

(25) 20 August 1801. Bishop John Carroll to Joseph Goldsmith, lease of lot 3 on the east side of Eutaw Street extended for a yearly rent of $20 (WG#72: 426).

(26) 9 August 1802. Bishop John Carroll to Thomas Connor, lease of lot 19 on the east side of Eutaw Street extended for a yearly rent of $25 (WG#74: 247).

---

[1]*And AAB, Miscellaneous Deeds.*

(27)   14 August 1802. Bishop John Carroll to Alexander Coulter, miner, lease of lot 18 on the east side of Eutaw Street extended for a yearly rent of $20 (WG#74: 595).

(28)   20 August 1802. This is a second recording for lot 3 [No. (25) above] (WG#74: 264).

(29)   17 June 1803. Bishop John Carroll to Bartholomew Faherty, lease of lot 14 on the east side of Eutaw Street extended for a yearly rent of $20 (WG#79: 36).

(30)   17 August 1803. Robert Sinclair to Rt. Rev. John Carroll and other trustees of the Female Humane Association [see Appendix 4], lot 69 of Cole's Harbor or Todd's Range on the west side of Calvert Street (WG#77: 225).

(31)   9 June 1804. Bishop John Carroll to Martin Griffith, lease of lot 17 on the east side of Eutaw Street extended for a yearly rent of $20 (WG#83: 64).

(32)   11 June 1805. Robert Sinclair to the Trustees of the Roman Catholic Church, for which Rt. Rev. John Carroll, president, "hath thereunto subscribed his name," ground at southwest corner of Charles Street and Pleasant Alley running west to Forrest Lane (WG#85: 247).[1]

(33)   17 August 1805. Robert Farrahar to Rt. Rev. John Carroll, lot on corner of Wilks Street [now Eastern Avenue] and Bond Street in trust for the use of himself, his wife, and children (WG#86: 241).

(34)   6 January 1806. Charles Carroll of Carrollton to John Carroll, for 5 shillings, lot 156 on northwest corner of North West Street [now Saratoga] and Charles Street (WG#88: 464).

(35)   4 April 1806. Charles Carroll of Carrollton to John Carroll, a deed of confirmation to deed No. (34) above (WG#88: 466). [See deeds in AAB as mentioned earlier.]

---

[1]*When this lot was purchased, a committee was appointed to have an episcopal residence built on it as soon as possible. The episcopal residence for the new cathedral, however, was not built until the time of Archbishop Whitfield, and it was not on the Sinclair lot, which was sold by the trustees, but in back of the cathedral. See Riordan,* Cathedral Records, *p. 58. Some early leases of this property by the trustees signed by John Carroll as president are found in WG#93: 633 (1807) and WG#95: 223 (1807).*

(36) 15 July 1806. William Stenson to Rt. Rev. John Carroll, tract called "Parker's Palace" on northwest side of Windsor Mill Road (WG#92: 248).[1]

(37) 21 October 1806. Bishop John Carroll to Joshua G. Pindell, lease of lot 11 on the east side of Eutaw Street extended for a yearly rent of $20 (WG#91: 501).

(38) 20 April 1809. Lewis John Mary Chevigné to Rt. Rev. John Carroll, a deed in trust, two adjacent lots of ground on Eutaw Street [south of Franklin Street] to indemnify Carroll for having acted as security for a loan to Chevigné from the Bank of Maryland (WG#101: 488).[2]

(39) 2 June 1809. Rt. Rev. John Carroll to Charles Carroll of Carrollton, mortgage of property leased by Carroll from John Eager Howard 21 October 1799 [see No. (8) above] because Charles Carroll became security for John Carroll in another transaction (WG#103: 205).[3]

(40) 10 November 1809. William Smith to Rt. Rev. John Carroll, trustee of the estate of James McAllister, deceased, lot on west side of Calvert Street "on the wharf extended" (WG#104: 523).

(41) 13 November 1809. Rt. Rev. John Carroll and MacAllister's widow and children, with Carroll as trustee for estate of James McAllister, to James Carey, deed of lot on west side of Calvert Street (WG#104: 525).

(42) 13 February 1810. This is a second recording for lot 7 [No. (21) above] (WG#106: 70).

(43) 4 February 1812. Rt. Rev. John Carroll to Jarrett Bull, for $1,221 deed for lot 1 on the corner of Eutaw and New [Franklin] streets, which had been leased to Anthony Livers [see No. (12) above] (WG#116: 516).

---

[1]*A long-time member of the cathedral congregation, William Stenson, widower, married at St. Peter's on 3 September 1806 Martha Hynson, widow of Samuel Eccleston Sr., thereby becoming the step-father of Samuel Eccleston Jr., fifth archbishop of Baltimore.*

[2]*And AAB, 11A-K-3. Chevigné was a mathematician who taught for a time at St. Mary's College in Baltimore.*

[3]*There is no mention of the subleases of this tract in the mortgage.*

There were at least eighteen other conveyances in which a John Carroll was either grantee or grantor. Some of these John Carrolls were probably the bishop, but in the absence of a title this can not be determined from the conveyances themselves. At least four other John Carrolls (one a free black) appeared fleetingly in the city directories that have been preserved.

Appropriately the first two land transactions that John Carroll negotiated as bishop in Baltimore County were for a seminary. In the first the tract he purchased was on what the deed called Turnpike Road. This was Reisterstown Road and is now at that point Pennsylvania Avenue. On it was One Mile Tavern, so called because it was a mile from the center of the city. This tract Carroll then sold to the Sulpicians, and One Mile Tavern became the first permanent seminary building in the United States.

The Reisterstown Road ended at Franklin Street, but most of the traffic continued on to Howard Street, a block east of Eutaw Street. This latter street Carroll opened up on the east side and the Sulpicians to some degree on the west side by leasing lots on Eutaw Street extended on tracts obtained from John Eager Howard.[1] This would account for the fact that the largest number of Carroll's leasees whose occupations were recorded were draymen or carpenters. The draymen, or carriage drivers, probably used their lots for stables. The carpenters were probably active in the construction of buildings in that part of Baltimore County then opening up north of the city line.

Carroll mentioned a number of the properties in his Baltimore County land transactions in his will of 22 November 1815.[2] "I am seized and possessed of certain estates real and personal in trust," he declared. To Bishop Neale his succes-

[1]For the Sulpicians see James Joseph Kortendick, S.S., "The History of St. Mary's College, Baltimore, 1799-1852" (M.A. thesis, Catholic University of America, 1942), appendix, "Epoques du Seminaire de Baltimore" by Jean-Marie Tessier.
[2]JCP, 3: 369-73.

sor he bequeathed "all houses, lands, lots and parcels within the United States vested in me, whereon are erected or are intended to be erected Churches or Chapels or graveyards to be laid off, Subject to the same trust or trusts on which I hold them respectively." Excepted was the lot in Boston, which Carroll bequeathed to his "most esteemed and respected friend" Bishop Cheverus his heirs and assigns.[1]

Excepted also was his "lease hold estate, renewable forever" on Eutaw Street subject to the payment of $200 annually for ten years "for the purpose expressed in a sealed paper signed by me." This he charged also to Neale. This was undoubtedly the land leased from Colonel Howard in 1799, in No. (8), subleased, in Nos. (13-29), (31), (37), (42), and then mortgaged to Charles Carroll of Carrollton in 1809, in No. (39). To Rev. Enoch Fenwick, rector of St. Peter's, he bequeathed land on the west side of Charles Street in trust forever for the purpose indicated also in the sealed paper. This was undoubtedly the Sinclair lot described in No. (32) intended for the residence of the archbishop. To Rev. Enoch Fenwick he bequeathed also the land conveyed by William Stenson, in No. (36), and all the property conveyed by Catherine Walsh O'Conner, in Nos. (5), (6), and (9).

The estates held in trust for churches, chapels, and graveyards certainly included those held by Carroll in his capacity as president of the board of trustees of the cathedral congregation, originally incorporated in November 1795 as "The Trustees of the Roman Catholic Church of Baltimore Town." The first board consisted of the Right Rev. John Carroll, Rev. Francis Beeston, Robert Walsh, James Barry, David Williamson, Charles Ghequiere, Charles O'Brien, Luke Tiernan, and George Rosensteel. At its initial meeting on 29 December 1795 the board elected Carroll president.[2]

---

[1] *Bishop Cheverus wrote to Daniel Brent, the executor, "I am more honored than I deserve by being mentioned in such terms in his will"* (Melville, Cheverus, p. 180).

[2] *Riordan,* Cathedral Records, *p. 19.*

On 10 April 1796 Beeston, as secretary, presented the following inventory of property belonging to the cathedral congregation:

1. A square at Dulaney and Wolfe streets given by William Fell to the Catholics of Baltimore for a burying ground.

2. Six lots on Philpot's Hill.

3. An organ, sacred vessels, and other church ornaments. The six lots on Philpot's Hill were soon enlarged to include the entire square of ground now lying between Granby and Stiles and Exeter and Gough. These were intended for the Cathedral Square.[1] In 1805 the plan to build a cathedral there was abandoned.

At the prompting of the Sulpicians Carroll decided to locate his cathedral just north of the then city boundary on land offered for sale by Col. John Eager Howard. On 19 April 1806 the latter deeded the Trustees of the Roman Catholic Church in the Town of Baltimore the ground between Franklin and Mulberry streets on the north and south and between Charles Street and a new street Howard would open up and call Cathedral Street on the east and west for $20,571.60. A fifth of this amount would be paid by 1 January 1807 and the rest with interest in four annual installments. The deed was signed by J. E. Howard, J. Carroll, and two other witnesses.[2] At the trustees' request Colonel Howard reduced the price to $20,000 when he graded Charles Street to the detriment of the land. Most of the payments were made by Luke Tiernan, trustee and one of the most generous contributors to the new cathedral.[3]

---

[1]*Ibid., pp. 19-21. Sales of this property by the trustees signed by John Carroll as president are found in WG#56: 188 (1798), WG#112: 155 (1810), and WG#115: 121 (1811).*

[2]*William D. Hoyt, Jr., "Land for a Cathedral: Baltimore 1806-1817,"* Catholic Historical Review *36 (1951): 441-45. This deed is not to be found in the Baltimore County land records.*

[3]*Ibid.; Riordan,* Cathedral Records, *p. 48.*

On 7 July 1806 Carroll laid the cornerstone for the edifice to be called the Cathedral of Jesus and Mary (but changed to the Cathedral of the Assumption before completion).[1] On 20 January 1807 the trustees for $563.33 deeded William Stenson a burial vault within the walls of the cathedral, the deed signed by "J. Carroll Pres[iden]^t of the Trustees of the R C Church."[2] In 1829 the trustees would purchase this vault from the estate of William Stenson.[3]

In 1812 the decision was made to sell, in eleven lots, the ground between an alley north of the cathedral and Franklin Street. On 18 May 1815 the three lots on Franklin nearest Charles Street and the three nearest Cathedral Street were sold. Two years later the five lots in the middle were sold but were repurchased by Rev. Enoch Fenwick in 1819. Later this land was also sold.[4] The sale of the lots on Franklin Street would in time become a matter of regret to the officials of the cathedral.

---

[1]*Spalding*, Premier See, *pp. 30-31; Riordan*, Cathedral Records, *pp. 25-26.*

[2]*Baltimore County land records, WG#92: 136.*

[3]*Riordan*, Cathedral Records, *pp. 103-4, claims that the land Stenson deeded Carroll in 1806, for which see No. (36), was for this vault. This is doubtful. The Stenson vault was apparently the one beneath the vestibule, in which was buried, according to tradition, "a lady distinguished for her virtuous deeds" and a child. The lady was possibly the stepsister of Archbishop Samuel Eccleston.*

[4]*Hoyt, "Land for a Cathedral," p. 442; Riordan*, Cathedral Records, *p. 48.*

APPENDIX 6

THE DU MOULIN LEGACY

An instructive episode in Carroll's life mentioned by none of his biographers was that of the Du Moulin legacy. On 20 March 1791 Sir Thomas Moore, baronet,[1] wrote Bishop Carroll from Paris. Mr. [Thomas] Talbot[2] had also written Carroll from London, he said, concerning the "saving of a soul," whom Divine Providence had placed in the baronet's care, his nephew, James Du Moulin. Though he was almost eighteen, his "character, bad dispositions, & vicious inclinations" had, despite the baronet's efforts, kept him even from being admitted to his first communion. Sir Thomas hoped that in a remote country and with good example he would change. He would be traveling with Mr. [Francis] Nagot [and the first Sulpicians], and Sir Thomas hoped that Carroll would receive him "as a misled sheep" and place him in college or apprentice him to a merchant. He was sending money with Mr. Nagot, and Carroll could draw upon Messrs. Wright and Company for his expenses in the same manner Carroll drew upon Mr. Talbot's account.[3]

The young miscreant was dumped upon Carroll without any prior consultation, but Carroll apparently accepted the responsibility without demur. No record has yet been found as to the manner in which he carried out the task. It is known only that young Du Moulin did not remain with the Sulpicians who brought him over. Dutifully Carroll received the baronet's annual payments and applied them to the nephew's needs.

---

[1]On 27 September 1790 Carroll had written Charles Plowden that Sir John Moore had just died, "I fear as he lived," and that his brother, now Sir Thomas, baronet, refused to go to the funeral (JCP, 1: 466-67). A footnote correctly identifies Sir Thomas as baronet of Fawley, with whose death in 1807 without issue the baronetcy was extinguished. Sir Thomas Moore does not appear in the Index despite his being mentioned five more times in the JCP (2: 101, 140, 209, 240, 269), all in connection with his nephew's expenses.

[2]Rev. Thomas Talbot, procurator for the former Jesuits of England, did not write Carroll until 5 May (AAB, 5-M-8).

[3]AAB, 5-M-10. For allusions to Sir Thomas and/or his nephew in the foregoing abstracts see Nos. 40, 53, 70, 74, 93, 102, 106, 132, 143, 146, 163, 192, 193.

In 1807 Sir Thomas died leaving his nephew £2,000. In 1810 the nephew told Carroll he needed a more ample allowance, and Carroll obligingly arranged the same (see No. 143). In November 1813, however, Carroll received a letter from Captain Andrew Du Moulin of the 1st Somerset Regiment dated Pendennis Castle, Falmouth, 29 June 1813.[1] The captain had wanted to write Carroll for some time but had waited in the hope that Mr. Selby (see No. 193) could supply him some information on his "poor unfortunate Brother," from whom he had not heard for more than twenty years. Having now heard that James was in "a state of derangement," the cause of which he could not fathom, he was extremely anxious. But knowing that he was under the care of "so great & worthy a Personage" as Carroll, he had no doubt that every attention was paid him. Mr. Selby, however, had told him that Carroll had not drawn on his brother's account for almost two years. If James had died, Andrew was anxious that his affairs be settled properly as he and his children were his nearest relatives.

Carroll undoubtedly informed Andrew of the state of James's health and "rejoiced" in 1815 when the captain wrote him to send his brother home. Carroll attempted to arrange the return but warned Andrew through Mr. Selby that it would be difficult to find a person endowed with the firmness and humanity needed to take him over, and he doubted that James would consent, since he "lives thro his own act so unconformably here" (see No. 193).

When Carroll died some four months later, James was still in Baltimore. It became the responsibility of Carroll's executor, his nephew Daniel Brent, to handle the remittances for Du Moulin, who apparently was incompetent to handle them himself. But it was the responsibility of Carroll's successors as archbishop to see to his proper care. In

---

[1]*AAB, 3-F-9.*

1814 Lady Anastasia Mannock, James's aunt, had died leaving him £1,950.[1] With this added to the legacy of his uncle, James Du Moulin was a wealthy man.

On 1 July 1819 Captain Du Moulin wrote finally from Bath to Archbishop Ambrose Maréchal.[2] Since Carroll's death the captain had made several inquiries but only recently was told that his brother had been transferred to Maréchal's guardianship. Family affairs made it imperative that he know at once whether James was still alive or not. If so, Andrew gave the archbishop full power to send him home by the first vessel sailing for Bristol. What could have been the motives of Sir Thomas Moore, their uncle and guardian, for sending his brother away when they were at school together he did not know. His brother showed promise of great genius, "but some unforeseen accident has worked I understand a most extraordinary change for the worst." Should James be unwilling to return, the captain concluded, "force ought to be used, as it is of the utmost consequence his coming to England as soon as possible."

Archbishop Maréchal did not do as requested. Perhaps at Maréchal's prompting or at that of Rev. James Whitfield, rector of the cathedral, James Du Moulin on 7 May 1821 asked Messrs. Wright and Company to transfer to the archbishop $5,000 of the money they held in trust for him.[3] The bankers thanked Whitfield for his kind attentions to Du Moulin and included a statement of his affairs. "We regret that Mr. Brent has delayed remitting him sufficient Funds for his support, as we duly acquitted his Bills in Mr. Brent's favor, last year, to the amount of £500 Stlg."[4]

---

[1]SAB, Record Group 3, Box 11A, Messrs. Wright & Co. to James Du Moulin, London, 4 September 1821.

[2]AAB, 16-C-13 (Maréchal Papers). Maréchal had evidently examined Carroll's papers for information on James Du Moulin. On the letter of 1813 from Captain Du Moulin (AAB, 3-F-9) he wrote, "Of no importance."

[3]See above, footnote 1. All correspondence hereafter cited is found in the Du Moulin/Brent papers in SAB, Record Group 3, Box 11A.

[4]Wright & Co. to Whitfield, London, 4 September 1821.

By the time the London bankers wrote these words, James Du Moulin was dead. In a will drawn 9 February 1821 and proved 14 August 1821 in Baltimore, he left £800 to his sister Barbara (Madame de Fages) and £700 to "my dear and much valued friend" Archbishop Maréchal and named his brother Andrew his residuary legatee. Rev. Alexius J. Elder (the Sulpician treasurer at St. Mary's College) was designated executor for his estate in the United States. The will was witnessed by John White, James Whitfield, and John J. Chanche.[1]

Elder began at once the settlement of the estate, but his demands for an accounting from Carroll's nephew for the £500 was met by a series of evasions. On 1 April 1822 Brent explained to Elder that his "unremitted employment" in the Department of State prevented his immediate compliance. He had, it turned out, used the money to pay his own debts. Finally, in 1825, Elder sued Brent to recover the £500. At the end of 1826 Elder's lawyer expressed a fear that it would be some time before the money could be got, as "Mr Brent has already been put to jail in another suit."[2]

In 1828 Andrew Du Moulin finally expressed his frustration over the long delay by an implied accusation. "I can hardly imagine," he wrote Elder, "that my brother in his lamentable situation could have suggested to anyone his desire of withdrawing so large a sum from the bankers in England. . . . Somebody must be accountable for placing the money in Mr. Brent's shallow hands." The archbishop, he felt, had received an exorbitant sum and should himself assume the responsibility of recovering the £500 for him.[3] No one explained to Andrew Du Moulin that it was Archbishop Carroll himself who was responsible for his nephew's involvement in the affairs of his brother James.

---

[1] *Elder was also fiscal agent for the Sulpicians. John White was a prominent layman, later a cathedral trustee. John J. Chanche, later bishop of Natchez, was on the faculty of St. Mary's Seminary and College.*

[2] *Lear to Elder, Washington, 6 December 1826.*

[3] *Du Moulin to Elder, London, 6 May 1828.*

To avoid imprisonment a second time Brent declared bankruptcy and placed his property in the hands of a trustee, his brother. It still took several years to divide the proceeds of the sale among the creditors and to settle the problem of receipts and releases on both sides. Andrew Du Moulin's last words to Elder, on 12 June 1839, were not cordial: "[Y]our demanding a release from me previous to the payment of the money seems to imply a want of confidence in my integrity far from flattering to my feelings."

Brent's legal and financial embarrassments apparently had little effect upon his reputation at the State Department. In the course of the suit against him, he was a central figure in the State Department's involvement in two important episodes touching the Catholic Church in the United States. In 1824 Charles Neale, the Jesuit superior in America, refused to obey an order from the Propaganda Fide and the Jesuit general that the American Jesuits surrender the better part of their largest estate to Archbishop Maréchal. Brent wrote Maréchal that Secretary of State John Quincy Adams had been asked by the American Jesuits to protest this order emanating from a foreign power. Brent would send a copy if such were written, but he suggested that any appeal to Rome on Maréchal's part would be impolitic. Maréchal sent an opinion of Roger B. Taney, to which Brent took exception, but he confided that Adams (perhaps at his own recommendation) would probably send no protest.[1]

In 1828 two Dominicans, ordered out of Philadelphia by their superiors abroad, complained to Secretary of State Henry Clay that their rights as American citizens were being violated. In Clay's absence Brent, as under-secretary, wrote at the president's direction to the American minister in

---

[1] *Hughes,* History, Documents, *pp. 1071-77.*

France to seek an explanation from the papal nuncio in Paris. Brent was also required to be the intermediary when the two Dominicans came to Washington to make a personal appeal to Clay.[1]

While Brent's performance at the State Department has often been cited with approval, no account mentions his unfortunate involvement in the Du Moulin controversy, his imprisonment, and his financial disgrace. In the end John Carroll's favorite nephew left the United States in 1834 to serve as consul in Paris, and there he died and was buried in 1841.

---

[1] *Peter Guilday,* The Life and Times of John England, First Bishop of Charleston (1786-1842), *2 vols. (New York: The America Press, 1927), 2: 234.*

ADDENDUM

The appearance of Ronald Hoffman's Princes of Ireland, Planters of Maryland: A Carroll Saga, 1500-1782 *in Spring of 2000 (University of North Carolina Press) revealed on page 152 still another important letter of John Carroll, too late to be placed in proper sequence. This one to his brother Daniel in 1760 is in the form of a partial quote in a letter from Charles Carroll of Annapolis (1702-1782) to his son Charles, later Charles Carroll of Carrollton (1737-1832).*

TO DANIEL CARROLL, Liège, 15 March 1760

John Carroll was enrolled in 1748 in the Jesuit college of St. Omer in French Flanders at the same time as his cousin Charles. There they were fellow students until 1753, when John entered the Jesuit novitiate at nearby Watten. As this letter attests, they kept in contact during their years in Europe. On 14 July 1760 Charles Carroll of Annapolis wrote his son Charles and at one point said: "Part of Jo: Carroll's letter from Liège Dated March 15th: 1760 to his Br Daniel Carroll in Maryland."

Carroll's cousin Charles Carroll has written him from London "with all the indifference of a Philosopher" unconcerned about news. "Mediocritas [the middle way], says he, is not that best?" What Mr. Carroll [the cousin's father] told Daniel of the result of his voyage to Europe was similar to what the son [cousin Charles] told Carroll when he saw him in September, that the father had not succeeded in Paris.[1] Of the motives, however, cousin

---

[1] *Charles Carroll, the father, had in 1757 gone to London first to convince the Lord Proprietor, Frederick, sixth Lord Baltimore, of the injustice of a double tax imposed on Maryland Catholics and then to Paris to inquire of the French government about the possibility of himself and other Maryland Catholics moving to the territory of Louisiana, where they could practice their religion freely. Charles, the son, was not enthusiastic at the prospect.*

Charles said nothing and John does not feel he should push his inquiries any farther. He had gone from Liège to Ghent just to meet cousin Charles on his way from Paris to London. Mr. [Henry ?] Rozier will give Daniel an account of the "Great improvement he [Charles] has made in France, & his Elegant way of living in London."

Carroll-McTavish Papers, MS 220, MHS.

WORKS CITED AND CONSULTED

Brent, Chester Horton. *The Descendants of Coll⁰ Giles Brent, Capᵗ George Brent, and Robert Brent,* ᴳᵉⁿᵗ, *Immigrants to Maryland and Virginia.* Rutland, Vt.: The Author, 1946.

[Brent, Daniel]. *Biographical Sketch of the Most Rev. John Carroll, First Archbishop of Baltimore.* Ed. by John Carroll Brent. Baltimore: John Murphy, 1843.

Browne, Patrick W., ed. and trans. *Beginnings of the Catholic Church in the United States, Being* Etat de l'Eglise Catholique ou Diocèse des Etats-Unis de l'Amérique Septentrionale, par Jean Dilhet. Washington, D.C.: Salve Regina Press, 1922.

Carey, Patrick W. *People, Priests, and Prelates: Ecclesiastical Democracy and the Tensions of Trusteeism.* Notre Dame, Ind.: University of Notre Dame Press, 1987.

Code, Joseph Bernard. *Dictionary of the American Hierarchy (1789-1964).* New York: Joseph F. Wagner, 1964.

Curran, Robert Emmett. "'Splendid Poverty': Jesuit Slaveholding in Maryland, 1805-1838." In *Catholics in the Old South: Essays on Church and Culture,* ed. by Randall M. Miller and Jon L. Wakelyn, pp. 125-46. Macon, Ga.: Mercer University Press. 1983.

———. *The Bicentennial History of Georgetown University: From Academy to University, 1789-1889, Volume I.* Washington, D.C.: Georgetown University Press, 1993.

Ellis, John Tracy, ed. *Documents of American Catholic History.* 2 vols. Chicago: Henry Regnery, 1967.

Fecher, Vincent J. *A Study of the Movement for German National Parishes in Philadelphia and Baltimore (1787-1802).* Rome: Gregorian University Press, 1955.

Finotti, Joseph M. *Bibliographia Catholica Americana: A List of Works Written by Catholic Authors, and Published in the United States.* New York: The Catholic Publication House, 1872.

Geiger, Sister M. Virgina. *Daniel Carroll II: One Man and His Descendants, 1730-1978.* Baltimore: The Author, 1979.

Guilday, Peter. *The Life and Times of John Carroll: Archbishop of Baltimore (1735-1815).* New York: The Encyclopedia Press, 1922.

———. *The Life and Times of John England: First Bishop of Charleston (1768-1842).* 2 vols. New York: America Press, 1927.

Hanley, Thomas O'Brien, S.J., ed. *The John Carroll Papers.* 3 vols. Notre Dame, Ind.: University of Notre Dame Press, 1976.

Hoffman, Ronald. *Princes of Ireland, Planters of Maryland: A Carroll Saga, 1500-1782.* Chapel Hill: University of North Carolina Press, 2000.

Hoyt, William D., Jr. "Land for a Cathedral: Baltimore 1806-1817," *Catholic Historical Review* 36 (1951): 441-45.

Hughes, Thomas. *History of the Society of Jesus in North America: Colonial and Federal, Documents*, vol. 1 in 2 parts. London: Longmans, Green, 1908, 1910.

Kauffman, Christopher J. *Tradition and Transformation in American Culture: The Priests of Saint Sulpice in the United States from 1791 to the Present.* New York: Macmillan, 1988.

Kenneally, Finbar, O.F.M., [ed.] *United States Documents in the Propaganda Fide Archives: A Calendar.* First Series, 7 vols. Washington, D.C.: Academy of American Franciscan History, 1966-1977.

Kortendick, James Joseph, S.S. "The History of St. Mary's College, Baltimore, 1799-1852." M.A. thesis, Catholic University of America, 1942.

Lemcke, Peter Henry, O.S.B. *Life and Work of Prince Demetrius Augustine Gallitzin.* Trans. by Joseph C. Plumpe. New York: Longmans, Green, 1940.

Lord, Robert H., John E. Sexton, and Edward T. Harrington. *History of the Archdiocese of Boston in the Various Stages of Its Development, 1604-1943.* 3 vols. New York: Sheed and Ward, 1944.

Madden, Richard C. *Catholics in South Carolina: A Record.* Lanham, Md.: University Press of America, 1985.

Maes, Camillus P. *The Life of Rev. Charles Nerinckx.* Cincinnati: R. Clarke, 1880.

Melville, Annabelle M. *Elizabeth Bayley Seton, 1774-1821.* New York: Charles Scribner's, 1951.

———. *John Carroll of Baltimore: Founder of the American Catholic Hierarchy.* New York: Charles Scribner's, 1955.

———. *Jean Lefebvre de Cheverus, 1768-1836.* Milwaukee: Bruce, 1958.

———. "John Carroll and Louisiana, 1803-1815," *Catholic Historical Review* 64 (1978): 398-440.

———. *Louis William DuBourg: Bishop of Louisiana and the Floridas, Bishop of Montauban, and Archbishop of Besançon, 1766-1818.* 2 vols. Chicago: Loyola University Press, 1986.

O'Neill, Charles Edwards. " 'A Quarter Marked by Sundry Peculiarities': New Orleans, Lay Trustees, and Père Antoine," *Catholic Historical Review* 76 (1990): 235-77.

Ridgeway, William H. *Community Leadership in Maryland, 1790-1840: A Comparative Analysis of Power in Society.* Chapel Hill, N.C.: University of North Carolina Press, 1979.

[Riordan, Michael J.] *Cathedral Records from the Beginning of Catholicity in Baltimore to the Present.* Baltimore: The Catholic Mirror, 1906.

Ruane, Joseph W. *The Beginnings of the Society of St. Sulpice in the United States (1791-1829).* Washington, D.C.: Catholic University of America Press, 1935.

Scharf, J. Thomas. *History of Baltimore City and County.* 2 vols. 1881. Reprint, Baltimore: Regional Publishing Company, 1971.

Shea, John Gilmary. *Life and Times of the Most Rev. John Carroll, Bishop and First Archbishop of Baltimore.* New York: John G. Shea, 1888. [Vol. 2 of *The History of the*

Catholic Church in the United States. 4 vols. New York: John G. Shea, 1886-1892.]

Sherman, Stuart C. "The Library Company of Baltimore, 1795-1854," *Maryland Historical Magazine* 39 (1944): 6-24.

Spalding, Thomas W. "John Carroll: Corrigenda and Addenda," *Catholic Historical Review* 71 (1985): 505-18.

————. *The Premier See: A History of the Archdiocese of Baltimore, 1789-1989*. Baltimore: Johns Hopkins University Press, 1989.

————. "The Carrolls of Maryland." In *The Encyclopedia of the Irish in America*, ed. by Michael Glazier, pp. 124-25. Notre Dame, Ind.: University of Notre Dame Press, 1999.

————. "John Carroll (1736-1815)." In *The Encyclopedia of the Irish in America*, ed. by Michael Glazier, pp. 121-23. Notre Dame, Ind.: University of Notre Dame Press, 1999.

Tilghman, Tench Francis. "The Founding of St. John's College, 1784-89," *Maryland Historical Magazine* 44 (1949): 75-92.

Van Devanter, Ann C., ed. *"Anywhere So Long As There be Freedom": Charles Carroll of Carrollton, His Family & His Maryland*. Baltimore: Baltimore Museum of Art, 1975.

INDEX

Boldface numbers indicate where a person or institution is identified in footnotes or introductions. The persons joined in marriage by John Carroll in Appendix 1 are not indexed unless they also appear elsewhere.